Childhood and Disability

Drawn from *Disability & Society* over the period 1997–2012, the 12 chapters in this book address a range of personal, cultural and institutional arenas in which challenges experienced by disabled children are played out. The book includes a mix of theoretical and applied material offering both powerful conceptual tools and practical insights, enabling readers to connect the work of recent decades to their own research and questions about disability and childhood. Readers will find this book an invaluable resource for understanding what we have learned about disability and childhood through the pages of the world leading international journal in the field. The collection makes available a well-informed understanding of conditions, policies and practices that create disability in children's lives so that we can further the struggle for a more inclusive future in which inequalities structured around impairment are challenged. The importance of children's own voices for resisting disablement in childhood is clearly foregrounded in this invaluable collection.

This book was originally published as a special issue of *Disability & Society*.

Sarah Beazley is Senior Lecturer at The University of Manchester, UK, and Consultant Speech and Language Therapist with deaf people and their families.

Val Williams is Head of Norah Fry Research Centre at the University of Bristol, UK. Her research is in disability studies, communication and policy, often working inclusively with people with learning disabilities.

Childhood and Disability
Key Papers from *Disability & Society*

Edited by
Sarah Beazley and Val Williams

Routledge
Taylor & Francis Group

LONDON AND NEW YORK

First published 2014
by Routledge
2 Park Square, Milton Park, Abingdon, Oxfordshire OX14 4RN

and by Routledge
711 Third Avenue, New York, NY 10017, USA

First issued in paperback 2015

Routledge is an imprint of the Taylor & Francis Group, an informa business

© 2014 Taylor & Francis

All rights reserved. No part of this book may be reprinted or reproduced or utilised in any form or by any electronic, mechanical, or other means, now known or hereafter invented, including photocopying and recording, or in any information storage or retrieval system, without permission in writing from the publishers.

Trademark notice: Product or corporate names may be trademarks or registered trademarks, and are used only for identification and explanation without intent to infringe.

British Library Cataloguing in Publication Data
A catalogue record for this book is available from the British Library

ISBN 13: 978-1-138-94916-4 (pbk)
ISBN 13: 978-0-415-72923-9 (hbk)

Typeset in Times New Roman
by Taylor & Francis Books

Publisher's Note
The publisher accepts responsibility for any inconsistencies that may have arisen during the conversion of this book from journal articles to book chapters, namely the possible inclusion of journal terminology.

Disclaimer
Every effort has been made to contact copyright holders for their permission to reprint material in this book. The publishers would be grateful to hear from any copyright holder who is not here acknowledged and will undertake to rectify any errors or omissions in future editions of this book.

Contents

Citation Information vii

Introduction
Val Williams and Sarah Beazley 1

1. Gone Missing? Disabled children living away from their families
Jenny Morris 5

2. Student Perspectives: Disabled Children, Parents and Professionals: partnership on whose terms?
Pippa Murray 23

3. Where Are the Children's Experiences? Analysing Social and Cultural Exclusion in 'Special' and 'Mainstream' Schools
J.M. Davis & N. Watson 39

4. 'I Value What You have to Say'. Seeking the Perspective of Children with a Disability, Not Just their Parents
Belinda Garth & Rosalie Aroni 56

5. Nothing to be had 'off the peg': consumption, identity and the immobilization of young disabled people
Bill Hughes, Rachel Russell and Kevin Paterson 72

6. 'Chocolate ... makes you autism': impairment, disability and childhood identities
Berni Kelly 87

7. Children's experiences of disability: pointers to a social model of childhood disability
Clare Connors and Kirsten Stalker 102

8. Notions of self: lived realities of children with disabilities
Vanessa Singh and Anita Ghai 117

9. Constructing 'normal childhoods': young people talk about young carers
L. O'Dell, S. Crafter, G. de Abreu and T. Cline 134

10. Not your average childhood: lived experience of children with physical disabilities raised in Bloorview Hospital, Home and School from 1960 to 1989
Tracy Odell 147

CONTENTS

11. Facilitating and hindering factors in the realization of disabled children's agency in institutional contexts: literature review
    Johanna Olli, Tanja Vehkakoski and Sanna Salantera   162

12. No safety net for disabled children in residential institutions in Ireland
    Pauline Conroy   177

13. Conclusion
    Sarah Beazley and Val Williams   191

    Index   195

Citation Information

The chapters in this book were originally published in *Disability & Society*, various volumes. When citing this material, please use the original page numbering for each article, as follows:

Chapter 1
Gone Missing? Disabled children living away from their families
Jenny Morris
Disability & Society, volume 12, issue 2 (1997) pp. 241–258

Chapter 2
Student Perspectives: Disabled Children, Parents and Professionals: partnership on whose terms?
Pippa Murray
Disability & Society, volume 15, issue 4 (2000) pp. 683–698

Chapter 3
Where Are the Children's Experiences? Analysing Social and Cultural Exclusion in 'Special' and 'Mainstream' Schools
J.M. Davis & N. Watson
Disability & Society, volume 16, issue 5 (2001) pp. 671–687

Chapter 4
'I Value What You have to Say'. Seeking the Perspective of Children with a Disability, Not Just their Parents
Belinda Garth & Rosalie Aroni
Disability & Society, volume 18, issue 5 (August 2003) pp. 561–576

Chapter 5
Nothing to be had 'off the peg': consumption, identity and the immobilization of young disabled people
Bill Hughes, Rachel Russell and Kevin Paterson
Disability & Society, volume 20, issue 1 (January 2005) pp. 3–17

Chapter 6
'Chocolate ... makes you autism': impairment, disability and childhood identities
Berni Kelly
Disability & Society, volume 20, issue 3 (May 2005) pp. 261–275

CITATION INFORMATION

Chapter 7
Children's experiences of disability: pointers to a social model of childhood disability
Clare Connors and Kirsten Stalker
Disability & Society, volume 22, issue 1 (January 2007) pp. 19–33

Chapter 8
Notions of self: lived realities of children with disabilities
Vanessa Singh and Anita Ghai
Disability & Society, volume 24, issue 2 (March 2009) pp. 129–145

Chapter 9
Constructing 'normal childhoods': young people talk about young carers
L. O'Dell, S. Crafter, G. de Abreu and T. Cline
Disability & Society, volume 25, issue 6 (October 2010) pp. 643–655

Chapter 10
Not your average childhood: lived experience of children with physical disabilities raised in Bloorview Hospital, Home and School from 1960 to 1989
Tracy Odell
Disability & Society, volume 26, issue 1 (January 2011) pp. 49–63

Chapter 11
Facilitating and hindering factors in the realization of disabled children's agency in institutional contexts: literature review
Johanna Olli, Tanja Vehkakoski and Sanna Salantera
Disability & Society, volume 27, issue 6 (October 2012) pp. 793–807

Chapter 12
No safety net for disabled children in residential institutions in Ireland
Pauline Conroy
Disability & Society, volume 27, issue 6 (October 2012) pp. 809–822

Please direct any queries you may have about the citations to
clsuk.permissions@cengage.com

Introduction
Val Williams and Sarah Beazley

Introduction

This book features a series of key papers about childhood and disability drawn from past issues of the journal *Disability & Society*. The papers were originally brought together for the first of a series of 'Virtual' Special Issues for which, as members of the journal's Executive Editorial Board, we were asked to take a retrospective view through the pages of past editions to select some of the most interesting and seminal papers on childhood and disability published over the years. Mindful of the privilege we had in identifying these articles, the task was an extraordinarily difficult one. For every paper included, there were many other strong contenders. However, we attempted to shape the collection around themes that shone out powerfully in the journal over time. The papers included should therefore be seen as tasters and signposts to encourage deeper exploration of issues concerning disability and childhood. In this collection of papers the focus is on childhood experiences both past and present and, as far as possible, disabled children's voices take centre stage.

Children's voices

Children's voices are not often heard in the social sciences or within sociology and other related disciplines and, as we consistently see through the pages of this book, disabled children are additionally marginalised by society's attitudes across historical and cross-cultural landscapes. However, from very early editions onwards, *Disability & Society* has played a key role in enabling readers to hear directly from disabled children across the world. This has challenged disability theorists to focus on the active agency of disabled children, rather than considering them only as passive objects of care. This critical agenda emerges in the first article featured in this book by Morris (1997), written on the cusp of change, and driven in part by an early UN Convention to ensure children were consulted about their own lives. Reflections on differences in the lives of disabled children in the 1960s, 1970s and 1980s are presented by Morris providing significant historical detail on exclusion and leading to demands that the voices of disabled children be systematically included in developments of policy and practice. Murray (2000) takes up this theme in a challenging and ground-breaking paper which gives the perspectives of parents. She shares analysis of difficult attitudes and experiences which oppress disabled children and their families and advocates a child-centred approach which must ensure disabled children are both listened to and thought of as members of families. The central role of families in the lives of disabled children has continued to be a strong theme in *Disability & Society* over the intervening years, making the journal a vital resource for those seeking to explore these fundamentally important issues.

Throughout the book, ideas about the 'normalcy' of childhood are questioned; the position of children within particular discourses and definitions of childhood can be interrogated in a variety of ways. To reinforce this, we include a paper which represents the views and perceptions of young carers (O'Dell, 2010). Young people in these pages talk about their own identity, their goals for the future and the barriers they face. Readers interested in international perspectives on these themes will find much in this collection that sheds light on cross-national matters, as well as the similarities and differences of children's aspirations across the globe, for example in India (Singh & Ghai, 2009) and in New Zealand (Kelly, 2005). The journal increasingly promotes global debate and cross-national dialogue on disability and childhood which we urge readers to pursue.

Researching disability and childhood

One of the themes threading through this collection is a methodological one, concerned with how to include children's voices in research and practice, and particularly how to raise the voices of children who experience communication differences and difficulties. Several of the papers offer insights into the complexity of this process. Garth and Aroni (2003) working in Australia gathered views of parents and children on medical consultations, finding imaginative ways to include input from children who were primarily non-verbal. Singh and Ghai (2009) included drawings to enable children to express their views, making plain that listening to any disabled child requires adults to step back from their own agenda and usual repertoire of communicative resources. Olli et al. (2012) in a review paper, refer to the need to avoid building 'otherness' in encounters with disabled children which can stem from applying supposedly objective, 'normative' criteria. Their review usefully brings together strategies for approaching children on an individual basis, listening to what they choose to talk about, and importantly, showing children that action will be taken based upon what they say. These approaches are important in producing genuine, child-centred interactions in which disabled children's views can be foregrounded. Many contributions to *Disability & Society* offer helpful concepts and practical tools for researching disability and we hope that inclusion of papers in this book that explore such methodological issues will encourage readers to participate in further advancing better practice through reading and contributing to the journal.

When children do speak up, of course they do not always say what we expect. Disabled children whose voices are represented in this book sometimes challenge received wisdom. Children who worked with Garth and Aroni (2003) perhaps surprisingly reported that they enjoyed aspects of their medical consultations in the same way as any child enjoys an outing. In a similarly thought-provoking vein, children demonstrated how personal and cultural values of teachers can pose disabling barriers in mainstream schooling as well as in special schools (Davis & Watson, 2001). Disabled children's own words and reflections may make us as practitioners, families and academics feel uncertain, but the papers remind us that it is important to find ways to allow honest talking. Connors and Stalker (2007) explored the views of 26 disabled children over two years. Having involved children as advisors for the design of their research they chose to use the format of a 'typical day in the life' to encourage children to talk about their experiences. Through a carefully executed child-led process, the authors learned that the children they worked with chose to focus on their similarities with other children, rather than dwell on differences or experiences of being disabled. There are many explanations for this, but one of them is certainly that disabled children seldom have the experience of an organised self-advocacy movement, in which they would be able to build their own politics and articulate a collective view. The ongoing salience of these discussions about disability and childhood convinces us as editors that this retrospective engagement with papers previously published in *Disability & Society* is vitally important as a foundation for future innovations and thinking.

Learning from disabled children

Much can be learned from the papers that make up this book about the range of experience that disabled children encounter. Of course, as is evident through the different disciplinary, personal and professional perspectives offered in this collection, there is no more a homogeneous group of 'disabled children' than any other set of people. All children have multi-faceted identities of which impairment is only one determinant. Kelly (2005) charges readers to consider the dual experience of living as a child and a disabled person, building strong theoretical reflections on the complexity of growing up with impairment. A postmodern discourse of fluidity does not always fit neatly with childhood experience of disability. Hughes et al. (2005) question whether disabled children's experience can be included within a brave new postmodern youth world, where clubbing, fast food and the 'casual culture of street and bedroom' allow most young people to reinvent themselves. Disabled young people by contrast face some intransigent barriers to engagement with these trends, which threaten to position them in fixed ways as dependent and defined by their impairment, a position that however is often left unspoken. Although the disabled children in Kelly's (2005) study did have views about the barriers they faced due to their impairments, these were seldom talked about within the family, nor at school; they faced the additional exclusion of silence.

Finally, we should remember that issues of over-protection and dependency can seem trivial when compared with the cruelty, abuse and violence faced daily by disabled children. In this book, papers by Odell (2011) and Conroy (2012) are relatively recent publications reflecting on the past history of institutionalisation and the ever present danger of abuse for disabled children. A 'disabled childhood', as Odell (2011) puts it, is 'not your average childhood'. Fourteen years after the paper by Morris that opens this book, about oppression of children sent away from their families, Odell writes as a former resident in an institution in Canada from 1960 –1989 basing her paper on the words of sixteen people with physical impairments who review some of their feelings about, and experiences of, institutional life. Despite their experience of abuse, including by peers, the commentators represent their experiences in a rich, nuanced way, reflecting the resilience of disabled children and describing the spaces they found for connecting with each other. Cruelty reported amongst and between children, and the hierarchies children constructed themselves in Odell's research, are characteristic of difficulties children continue to face and transparency and discussion of such issues is essential. Conroy (2012) reports on physical, psychological and sexual abuse of disabled children living in religious institutions in Ireland, and discusses children's testimonies in the light of the UN Convention on the Rights of Persons with Disabilities, 2007,

Article 15 *'freedom from torture or cruel, inhuman or degrading treatment or punishment'* and Article 16 *'freedom from exploitation, violence and abuse'*. Loss of identity, creation of new impairments and absence of respect are the prominent and dreadful consequences of institutionalisation, and stand as a warning to all those wishing to make child-centred provision for disabled children safe.

We hope that as readers look through this selection of papers from *Disability & Society*, they gain fresh perspectives on their own thoughts on childhood and disability and impetus for driving forward further much needed research and change. We know that many topics of contemporary significance in disabled children's lives are not present within this book, such as new challenges and forms of resistance associated with global conflicts and crises or with constantly developing technologies which expose ever younger children to internet violence and pornography. Forthcoming issues of the journal include coverage of these matters and we warmly invite readers to contribute new work to *Disability & Society* that will build on the platform of this retrospective, to evolve new approaches to understanding childhood and disability in an ever-changing world. This book is important for continuing debates of critical importance to the combined interests of researchers, practitioners, policy makers and academics, as well as those disabled children and their families affected by their work. It is our hope that increasingly material published in *Disability & Society* will forge a new direction of travel, so that the voices of disabled children and their families will shape the work of the journal's readers.

Acknowledgements

We are grateful to all the authors whose papers feature in this collection and to the Editorial Board whose high-quality refereeing enables the journal to publish its influential work. Helen Oliver has provided invaluable, friendly and efficient administrative support which is much appreciated. Also our thanks are extended to the publishers who offer consistent support to the journal and its production.

Gone Missing? Disabled children living away from their families

JENNY MORRIS
c/o Disability & Society, Division of Education, University of Sheffield, 388 Glossop Road, Sheffield S10 2JA, UK

ABSTRACT *Many disabled children spend most of their childhood in 'care', but not formally 'in care'. Research concerning disabled children has been dominated by a medical model of disability and by a failure to include the subjective reality of children themselves. There is also inadequate statistical information available concerning children who spend most of their time away from a family setting. The article looks at what we do know about such experiences, identifying some issues for future research.*

Disabled children often experience patterns of care which would never be tolerated for non-disabled children. Many of them spend much of their childhood away from their families—in boarding schools, 'respite care', hospitals and other residential settings—yet this separation, the reasons for it and its consequences are often unacknowledged [1].

In Britain, the implementation of the Children Act 1989 offers important opportunities to challenge and change this situation. The 'children first' principle which underpins the legislation has, for example, prompted many social services departments to relocate responsibility for disabled children from specialist disability sections to their children and families sections. Such developments are promoted by a recognition that disabled children share many needs in common with their non-disabled peers.

Another requirement laid down by the Children Act is that of consulting and involving children in decisions which affect their lives. This reflects Article 12 of the United Nations Convention on the Rights of the Child which states that 'States Parties shall assure to the child who is capable of forming his or her own views the right to express those views freely in all matters affecting the child, the views of the child being given due weight in accordance with the age and maturity of the child'. Children generally, and disabled children in particular, have rarely been consulted about the decisions which adults make about their lives. Policy guidance issued to local authorities by the Department of Health seeks to bring about a change in this situation.

> Learning to make well-informed choices and making some mistakes should be part of every child's experience. Children and young people should be

given the chance to exercise choice and their views should be taken seriously if they are unhappy about the arrangements made for them. (Department of Health, 1991, p. 14)

Research has an important role to play in examining and highlighting the nature and consequences of policy and practice. Unfortunately, much research concerning disabled children has been characterised by two major inadequacies: it has been based on a medical model of disability; and it has failed to concern itself with the experiences of disabled children, focusing instead on that of service providers and parents.

This article looks at these two criticisms and then goes on to identify some important issues for future research.

Disabled Children and the Medical and Social Models of Disability

Most definitions of disability within existing research and policy development are based on a medical model of disability rather than the social model which has been articulated by the disabled people's movement. Within the medical model, the term 'disability' refers to physical, sensory or intellectual impairment and both the problem and the solution are defined in terms of a person's impairment.

> People become individual objects to be 'treated', 'changed', 'improved', made more 'normal'.... The overall picture is that the human being is flexible and 'alterable' whilst society is fixed and unalterable. We must adapt to a hostile environment. (Mason & Rieser, 1992, p. 13)

In contrast, within the social model of disability, 'disability' does not refer to impairment, but to the social factors which create barriers and deny opportunities. These factors include prejudicial attitudes and institutional discrimination, such as the failure of schools to provide the kind of support and facilities that children with impairments require.

The disabled people's movement therefore use the word disability to refer to prejudice and discrimination, just as racism and sexism refer to the prejudice and discrimination experienced by Black people and by women. While the disability movement does not deny the value of using medical and rehabilitation skills to maximise each person's physical and intellectual potential, it is the medical model's exclusive focus on the cure and treatment of impairment and its failure to locate the problem and the solution in social barriers which is objected to.

The phrase 'children with disabilities' is often defended as being based on the 'children first' principle. However, its use means that children are identified and defined in terms of their impairments (because here the term 'disability' is taken to mean impairment), and this can inhibit a recognition of the social context in which they experience impairment.

Unfortunately, the most commonly accepted method of classifying disabled children has been based on the medical model. The World Health Organisation's (WHO) International Classification of Impairment, Disabilities and Handicaps uses the following definitions:

Impairment: 'Any loss or abnormality of psychological, physiological or anatomical structure or function.' In other words, parts of the body which do not work at all or incompletely.

Disability: 'Any restriction or lack (*resulting from an impairment*) of ability to perform an activity in the manner or within the range considered normal for a human being' (my italics). In other words, things that someone cannot do or has difficulty doing.

Handicap: 'A disadvantage for a given individual, *resulting from an impairment or disability*, that limits or prevents the fulfilment of a role (depending on age, sex and social and cultural factors) for that individual' (my italics). In other words, the part that an individual can play in society and the kind of relationships which s/he can enter into.

The WHO classification explicitly states that the restrictions on what someone can do (their 'disabilities'), the part they can play in society, and the relationships they can enter into (their 'handicaps'), solely result from impairment. There is no room here for recognising that the inability of a 15 year old, who has speech difficulties as a result of cerebral palsy, to be part of the local teenage sub-culture is created by the prejudicial attitudes and inaccessible environments which restrict his or her activities rather than cerebral palsy or speech difficulties in themselves. There is no room for recognising that two people with the same level of impairment may have contrasting experiences, depending on the attitudes, the support and the environment which are a feature of their daily lives.

Most importantly, within this classification and this way of defining people, there is no room for measuring the things that make a difference to people's lives. Research which uses the WHO classification cannot measure the disabling attitudes which create misery and anger amongst some disabled children attending mainstream schools, nor can it measure the enabling actions of those whose ability to communicate with multiply impaired children mean that opportunities are created which would not otherwise exist for such children.

A further criticism of the medical model approach concerns the way that there is no room for measuring the extent to which the child's experience (rather than their impairment in itself) has, in fact, inhibited development and ability. This is particularly important when researching the experience of disabled children in institutional settings. There has long been an understanding that institutional practices can stunt a child's emotional, intellectual and physical development. An early example is the study by King, Raynes and Tizard of children with comparable levels of impairment in institutions with differing management styles. They concluded that 'those in child-oriented units were significantly more advanced in speech and feeding than those in institutionally-oriented units' (King *et al.*, 1971, p. 198).

Indeed, most theory and practice concerning the development of children who do not have any physical, sensory or intellectual impairments has as one of its central tenets that the amount of stimulation, interaction, security and love which a child receives has a fundamental effect on their development. Life for many children with impairments is dominated by a lack of stimulation, interaction, security and love—

and research on their experiences must therefore use measurements of disability which encompass this. To assume that all communication, mobility and behavioural difficulties are solely caused by impairment is to further disable these children by failing to recognise their actual experiences.

The Invisibility of Disabled Children's Experiences

This brings us to the second criticism of research in this area, namely that, associated with the medical model of disability, there has been a failure to base research on children's experiences. The largest and most comprehensive study of disabled children carried out in Britain to date—that conducted by the Office of Population Censuses and Surveys—undertook 1019 interviews with carers of children in residential care. In only 13 cases were children even present at the interviews (Loughran *et al.*, 1992, p. 9). This failure to gather information from children themselves about their experiences is very common.

Bryony Beresford's review of research concerning disabled children found that children *generally* have not been directly asked about their experiences—'children's opinions have been consistently ignored by researchers and practitioners, and services and interventions for children have been instigated without consulting the children themselves' (Beresford, 1997). Disabled children, she concludes, 'belong to two groups who have consistently been refused a direct voice in research. Methological and ethical arguments have precluded children from being involved in research, and having a disability [i.e. impairment] marginalises disabled children even further'. Ruth Marchant in a recent review of 'user views' on services for disabled children and young people confirmed while there has been 'an explosion of interest' in recent years in the views of parents of disabled children, 'in comparison there is very little yet published on what disabled children and young people say' (Marchant, 1996, p. 1).

Yet the research world is beginning to acknowledge the failure to consider the views of children. Beresford states that 'In recent years researchers from a wide variety of disciplines have acknowledged their failure to consult directly with children.' We are now starting to see the development of research methods which focus on non-disabled children and young people's subjective experiences (see, for example, Alderson, 1995; Hazel, 1995) and it is vital that researchers concerned with *disabled* children adopt the explicit aim of recording children's own experiences.

Since many disabled children who are most at risk of spending large amounts of time away from their families have significant communication impairments, researchers will have to acquire new skills and develop new ways of gathering information. Some progress has already been made in this field (see, for example, Hirst *et al.*, 1990; Minkes *et al.*, 1994; Hirst, n.d.; Roberts n.d.). Social researchers may also learn from innovatory practice in the field of inspecting and evaluating services, in particular two examples (London Borough of Richmond, 1994; People First, 1994) where people with learning difficulties carried out evaluations which involved communicating with people with significant communication needs.

Pioneering work has also been done by Ruth Marchant and Marcus Page in their investigations concerning children with multiple impairments who have experienced abuse (Marchant & Page, 1992). In addition, initiatives such as Pat Fitton's detailed account of her daughter's life illustrate the way that detailed knowledge, love and concern creates methods of communication (Fitton, 1994). Researchers will need to find ways of using such relationships as a resource but, of course, may find that children living away from their families do not have anyone who knows them well enough.

We will now go on to look at what is known about disabled children's experiences of living away from their families, looking first at what statistical information is available and then focussing on some messages which come from what disabled adults who have had this experience say about it.

How Many Disabled Children Experience a Childhood Dominated by Institutional Provision?

A statistical breakdown of children living away from their families which is commonly cited is that given by Philippa Russell, taken from a number of different sources.

Children in residential schools or children with special educational needs	16,550
Children in maintained residential schools	5000
Children in non-maintained or independent residential special schools	11,000
Children in EBD schools (maintained and non-maintained)	8000
Children living in 'communal provision'	5500

(Russell, 1994, p. 32.)

The last figure given here, concerning children in 'communal provision' comes from the main source of statistical information about the disabled population in Britain—the OPCS survey referred to above. This concluded that, in 1988, there were 5564 disabled children between the ages of 5 and 15 living in communal establishments who returned to their (birth or foster) family less than once a fortnight (Bone and Meltzer 1989). Although carried out some years ago, the OPCS survey remains an important, and much-used, source of information about disabled children, and it is worth looking in some detail both at what the survey found and at its inadequacies, particularly as these contain important lessons for future research.

The OPCS researchers carried out a census of all residential establishments catering for children. Each establishment was asked whether they had any disabled children and were informed that, 'A child should be regarded as disabled if he/she has difficulties with everyday activities because of a long-term health problem. This included physical, mental and behavioural problems which are chronic in nature' (Bone & Meltzer, 1989, p. 44).

Important though the survey is as a source of information about disabled children in institutional settings, it has significant limitations because:

- it included children who would not generally be classified as 'disabled', although in educational terms they may well be classified as having 'special needs'.
- it did not include disabled young people between the ages of 16 and 19;
- it excluded large numbers of disabled children whose childhood was dominated by residential provision, the most important group being those at boarding schools.

The OPCS inclusion of 'behavioural problems' as a 'disability' resulted in a large group of children being included who had no physical, sensory or intellectual impairment. While the survey grouped their sample solely according to severity, Loughran et al. carried out a secondary analysis of the same data and grouped the sampled children into 10 clusters which were based on both severity and type of impairment (Loughran et al., 1992, p. 23). In this secondary analysis Cluster 1—which makes up 42% of all the children included, the great majority (91%) only had behavioural difficulties (p. 34). Loughran et al.'s description of this group is illuminating:

> The behaviour problems presented by this group were largely those of conduct and delinquency, although a significant minority showed signs of depression.... The children in this cluster were those most likely to take part fairly regularly in some form of substance abuse (getting drunk, taking drugs or sniffing glue). Just over a fifth of them engaged in such activity at least once a month. Nearly half were involved in lying or stealing at least once a week.... Just over a third had outbursts of violent temper or aggression at least once a week and a similar proportion were described as over-active and usually unable to concentrate. Just under a third were described as being miserable, afraid, or worried most of the time every day and this group had the second highest rate[2] of threatened or attempted suicide (eight per cent at least once per month).

While these children are certainly experiencing barriers to a good quality life, it is questionable whether they should have been defined as disabled children since we generally associate the term with physical, sensory and intellectual impairment. This is confirmed by the fact that, when staff were asked to record what 'complaints' caused children's disability, those looking after children with predominantly behavioural and emotional problems tended not to respond. 'This was because [they] did not want to classify their children as "disabled". They preferred to describe the children simply as having severe behavioural, learning or emotional problems' (Bone & Meltzer, 1989, p. 31).

The classification of behavioural and emotional difficulties (and associated learning problems) as a 'disability' creates significant analytical and methodological problems. Indeed, the survey's authors recognised that 'the fact that children are in residential care can cause or exacerbate behavioural or emotional problems' (p. 31). Moreover, the fact that staff recorded whether the children had behavioural problems, and how severe they were, means that such difficulties were inevitably measured in terms of the problems the behaviour caused for the staff rather than for the children themselves.

Unfortunately, other research (such as the *Pathways to Adoption* survey, Murch *et al.*, 1993) has followed the OPCS classification and included 'emotional and behavioural difficulties' as a 'disability'. This sometimes has the effect of obscuring the experience of children with physical, sensory and/or intellectual impairments because children who *only* have emotional/behavioural difficulties are the largest group.

As mentioned above, a further limitation of the OPCS survey is that disabled young people between the ages of 16 and 19 who are living in some form of institutional provision are unlikely to have been included in any of the four parts of the survey. The researchers calculated that this meant that approximately 3600 disabled young people were 'missing' from their statistics (Bone & Meltzer, 1989, p. 44).

Yet another limitation is that, even within the 5–15 age group, 'The OPCS survey... tends to understate the importance and size of residential care provision for these children' (Loughran *et al.*, 1992, p. 14). This came about because of the exclusion of boarding schools and of children in residential establishments who went to stay with their parents at least once a fortnight.

As secondary analysis of the study pointed out,

> Boarding schools emerge as the most important form of residential provision, yet the inclusion of their pupils in the private household survey [of disabled children] obscures this fact. Although for boarding pupils 'home' is usually elsewhere, they spend the majority of any year, and sometimes a significant proportion of their childhood, away from home. (Loughran *et al.*, p. 14)

We will further consider the role of boarding schools later in this article. A final point on the question of who was and was not included in the OPCS data concerns children with physical and/or sensory impairments. Secondary analysis of the OPCS survey of disabled children in residential establishments (including residential schools) who went home (to either birth parents or foster carers) less than once a fortnight shows that there were no children who only had physical and/or sensory impairments in this situation (Loughran *et al.*, 1992). Yet anecdotal evidence tends to contradict this; a question mark must remain therefore over whether this group of children are entirely 'missing' from the OPCS survey of children in 'communal establishments'. One explanation may be that, as the Looking After Children project commented, 'many children with physical disabilities are mistakenly regarded as having impaired intellectual capacities' (Looking After Children, 1993, p. 1). If this were the case, then the value of the OPCS survey for what it tells us about service requirements is even more limited.

What Do We Mean by the Phrase 'Living Away From Home'?

This is an important question for any attempt at a general picture of the experiences of disabled children. Of course, for the adults who shared their 'life stories' in *Gone Missing*, the answer to this question is obvious: they spent a large part of their childhood in an institutional rather than a family setting. However, in the world of statutory and voluntary agencies concerned with disabled children, the meaning of words and phrases is often bound up with legislation, administrative practices and professional frameworks. The Department of Health's guidance on implementing the Children Act as it concerns disabled children appended a useful glossary of terms which included the following definitions:

> *Accommodation:* being provided with accommodation replaces the old voluntary care concept. It refers to a service that the local authority provides to the parents of children in need, and their children. The child is not in care when s/he is being provided with accommodation: nevertheless, the local authority has a number of duties towards children for whom it is providing accommodation, including the duty to discover the child's wishes regarding the provision of acommodation and to give them proper consideration.
>
> *Care order:* an order made by the court under Section 31 (1) (a) of the Act placing the child in the care of the designated local authority. A care order includes an interim care order except where express provision to the contrary is made.
>
> *Children living away from home:* children who are not being looked after by the local authority but are nevertheless living away from home, eg, children in independent schools. The local authority has a number of duties towards such children, eg, to take reasonably practicable steps to ensure that their welfare is being adequately safeguarded and promoted.
>
> *Looked after:* a child is looked after when s/he is in local authority care or is being provided with accommodation by the local authority.
>
> (Department of Health, 1991, pp. 68–71)

If we are looking at the experiences of children who spend large amounts of their childhood away from a family setting, we are therefore concerned with

- children who are subject to a care order and placed in residential establishments;
- children who are subject to a care order and placed with foster parents, but who spend most of their childhood at boarding school and/or other forms of residential provision;

- children who have either of these two experiences, but are not actually subject to a care order;
- children who spend most of the year away at boarding school and/or other forms of residential provision;
- and children who spend long periods of their childhood in hospital or other health settings.

Some children, of course, have a combination of these experiences.

Although the Department of Health classifications given above are helpful, the way that statistics are gathered concerning disabled children is not. None of the data gathered by central government from local authorities enables the identification of the total number of disabled 'accommodated' or 'looked after' children or those subject to care orders (Department of Health and the Welsh Office, 1993, 1994; Department of Health, 1994). Nor is there any data on disabled 'children living away from home'. There are only two sorts of statistical information concerning disabled children. One relates to service provision, in that local authorities are asked to record numbers of children looked after in specialist residential provision (including residential homes, schools and 'medical or nursing care'). A major problem with this set of information is that disabled children looked after may fall into other categories of residential provision.

The second set of information relates to 'Reason for being looked after'. Guidance to local authorities issued by the Department of Health instructs them to record separately 'Children with Disabilities' who are looked after, broken down into three categories

- child with learning difficulties alone, to meet his/her family's needs;
- child with physical/sensory disabilities alone, to meet his/her family's needs;
- child with both learning and physical/sensory disabilities, to meet his/her family's needs.

For non-disabled children there are 17 categories of 'Reason for being looked after' including abuse, family homeless, child abandoned and preventive work with family for child arising from concern for child's welfare (Department of Health, 1995). Methods of recording and measuring therefore obscure disabled children's experience once again.

At a local level there seems to be no clearer picture of how many disabled children are spending long periods of time away from a family setting. Although each of a sample of eight local authorities said that they knew how many disabled children were in full-time residential provision, it was also evident that there were limits to how available, or how useful, this information was. Even the recording of the numbers was sometimes uncertain, as indicated by the following response from one authority:

> If you asked [whether we have a record of how many children are in full-time residential placements] at a corporate level the answer would be 'yes'. But if you then asked for numbers they wouldn't be able to put their hands on it. They would have to look at files held by education, social

services teams, commissioning and the people who pay the bills. We're currently trying to incorporate all these lists on one computer database. (Morris, 1995, p. 44)

Another respondent recounted how, when trying to track down how many out-of-county placements there were concerning disabled children, he had to refer to 'half a dozen lists and make about 20 different phone calls—and then I had to query their definitions of disability because they gave me details on children with behavioural difficulties who don't have impairments'.

It might have been hoped that the setting up of Disability Registers, required by the Children Act, would enable a more comprehensive picture of the number of disabled children in residential settings. However, evidence from the sample of local authorities indicated that:

- There were variations between local authorities in how they defined 'disability'.
- there were significant variations in what information was collected when registering a child in each local authority. This limits the usefulness of the registration system as a source for collecting data across local authority areas.
- Most Disability Register forms assumed that the child lived with their family and there is therefore a question mark over whether children in residential settings would be included on the Register.

We do not know enough, therefore, about either the numbers nor the circumstances in which disabled children enter a range of residential provision—whether run by education, health, social services or by independent sector organisations. The situation is unlikely to improve as statistics on 'looked after' children and those 'accommodated' under the Children Act 1989 do not separate out disabled children. The data available on disabled children collected through Disability Registers, is also unlikely to be able to separate out those in residential provision. It is currently impossible for planners and policy-makers properly to address their needs when so little is known about the size of the population concerned and the nature of their experience.

One complicating factor in any discussion about what we mean by 'children living away from their families' concerns the experience of 'respite care'. For most disabled children 'respite care' will be experienced as a few days or weeks away from the family home. However, research carried out before the implementation of the Children Act indicated that some children experience an *extensive* use of respite services, while others experience a *multiple* use of services (Robinson & Stalker, 1993, p. 56).

As Robinson & Stalker (1993) identified, 'it is in hospital and health authority units that children are most likely to have extended stays' (p. 60). The Children Act requires health providers to inform the relevant social services authority if a child is accommodated for more than three months but there has, as yet, been no national monitoring of whether this information is being passed on or how many children are involved. Evidence from the small local authority sample carried out for the *Gone Missing* research indicated that such notification was patchy.

There is also some evidence that hospices are increasingly being used to accomodate children who are not terminally ill, but who have significant impairments which require life-saving nursing care (Stein & Woolley, 1990) [3].

Research concerning disabled children who spend a lot of time away from their families needs to use the experience of childhood rather than service provision as the starting point. Gathering information from service providers tends to result in 'snapshot' pictures of services. This method is useful in that purchasers and providers will want to know levels of occupancy of and demand for, say respite care schemes, and the characteristics/needs of service users. However, if we are really to find out about disabled children's experiences, longitudinal or retrospective studies will tell us more because they enable us to track a child's experience.

It will also be important that these experiences are not totally defined in legislative or administrative categories. For example, a child who attends a boarding school and goes to some form of respite care during much or all of the school holidays may be recorded by the social services authority who pays for the respite care as receiving short-term care. Seen from the child's perspective, however, the experience is one of long-term care.

This latter point illustrates the importance of developing research methods which put the child's experience at the centre of what is being recorded. The remainder of this article concerns three important issues which emerged from the ten life stories contained in the *Gone Missing?* report—in other words issues which came out of the direct experience of adults who, as children, had spent most of their time away from a family setting.

Disabled Children are Often in 'Care' but not Formally 'In Care'

This statement reflects a common experience amongst the ten life stories. It appears that many disabled children find that their childhoods are dominated by being in residential provision of some kind, but their local authority has not formally taken parental responsibility for them.

Jake, for example, was taken into hospital when he was 2 years old, 'basically because there was nowhere else to go and they wanted to find out what was wrong with me'. He went on to explain

> Then my father died and my mother was left with my two brothers and two sisters to look after. She had no choice but to put me in residential care. There were just no facilities for disabled children. When I was two and a half they put me in another hospital where there was no medical care but where they just looked after you. I was there for 16 years.

Terry also 'went into care' at an early age, when he was 5 years old.

> I think it was to do with my parents that I got sent away. My parents are divorced now—they didn't get on too well and I think my mother

particularly just couldn't cope with having a disabled child. But at the time, I just thought it was normal to be sent away, I never gave it much thought ... Once I went away, first to the hospital school and then to the residential schools, I didn't see my parents at all, they didn't come to see me and I didn't go home in the holidays. You were just there and the years just went past.

And Laura explained,

> I spent a lot of my childhood in and out of hospital, in and out of children's homes, for one reason and another... I can't remember why I first went into a children's home but later on it was because my mum couldn't cope. The home I first went to didn't have any other disabled children but the one I went to when I was 13 did... I can remember being hit at my first home. That was bad because my dad used to hit me as well. I thought, well one place is as bad as another. He was horrid to my mum as well. I think they knew, social services, but I don't know what they did about it. My mum used to ask them to take me in.

These three accounts concern experiences in the 1960s, 1970s and 1980s, respectively. Given the similarities over a period of 30 years, can we be confident that things have changed in the 1990s?

In order to answer this question, we need further investigation of the circumstances in which disabled children enter residential provision. Secondary analysis of the OPCS study found that the more significant their impairments the less likely it was that children in residential provision were formally in care. Whereas 95% of those in Cluster 1 were formally in care (with only 24% of these being in care on a voluntary basis), 54% of those in Cluster 10 were formally in care (and 59% of these were in care on a voluntary basis).

The more significant the impairment the more likely it is that residential provision is a reaction to the parents' need for help with looking after their child and such a situation is—quite rightly—unlikely to result in the social services authority taking parental responsibility. An important research question is whether family based support services and local, mainstream education provision would make it unnecessary for disabled children to leave their family home—and whether such developments are taking place.

There is also evidence that many disabled children whose childhoods are dominated by institutional provision are unnecessarily denied the same opportunity as non-disabled children of a family life through fostering or adoption. This happens partly because their parents will not agree to fostering or adoption even though they cannot offer their children a family life and partly because social services authorities have failed to take appropriate action. Christina Lyon concluded from her research on the legal status of disabled children in hospital and residential settings that 'rarely, if ever, was the issue of family placement raised' and she was left 'with the feeling that any detailed consideration of their right to normal family living was being discarded' (Lyon, 1990, p. 83).

Jake talked about what this kind of situation meant for him:

> There was no talk about fostering or adopting because my family were around. But no-one talked about helping my mother look after me at home. She didn't have the support, she couldn't afford to stay home from work—she had to work because my father had died.

Suba remembers wanting to go to a foster family when she was at a residential school

> I remember when I was about 14 they had a case conference and there was some discussion about me being fostered, about me going to live with a family. I really really wanted it but my dad wouldn't agree.

In the case of each of the 10 'life stories'. It was unclear whether anyone in the child's life was taking responsibility for the kind of role which parents play—of fighting to get the best education for their child, the best health care, the most choices as they enter adulthood.

Terry illustrated this experience when he said

> I think also there's a question of who's got responsibility for you. If you don't see your parents from one year to the next you don't know who's responsible for you and as a child you get mixed up. There's this big massive institution—I never felt anyone was responsible for me. I always felt I was responsible for myself. I didn't feel as if anyone loved me.

The Role of Residential Education in Separating Children From their Families

Follow-up research on the OPCS survey by Sally Baldwin and Michael Hirst found that

> ... three times as many disabled as non-disabled young people were attending a residential educational establishment or had done so in the past (18 and 6 per cent respectively). Further, the most severely disabled young people were far more likely than those whose disabilities were less severe to go away to school or college. (Hirst & Baldwin, 1994, p. 19)

Parents often find that the kind of educational provision that their child requires cannot be provided locally and that residential education, sometimes many miles away, is the only thing on offer. There is also anecdotal evidence that professionals sometimes feel that sending a disabled child away to boarding school is an acceptable response to the daily hard work which often confronts parents. As one mother wrote,

> The reaction of one doctor to the worsening of Kim's condition has been 'Send him to boarding school and have him home at weekends. Then your life won't be so hard.'... When I say that this wouldn't solve any problems, I am accused of having a 'separation problem'... I find it difficult to accept

that Kim is being treated as something other than an 8-year-old child. He is *not* 'an epileptic', he is a child who has epileptic fits. *Of course* I have a 'separation problem' about the idea of my 8-year-old child going away to boarding school. (Murray, 1992, p. 146.)

There is anecdotal evidence (such as that contained in the life stories in the *Gone Missing?* report) that residential special school provision sometimes masquerades as education, but is, in fact, social care; in other words some disabled children are sent away to boarding schools because of their care needs rather than their educational needs. Moreover, boarding school provision is sometimes a response to family breakdown and/or parental rejection.

Suba, who had been rejected by her mother at birth, and experienced emotional and physical abuse throughout her childhood, felt that she was sent away to boarding school for social, as well as for educational, reasons. As an adult she feels angry that the professionals who were in contact with her did not confront the abuse she experienced.

> They knew I was in grave physical danger as a baby and they knew that things weren't right throughout by childhood but they didn't have the guts to do anything. I thought emotional and physical abuse was normal.

Sue Trickett and Frances Lee, in their work as social workers in a boarding school for children with significant learning difficulties, also found that educational provision is sometimes used as a response to social needs. They argue that, in these circumstances,

> local authorities do not follow the normal childcare principles and practice used for non-handicapped children. We have found that local authorities use boarding schools as a substitute for care, and to avoid taking responsibility for the child and provide suitable alternative provision. (Trickett and Lee, 1989.)

They describe situations where *ad hoc* and varying arrangements are made to accommodate children during the school holidays, commenting

> The intellectual impairment suffered by these young people makes it impossible for them to have any understanding of what is happening to them. The fact that their confusion and anxiety leads to their exhibiting disturbed and aggressive behaviour is hardly surprising. It compounds the difficult situation because it often leads to their rejection by holiday placements and sometimes by the school.

Anecdotal evidence suggests that 52-week placements in residential schools are increasing, a point made a number of times by Philippa Russell in her various assessments of current developments concerning disabled children (Russell, 1993, 1994). One voluntary organisation with whom contact was made during the course of researching *Gone Missing?* confirmed that one of their residential schools had recently opened a '52 week unit' in response to 'demand'. Moreover, in the course of my current research I have found that a third of schools held on a regional database of residential establishments offer 52-week placements. This same database found that some social workers were seeking residential education placements because 'the school term structure was not appropriate for the child because parents could not cope for the whole of the school holidays' (Carebase, 1993, para. 3.9). This comment reflects two phenomena: that the schools concerned were open for longer than the normal school terms; and that boarding school placements are sometimes made for social care reasons rather than educational reasons.

I am not aware of any other research which would confirm whether there is currently an increase in establishments offering 52-week placements, or explain why it is happening. If it is the case that 52-week placements are increasing, then a number of other issues also need to be put on the research and policy agenda. These include the question of whether children in 52-week placements have a social worker or other professional who regularly visits them and who will take responsibility for what is happening to them. Children who are in boarding schools may not be accorded the protection of the Children Act and may be truly 'lost' to the systems which are supposed to protect them.

For Some Disabled Young People the Question of 'Leaving Care' Never Arises

Those who are in residential provision of some kind as children often find that there is no option when they reach adulthood other than moving into adult forms of residential provision. Jake, for example, went from residential school to residential college and then, at the age of 21, found that

> After I left college, there was no other option but to go into another residential home. I thought it was the end of my life.

Laura described her experience of entering adulthood

> I came here when I was 18. They had a meeting with my mum and dad and asked me about my future. I didn't know what was on the cards. They said, there's this new place we're opening up for young people. They turned out not to be so young. There's just me and this other girl, the others are older—I think they all came from a home that had been closed down.

Paul, who had entered residential care following an accident when he was very young, found that the only thing offered to him at the school-leaving age was a home run by a major charity.

> I was very isolated again because I was the only Black person. It was a very traumatic experience being there... I was only vegetating. We had to go to a work centre during the day time—there was no choice about it. We had to do demeaning things like put string into labels.

While the 1994/95 campaign on care-leavers launched by the social work magazine *Community Care* emphasised that young people in care leave residential or foster care at a much earlier age than young people leave their family home, for disabled young people the issue is much more about the barriers to leaving residential provision at all. The failure of this campaign to include any mention of disabled young people leaving care reflects the general invisibility of this as a policy and practice issue.

We need to know more about whether local authority practice is enabling disabled young people, whose childhoods have been dominated by institutional provision of one form or another, to live independently within the community. In particular, we need to know whether the rights which disabled young people have under existing legislation, such as the 1970 Chronically Sick and Disabled Persons Act, are being accessed to enable them to live in their own home and participate within the community.

A major barrier to living independently experienced by disabled young people themselves is the fact that they often have little contact with disabled adults living independently, so they have limited expectations of what they might be able to do as adults. Moreover, the dominant notion of independence concerns doing things for yourself—and this is reflected in, for example, the Looking After Children assessment forms which are promoted as good practice by the Department of Health. This kind of assumption inhibits the ambitions for independent living which non-disabled adults have for disabled young people and the ambitions of the young people themselves.

Even for those who do manage to leave institutional provision, their childhood experiences can significantly affect their adult lives. All of the 10 people whose life stories appear in *Gone Missing?* spoke of the emotional distress which was a legacy of their childhood experiences, and three of them have received in-patient psychiatric treatment. Fiona said,

> ... the emotional damage of those earlier years continues to disable me in many ways. I still suffer particularly from long periods of depression and I find it hard to nurture myself and to reach out and make close relationships with people.

Many disabled young people who are in residential provision feel rejected and abandoned by their parents. This is commonly unacknowledged and people often grow into adulthood with significant emotional damage, particularly if they have also been abused within residential provision—as many of them have. They experience the kinds of anger, depression and sometimes serious mental health problems which non-disabled adults seek help with—yet most psychotherapists, counsellors and mental health facilities are not physically accessible for anyone with a mobility impairment and panic at the idea of providing a service for a disabled person. If that person has a communication impairment and/or learning difficulty they are particularly unlikely to receive support of this kind. Research concerning mental health services and their use needs to highlight these important issues.

Conclusions

The purpose of this article has been to generally raise questions relating to the experience of disabled children whose lives are dominated by being away from their families.

The inadequacies of most of the information and research currently available about disabled children stem primarily from the common use of the medical model of disability and the failure to include the subjective experience of children themselves. Urgent attention needs to be given to the collection of information about disabled children living away from their families to enable service planners, purchasers and providers to have a clear idea about the experiences and needs of the children concerned.

We need to know much more about the experiences of disabled children and young people, and such research must offer an opportunity for their accounts to be heard. Only when this happens will policy and practice be driven more clearly by the interests of disabled children themselves.

NOTES

[1] This was the conclusion reached by a review of research and policy concerning disabled children living away from their families (Morris, 1995). The article draws on this report and is also informed by the author's current research, funded by the Joseph Rowntree Foundation, which looks in more detail at both policy and practice concerning disabled children, and at their experiences of residential care.
[2] The highest rate of threatened or attempted suicide was found amongst the group of children who experienced fits, and who had severe behavioural difficulties and were likely also to have intellectual impairments (Loughran *et al.*, 1992, p. 37).
[3] The Joseph Rowntree Foundation has recently funded a research project, to be carried out by Dr Carol Robinson at the Norah Fry Research Centre, Bristol, to look at this issue.

REFERENCES

ALDERSON, P. (1995) *Listening to Children: children, ethics and social research* (Ilford, Barnardos).
BERESFORD, B. (1997) *Personal Accounts: involving disabled children in research* (London, HMSO).
BONE, M. & MELTZER, H. (1989) *OPCS Surveys of Disability in Great Britain, Report 3: The prevalence of disability among children* (London, HMSO).
CAREBASE PLACEMENT MATCHING AND INFORMATION SERVICE (1993) *Annual Report* (London, Carebase).
DEPARTMENT OF HEALTH (1991) *The Children Act 1989, Guidance and Regulations: Volume 6, children with disabilities* (London, HMSO).
DEPARTMENT OF HEALTH (1994) *Key Indicators of Local Authority Social Services 1991–2* (London, Government Statistical Service).
DEPARTMENT OF HEALTH (1995) *Children Looked After by a Local Authority: 1 April 1995 to 31 March 1996: Guidance Notes (Draft)* (London, Department of Health).
DEPARTMENT OF HEALTH AND THE WELSH OFFICE (1993) *Children Act Report 1992* (London, HMSO).
DEPARTMENT OF HEALTH AND THE WELSH OFFICE (1994) *Children Act Report 1993* (London, HMSO).
FITTON, P. (1994) *Listen to Me: communicating the needs of people with profound and multiple disabilities* (London, Jessica Kingsley).
HAZEL, N. (1995) 'Seen and Heard?': an examination of methods of collecting data from young people, Dissertation submitted for the Degree of Master of Science in Applied Social Research, University of Stirling.
HIRST, M. (no date) *National Survey of Young People with Disabilities: end of project report* (York, Social Policy Research Unit, University of York).

HIRST, M. & BALDWIN, S. (1994) *Unequal Opportunities: growing up disabled* (York, Social Policy Research Unit, University of York).

HIRST, M., JONES, L. & BALDWIN, S. (1990) Communication Skills and Research, in: D. ROBBINS & A. WALTER (Eds) *DH Yearbook of Research and Development 1990*, pp. 78–81 (London, HMSO).

KING, R.D., RAYNES, N.V. & TIZARD, J. (1971) *Patterns of Residential Care: sociological studies in institutions of handicapped children* (London, Routledge and Kegan Paul).

LONDON BOROUGH OF RICHMOND (1994) *Inspection of Avenue Day Centre and Normansfield Day Service: user assessor report* (London, Change).

LOOKING AFTER CHILDREN PROJECT (1993) *Bulletin No. 4: concerning disability* (Dartington, Dartington Social Research Unit).

LOUGHRAN, F., PARKER, R. & GORDON, D. (1992) *Children with Disabilities in Communal Establishments: a further analysis and interpretation of the OPCS' investigation* (Bristol, Department of Social Policy and Social Planning, University of Bristol).

LYON, C. (1990) *Living Away from Home: the legal impact on young people with severe learning difficulties* (Keele, University of Keele/Barnardos North West).

MARCHANT, R. (1996) User Views on Services for disabled children and young people and their families: Literature Summary, unpublished, prepared for Northumberland County Council.

MARCHANT, R. & PAGE, M. (1992) *Bridging the Gap: child protection work with children with multiple disabilities* (London, NSPCC).

MASON, M. & REISER, R. (1992) The medical model and the social model of disability, in: MASON, M. & REISER, R. (Eds) *Disability Equality in the Classroom: a human rights issue* (London, Disability Equality in Education).

MINKES, J., ROBINSON, C. & WESTON, C. (1994) Consulting the children: interviews with children using residential respite care services, *Disability & Society*, 9, pp. 47–57.

MORRIS, J. (1995) *Gone Missing? a research and policy review of disabled children living away from their families* (London, The Who Cares? Trust).

MURCH, M., LOWE, N., BORKOWSKI, M., COPNER, R. & GRIEW, K. (1993) *Pathways to Adoption* (London, HMSO).

MURRAY, P. (1992) 'Jessie and Kim' in: J. MORRIS (Ed.) *Alone Together: voices of single mothers* (London, The Women's Press).

PEOPLE FIRST (1994) *Outside but not Inside ... Yet! Leaving Hospital and Living in the Community: an evaluation by people with learning difficulties* (London, People First).

ROBERTS, D. (no date) *Development and Piloting of an Interview Schedule for Use with Young People with Mental Handicap* (York, Social Policy Research Unit, University of York).

ROBINSON, C. & STALKER, K. (1993) Patterns of provision in respite care and the Children Act, *British Journal of Social Work*, 23, pp. 45–63.

RUSSELL, P. (1993) *Children with Disabilities: some current issues in residential care* (London, National Children's Bureau).

RUSSELL, P. (1994) *The Children Act 1989: children and young people with learning difficulties—some opportunities and challenges* (London, Council for Disabled Children).

TRICKETT, S. & LEE, F. (1989) Children First?, *Community Care*, 26th January pp. 11–12.

STUDENT PERSPECTIVES

Disabled Children, Parents and Professionals: partnership on whose terms?

PIPPA MURRAY
University of Sheffield, Department of Educational Studies, 388 Glossop Road, Sheffield S10 2JA, UK

ABSTRACT *Taking a parental perspective, this paper explores the experience of partnership between parents of disabled children with learning difficulties and educational professionals. It is argued that until policy, legislation and practice moves from its present perspective of viewing disability as the failure of the individual to that of a perspective embracing equality of value for all, relationships between parents and professionals will be fraught with difficulties. Furthermore, it is argued that until disabled children are centrally and positively placed within the relationship between parents and professionals, the existing prejudice and oppression experienced by disabled children will dominate the relationship.*

Introduction

It is a widely held belief that within education generally and within special education in particular, a partnership between parents and professionals is both desirable for and beneficial to a child's education. Taken from a parental perspective, this paper looks at the relationship between parents of disabled children with learning difficulties and educational professionals. From the age of 5, when my disabled son first went to school, until his death at the age of 15, my son and I were involved with many educational professionals. Of those many relationships we had few partnerships.

As I shall show in this paper there is, within the literature covering home–school relationships, much speculation as to what constitutes a partnership (Mittler & McConachie, 1983; Bastiani, 1987; Pugh *et al.*, 1994). In using the term here, I am referring to relationships within which my son was positively valued in addition to being central and of foremost importance; where, in the light of his medical condition, his learning and communication difficulties, my parental knowledge was seen as crucial to forming and maintaining a relationship with him; where different roles with regard to my son were recognised and the boundaries between those roles respected by all parties; and finally, and most importantly, they were relationships with which my son was happy.

It is interesting to note that in our experience partnerships were only formed with my son's support workers—the professionals with the lowest status, least power and, in our particular case, the least professional experience. The role of the professional in preserving dominant ideology is explored by Fulcher (1999). In using the term 'educational professional' throughout this paper I am referring to relationships within a disabled child's life which involve payment by an education authority.

Although not every relationship with a support worker became a partnership, partnerships were formed with those support workers who my son and I were involved in appointing. This raises the question of who is partnering who and to what end. On reflection, in our particular case, it is evident that on the occasions that a partnership was established, it was my son who was in the role of 'chief partner' with the rest of us going alongside him in our different roles. This was also true of partnerships established, all be it rarely, outside the educational arena.

It is, of course, impossible to draw conclusions from such limited experience, but individual cases presented in a critical way can offer not only direct insight into the experience in question, but also some degree of explanation of the experience (Cohen & Manion, 1980; Yin, 1984; Merriam, 1991; Stake, 1998). In addition, individual case studies, either on their own or as part of a group, can highlight areas requiring further investigation (Morris, 1995).

In order to examine the relationship between parents of disabled children and educational professionals I shall first look at the relationship between parents and their disabled children. Parents have over the years, been considered to be part of the system of oppression affecting their experience as disabled children (Aspis, forthcoming, 2000; Campbell & Oliver, 1996). Simultaneously, parents have described the experience of family oppression on the basis of having a disabled child (Goodey, 1991; Murray & Penman, 1996; Rose, 1997). I am aware that this is a very sensitive area and, as such, has to be treated with great caution. Our disabled children are central to any relationship we, as parents, have with professionals. To ignore the nature of the relationship limits the understanding we can have of legislation, practice and policy as it has developed.

Our relationships with our disabled children are subject to the huge pressures of prevailing prejudice towards disabled people in general (Mason, 1995). In the main, our children, under the dominant medical model of disability which views disabled people as being less than perfect as a result of their impairment, are seen as intrinsically defective. How we as parents, particularly as non-disabled parents, respond to and view our children will certainly impact upon relationships we have with professionals. Such divergence is evident in literature written by parents—the demands of parents who view their disabled child positively (Goodey, 1991; Murray & Penman, 1996) are very different from those who struggle with accepting their disabled child (Hannam, 1988; Meyer, 1995). Traditionally, the way that theorists (Bowlby, 1989, 1990) have described the relationship between parent and child as an important conditioner on all relationships has placed the onus of the child's acceptance or rejection on the shoulders of the parents. This apportioning of blame is not a helpful analysis because it ignores the role of society in creating inclusion and exclusion. In this paper I shall be taking a more holistic explanation for existing mechanisms of inclusion/exclusion as a precursor to developing more inclusive alternatives.

Past Experience

What Happened to Disabled Children and their Parents in the Past?

The large scale definition of disabled people as 'sub-human' is to be found early on in the twentieth century in the great interest from medical scientists throughout America and Europe to eliminate genetic 'defects' (Oswin, 1998; Rieser, 1990; Morris, 1991). The strength of attitudes growing out of this definition was nowhere more cruelly displayed than in Germany in the 1930s where the Nazis, in their desire to create a pure master race, organised a mass euthanasia programme for disabled adults and children. This programme was the forerunner to the more infamous mass killings of Jews and Gypsies.

The complex legacy of past attitudes and practice towards disabled people in shaping present experience and expectations of parents today is evident in the following newspaper clip:

> Fatherly Love
>
> A father was spared prison and given a two-year probation sentence after trying to kill himself and his 20-year old autistic son because of pressure at home and at work. Stephen James, 48, was found not guilty of attempted murder at Manchester crown court in June.
>
> The dental technician from Rochdale was rescued by two passers-by who pulled him and his son from a car filled with exhaust fumes. (*Disability Now*, August, 1999, p. 6.)

In sharp contrast to this portrayal of parent as martyr is the equally common place picture of parent as saint—the 'exceptional mother' or the 'uncommon father'.

The images presented have little to do with individual parents, rather they are a reflection of the dominant view of our disabled children with learning difficulties as being intrinsically defective and, therefore, sub-human. From this point of view, the largely taken for granted, loving emotions a parent has for a child are distorted by others who perceive the disabled child as being unlovable. Such distortion also serves as a means of distancing others from the experience, so making parents of disabled children different from other parents. I recall the early days of my son's diagnosis as having a brain injury; a common reaction of friends on hearing of his impairment was that, while they were sure they could not 'cope' I had the necessary qualities to 'deal with it'.

To return to the historical analysis, it was common practice for parents in the late 1950s to take the advice given to them by professionals to leave their disabled children with learning difficulties in the hands of those who considered that they knew best how to look after and care for their children (Dyer, 1996; Barron, 1996). Parents were frequently told that if there was any hope for a cure for their child it would be in a hospital setting. Such policy and practice resulted in many disabled children with learning difficulties living in large institutions:

> Thirty or forty years ago the stigma of mental handicap was so marked that relatives were positively encouraged to abandon them in hospital. 'Go, and don't look back; we are the experts, we will look after her', and 'She'll be all right here; give us a ring in three months and see how she is getting on,' are the comments quoted to me by parents whose children went into hospital when the difficulties of home care became insufferable and family break down was imminent or established. (Dyer, 1996, p. 1.)

It is perhaps too easily assumed that parents leaving their children in such institutions were heartless and unloving. Children who went through the experience and lived to tell their stories report feelings of abandonment and rejection (Pugh, 1995; Barron, 1996; Hevey, 1999). At the time that the institutions were at the height of their popularity, disabled people were regarded as sick, and in need of nursing care and protection. Custodial care offered parents the relief of day-to-day care and removed the stigma of having a disabled family member. For families on low incomes it was often the only option available to them (Dyer, 1996; Hevey, 1999). Parents taking this choice had to leave their child in the hands of the experts trusting that they were doing the best thing for their child as there was little communication between the home and the hospital:

> Parents were limited to 'contact' with their child and knew little or nothing of the hospital in general. Accidents, treatment changes, ward changes and other happenings were regarded exclusively as hospital responsibility and only the very confident and self-assured would go beyond the authority of the ward sister and ask to see the consultant. Challenge of this authority by parents was seemingly unknown; they knew the system and accepted it. Their role was limited to being a Friend of the Hospital and raising money for patients' welfare and outings. (Dyer, 1996, p. 2.)

It is clear that parents did not have the right to know what was going on for their child nor to have a say in their child's treatment or lifestyle. The prevailing view was that professionals knew best. Dyer describes the way in which parents colluded with this view and in so doing repressed their feelings of guilt, shame and embarrassment:

> But in those days conversations between parents were very limited. We accepted the good fortune that our 'sick' children were being nursed; we and our families were relieved of a burden destructive to normal family life, and we colluded with the view, proffered by medical and nursing staff, that this was the best possible place and care which we would have for our children. It certainly was as far as I knew; I never doubted at this time, or after, the decision for hospitalisation for Hilary in what I had been told was the journey to her death, but where, if anywhere, I hoped a cure might ultimately be found for her condition, (Dyer, 1996, p. 34.)

Literature concerned with the family experience of having a disabled child frequently refers to parental feelings of guilt, shame and even hostility (Featherstone, 1980; Horwood, 1988; Dyer, 1996). The personal account of Hannam (1988) makes painful reading at times when he, alongside other parents, describes their feelings towards their disabled children with learning difficulties:

> I am trying to sort out my relationship with David. It was certainly never a good one, for frequently he bored me, disgusted me and even his harmless little tricks got on my nerves and could make me angry more quickly than I have believed possible. (Hannam, 1988, p. 37.)

As a counter point to negative mainstream attitudes, however, it is increasingly possible to find accounts in the literature by parents who hold a more positive view:

> There was a vacancy at the local mental handicap hospital and 'A' could be admitted that day, the almoner was prepared to take us to one, we were lucky to be offered this opportunity as places did not come up very often and with 'A' in the hospital I could go home and have another baby. I declined her offer. I had a baby. 'A' was the one I wanted not another one. (Name withheld, Murray & Penman, 1996, p. 8.)

Over the years policy and practice changed with regard to the use of long-term institutions. Public opinion and policy debates in the 1960s and 1970s, primarily formed by studies on the damaging effect to individuals of institutional life (Barton, 1959; Goffman, 1963) created a shift from large segregated institutions to smaller community-based institutions. It has been suggested that such a move was not solely based on a desire to provide a better service but was also motivated by economic considerations (Oliver, 1990; Barnes, 1991). At the same time the developing philosophy of 'normalisation in human services' influenced the ideas surrounding the transition of children and adults with learning difficulties from long stay hospitals to community care (Wolfensberger, 1972).

In the field of education corresponding changes took place. One small group of children had been excluded from the 1944 Education Act. In an attempt to rectify this the 1970 Education Act stipulated that the notion of 'ineducable' disappear from educational language and be replaced with the term 'ESN(S)'—severely educationally subnormal. This change of terminology was accompanied by a corresponding shift of responsibility for these disabled children from the health service to education departments.

Post-war Legislation

How Did the Legislation Affect the Relationship Between Parents and Professionals?

Compensatory ideology has dominated theory, policy, legislation and practice in the home–school field for a long time in post-war Britain (Bastiani, 1987). The Plowden Report of 1967, which has set the scene for policy and practice of home–school relationships, developed the idea that it was the attitude of parents and the interest they showed in their child's educational progress which outweighed external factors such as family income in influencing a child's educational career:

> ... if the least co-operative parents rose to the level of the most co-operative, the effect would be much larger than if the worst schools rose to the level of the best or the least prosperous parents to the level of the most prosperous ... (Plowden Report, cited in Bastiani, 1987, p. 92.)

The Plowden Report gave official sponsorship to the belief that the reform of home–school relationships and practices was important, and that improved communication between parents and schools could lead to the significant improvement in the school performance of many children, particularly those who were then regarded as 'underachieving'. Thus, whilst schools had the primary task of educating children, they were also given the task of compensating for those home circumstances and home environments which were perceived as providing little support or stimulus for learning. In locating the problem of 'failing' pupils out of the school and within the family, schools were legitimately able to avoid taking responsibility for pupils who were not succeeding within the education system. Taken to an individual level, teachers were given the room to avoid self-critical reflection of their teaching practice, and simply blame the parents for the failure or disaffection of their child.

The Warnock Report of 1978 took the concept of home–school relationships further by emphasising the importance a partnership between professionals and parents could have on the education of disabled children. In keeping with the ideology behind the Plowden Report, such a relationship is based upon the notion that it is the professionals who carry the knowledge and expertise:

> These teachers will be responsible for devising programmes which are suitable for the parents to carry out. They will help parents to work with their children. By working directly with the children they will themselves provide a model of how such programmes can be effectively carried out. (Warnock Report, 1978, p. 152.)

The expectation that parents should take on an educational role, based on professional advice, with regard to their disabled child was in keeping with expectations of all parents (Pugh *et al.*, 1994). Warnock added to this with regard to disabled children, however, as she also gave teachers the task of helping parents love their disabled child. There is here an echo of some of the difficulties we saw earlier which can arise between a parent and their disabled child within our present culture:

> Parents of an ESN child may be assailed by guilt, shame, frustration and disappointment but almost always they will want to listen to someone who is on their side in efforts to love and understand the child. (Warnock Report, 1978, p. 15.)

The Warnock Report reinforced the idea not just of the professional as expert but also that of the intrinsic deficit nature of disability. Viewed in this way disability becomes the problem and therefore the responsibility of the individual:

Some children with disabilities are more resilient than others in striving to overcome them. (Warnock Report, 1978, p. 151.)

It has also left a legacy whereby it is almost impossible for children unable to show that they are learning or for children who have degenerative conditions to succeed within the education system. The notion of educational progress, however slow, is central to the report:

> The purpose of education for all children is the same; the goals are the same. But the help that individual children need in progressing towards them will be different. Whereas for some the road they have to travel towards the goals is smooth and easy, for others it is fraught with obstacles. For some the obstacles are so daunting that, even with the greatest possible help, they will not get very far. Nevertheless, for them too, progress will be possible, and their educational needs will be fulfilled, as they gradually overcome one obstacle after another on the way. (Warnock Report, 1978, p. 5.)

Such a view of education, with the emphasis on the acquisition of new skills and the achievement of certain goals was reinforced by Warnock in 1985, when she emphasised the notion that education is about the tangible achievement of new skills:

> But that he can do something he couldn't do before is proof that he is really being educated: and this is as true whether his new skill is as complicated as building an aeroplane or as simple as tying his own shoe laces. (Warnock, 1985, p. 6.)

To have this as the basis for the education system is to create a tension between some children and their schooling experience as it is simply not possible for certain disabled children to be seen to be achieving. Parents are then placed in a position of having to ally themselves with a system which views their child as failing thereby jeopardising their relationship with their child, or to ally themselves with their child and thereby introduce an element of struggle in their relationship with the education system. Whichever choice they make will undoubtedly have an effect not only on their relationship with their child, but also on their relationships with individual professionals.

Later Education Acts have given parents greater involvement in the education system. The 1981 Act gave parents of disabled children rights to be involved with the assessment procedures by informing them of and including them in: pre-referral discussions; referral procedures; assessments; decisions over placement and provision and review processes. Local Education Authorities (LEAs) were given the duty of seeking parental advice and consulting with parents before making a decision on which school a child should attend. The Act also promoted the integration of disabled children by stating that more disabled children should be educated in their local mainstream school. However, LEAs were given three caveats which have been widely used in decisions over placement when parental wishes conflict with their own. These caveats are that a child should attend their local mainstream school if it is thought to be:

(1) in the best interest of the child's education;
(2) the most efficient use of resources;
(3) does not have a detrimental effect on the education of the other pupils in the class.

Subsequent legislation, although appearing to give parents a greater say in matters concerning their child's education, has left these three stipulations. For parents of disabled children with perceived severe learning difficulties, communication impairment and/or emotional and behavioural difficulties these three points remain a stumbling block to the practice of partnership (Mason, 1998).

Embodied within these caveats is one of the major problems with the concept of parents as partners, i.e. that of power. Whilst LEAs and their professionals have legislative backing for any decision they make, parents can have little influence in cases where they disagree with decisions made by the LEA. This was clearly demonstrated in 1997 when the High Court backed the LEA in the case Crane v Lancashire (Brandon, 1997). In this case, the parents of a 14-year-old disabled boy with learning difficulties were trying to secure a mainstream education for their son. Having failed in their attempt to secure this through the tribunal system they took the case to the High Court. In his summing up statement Mr Justice Popplewell dismissed the case as follows:

> ... it seems to me that the tribunal, which is a specialist tribunal presided over by somebody with some legal qualification, have, in fact, in a short and summary conclusion arrived at a decision which is unchallengeable before me. It is not necessary to explain to the Bar, but it may be necessary as there are lay clients involved, that I should say I do not sit as an appeal myself having to decide whether The Elms or the Tarleton is the appropriate place. That is for the Tribunal and initially for the education authority, the tribunal having heard all the evidence and all the arguments. Only if I find that the law has been misapplied, or it is a conclusion to which no tribunal could have come, can I interfere. Accordingly I shall dismiss this appeal. (Court Transcript, 1997, p. 20.)

It is interesting to note that a main thrust of the Tribunal's argument that Niki should not be placed in a mainstream school was based on his inability to keep up with his peers:

> The LEA said that the professionals in the form of the Head Teacher, the Support Teacher, the Special Support Assistant and the Special Needs Adviser all had reservations as to the success of Niki's integration into mainstream primary schooling. The gap between the work Niki was doing and his attainments in them, compared to what his peer group was achieving, was widening. (LEA's Tribunal Submission cited in Court Transcript, 1997, p. 9.)

The parent's voice was small and, in the end, insignificant in the face of the power of the professionals backed by the legislation and the legislative process.

The 1988 Education Reform Act made parents consumers through their right to choose which school their child went to, but it also made schools more selective of their pupils with the establishment of a National Curriculum, and a programme of assessment and testing for all pupils in maintained schools, including special schools. Results of teacher's assessments and standardised national tests are fully reported to parents together with information on the average results attained both in their locality and nationally (ACE, 1996). The 1993 Education Act and Code of Practice on the Identification and Assessment of Special Educational Needs (DfEE, 1994) highlighted areas relating to special needs provision. Superficially, it appeared that parents were being given some power by the establishment of independent tribunals which were set up to deal with intractable disagreements between parents and LEAs. In practice, however, an increase in the power of parents in one area was eroded by changes in legislation and practice in other areas, e.g. league tables, local management, increasing selection and opting out of LEA control (Jordan & Goodey, 1996). In this context, we can see how parents are actually being put against each other in order to compete for resources. Such fragmentation can only lead to diminishing power for all parents.

It is evident that while post-war legislation has given us a rhetoric of 'partnership', 'participation' and 'co-operation' it has also given Local Authorities, and their employees a free hand in the management and distribution of resources. Whilst this does not necessarily preclude partnership it suggests that partnerships can only exist where parents agree with placement decisions. I would argue that such a fragile agreement does not constitute partnership.

Prior to relationships with educational professionals, parents of disabled children will have come into contact with professionals from health and/or social services. The following section explores the early parental experience of relationships with non-educational professionals.

Parental Experience of Professionals

What Happens to Parents Before we Meet Educational Professionals?

It is well documented that the time of diagnosis of impairment is often very traumatic for parents (Jupp, 1992; Mason, 1995). This is hardly surprising in light of the apparently natural instinct that we have children who are healthy, happy and progress easily through the different stages of childhood into adulthood:

> There are too the traditional concerns of generations of parents: that children should be healthy and have access to a good education, developing skills that will enable them to get a job and become independent adults ... (Pugh *et al.*, 1994, p. 9.)

The corresponding shock we get on hearing the news that our child has an impairment may be compounded by the way in which we are told and the treatment we receive from professionals at this time:

> Hannah was born in the middle of the night and shortly after went blue and was sent to the special baby unit. The following morning nobody would tell me anything and they wouldn't let me see her. So I went and sat outside the special baby unit. Somebody put their head round the door and said, 'Where's the little Mongol?' Two junior doctor came in and examined the baby, and talked about things like lines on the palms, and I wondered what he meant. My husband arrived in afternoon with my other daughters and he was whisked away. He came back and asked me to go for a walk with him. As we went down the corridor he said, 'She's got Down's Syndrome'. I said, 'God, is that all', because I'd got her dead and buried by then. The junior doctor who told us was virtually in tears. He hadn't told parents before. When Hannah was born they suggested we go home and leave the baby in hospital whilst we thought about whether we wanted to keep the baby. (Evans, 1996, p. 22.)

On reading this it is easy to think that we are hearing about the account of a parent's experience that dates back 30 or 40 years or more; in fact, Hannah is now only 12 years old.

Due to the fact that we are all the products of a segregated education, as non-disabled parents we may have had little or no contact with disabled people before having a disabled child. This puts us in a vulnerable position when we come into contact with professionals who we assume have more experience and knowledge than us:

> At that time I didn't know anything about a handicapped child, and so everything they was telling me I thought well, they must know what they're talking about, so I put my trust in them and just followed whatever they said. (Goodey, 1991, p. 106.)

Coming from any one perspective as I am presently doing, it is easy to ignore other perspectives unless we hold a larger picture in view. In this case the larger perspective is the way in which disabled people have been systematically oppressed throughout the ages. Another perspective which I might easily ignore is that of the professional who will also have been influenced by the prejudice and oppression embodied in the medical model of disability. Professionals, by the very nature of their status, are thought to hold knowledge particular to their profession, which non-professionals do not have easy access to. When a professional view is challenged, then the very basis of the professional identity is at stake. It is very easy in such a situation for conflict to arise:

> They distrusted my word, they didn't believe me, so then I started distrusting them. That was when it really all started, and I think Miss P's got me down as a trouble maker ... (Goodey, 1991, p. 108.)

Vincent argues that the mixed messages about our children we receive from a range of professionals may lead to the increased likelihood of conflict with all professionals:

> The sense of having to battle to improve or just protect one's position and belongings, increases the likelihood of conflicts between parents and teachers starting because the parent is defending his/her child on non-educational matters. (Vincent, 1996, p. 81.)

Such conflict has arisen in spite of legislation and policy advocating the benefits of partnership, particularly between parents of disabled children and professionals:

> We have insisted throughout this report that the successful education of children with special educational needs is dependent upon the full involvement of their parents; indeed, unless the parents are seen as equal partners in the educational process the purpose of our report will be frustrated. (Warnock, 1978, p. 150.)

The complexities of parent/professional partnership are enormous—it appears that parents have an expectation of professionals being able to help and support them, professionals want to give help, the language of the legislation encourages us to think this will be possible and yet, in practice, there is frustration and confusion on both sides of the relationship (Goodey, 1991; Murray & Penman, 1996; Warnock, 1985).

The following section looks at what is meant by partnership and the different models of partnership which have developed in the education system.

Partnership

What Do we Mean When we Talk of Partnerships Between Parents and Professionals?

Within the realm of education it is now the ordinary experience of parents of young children to have frequent contact with their child's school. Such contact typically decreases as the child grows older with parents attending yearly 'parent/teacher' evenings. This contact, whilst perhaps being pleasant, informative and helpful for both parents and teachers, is not necessarily partnership.

Partnership is a term that is used to describe many different kinds of relationships. It is used both in personal relationships such as marriage and in business-like relationships such as between lawyers and doctors. People enter into temporary and permanent partnerships. Some partnerships are based on informal agreements, whilst others have formal legal contracts and obligations. Some partnerships include the notion of a power differential, e.g. senior and junior partner in a law firm. Most partnerships imply a common goal or interest whether or not that goal is specified or remains vague. Most partnerships imply some degree of choice: if for any reason one of the parties wants to change the arrangement then this is seen as possible, if not always desirable, by the other.

Partnerships between parents and educational professionals do not fit into any of these categories. Neither the parent nor the teacher necessarily chooses the partnership—we certainly do not choose it on an individual basis as both parents and teachers are 'given' each other. We cannot end the relationship when and if we might want to, neither can we extend it if we think it is working well; within the relationship it is assumed that our common goal is one of in 'the best interest of the child'—as this is an entirely subjective matter it is a goal that cannot be assumed. A complicating factor for a partnership between a parent and a professional is that of the different nature of their long-term responsibilities within the partnership. A parent is a parent for life and has to assume responsibility for many aspects of their child's life. A teacher is in relationship with a child and his/her parent for a matter of years at the most with the main professional responsibility lying within the school. In addition, a teacher holds only educational responsibility. Such differences of the very nature of the relationship with the child are bound to have an effect on the relationship formed between parent and professional.

Jones (1998) describes five parent/partnership models which have developed over the last twenty years: the 'expert model', the 'transplant model', the 'consumer model', the 'empowerment model' and, finally, the 'negotiating model'. In following the outline of these models it becomes apparent that there has indeed been a shift of perspective from that of the professional giving knowledge and the parent being the passive recipient of information to that of a process of negotiation taking place between parent and professional. In spite of this development Jones concludes that:

> ... the definition of need is still predominantly based on addressing what is viewed as an individual problem. This pervades the teaching process, the categorisation of children, assessment and the professional practice. The rhetoric of 'partnership' and legislation may leave underlying value judgements unchanged. (Jones, 1998, p. 53.)

It is perhaps useful at this stage to look at practice which is considered to be compatible with the rhetoric. Reports from the Office for Standards in Education (OFSTED) have praised schools for their partnerships with parents when they have shown evidence of responding to parental requests quickly. When parents have received regular newsletters with notice of forthcoming events which might be of interest to parents. Where schools have given responsibility to one member of staff for developing home-school liaison. Where parents are given clear information on their child's progress with the opportunities for follow-up discussion should the parent desire. Where there is good use of home-school contact methods such as regular use of home-school diaries. Where there is development of parental involvement in the teaching of their child through the setting up of libraries for books, toys and games (Blamires, 1997). Although such practice is time consuming for teachers who are presently hard pressed with large class numbers and the delivery of a national curriculum it is relatively easy for schools to implement without affecting the status quo with regard to the power relationship between parents and schools. There is room here for confusion and friction to arise between parents and teachers. On the one hand, whilst teachers are perhaps putting time and effort into projects they define as encouraging parental involvement it is possible that parents feel that their child's needs are not being met. The resulting mutual incomprehension of each others situation serves as a barrier to partnership.

Another crucially important factor when considering the nature of home-school relations is that the person of chief concern, the person about whom the partnership is founded, is missing from the partnership equation. Although some attention has been paid to children's rights within the education system and reference made to the child in the legislation (Armstrong, 1995) the notion of exploring partnership with the child central to the relationship has so far been ignored.

Ways Ahead

Might There be a Better Way of Doing Things?

It is commonly assumed that children in general, and disabled children with learning difficulties in particular, should not be concerned with the nature of their education; rather they should passively receive what is put in front of them. The final section of this paper looks at the possibility of placing the child with learning difficulties in the position of 'chief partner'.

In a study on the relationships between children with serious medical conditions, parents and their teachers it was found that some children, 'despite sometimes extensive absences and poor prognosis, were fully included in their school community' (Norris & Closs, 1999). The majority of children and their parents, however, felt excluded or marginalised. Of those children who were fully included, good relationships between teachers and pupils, and teachers and parents were seen to be a fundamentally necessary ingredient. The issues highlighted by this study are of relevance to all children: a poor medical prognosis for a child simply throws the questions and concerns for all children into a sharp focus. A major impediment to a child's inclusion in the class and, therefore, the school, were the fears and anxieties of the teacher concerned. Such fears and anxieties, although perhaps understandable, are allowed to dominate in a system which does not value all children equally. It seems that a relationship between a number of adults, in whatever their role, can only begin to come near to being a 'partnership' if respect for the individual child is at the heart of all the adults concerned.

> She (headmistress) said to me, 'I've learnt a little bit along the way, from John. There was something I didn't know before and now I know it, so I've had an education. That is what education is. (Goodey 1991, p. 38.)

The mutuality of the relationship between head teacher and pupil expressed here places the disabled child with learning difficulties at the centre of the educational relationship.

Conclusions

As has been shown in this paper, the relationship between parents of disabled children with learning difficulties and educational professionals is one which is fraught with issues of social conditioning and power. The word partnership has been used and misused within this context to such an extent that it now carries little real meaning. The length and breadth of the distance we have to go to even begin to approach a meaningful relationship between parents and educational professionals which benefits our children is enormous. In my own parenting experience I recall the confusion of the early years; confusion emanating from the conflict between the natural bond I had with my son, the proof I had that, simply by his existence, he was of equal value to any other human being. This stood in sharp contrast to my own past segregated experience based upon the predominant ideology within our culture that to be disabled with learning difficulties is to be 'lesser than'. I was fortunate that my early years of parenting coincided with the time that disabled adults were developing and publicising the social model of disability which states that people with impairment are disabled, not by their bodies, but by society. Through this explanation I was able to begin to understand the different strands at play—my positive experience of relationship with my son alongside my past more negative assumptions and the wider, generally negative, messages about him I was receiving at that time. Our experience was that it was only possible for partnerships to be formed when professionals, whilst simultaneously doing their very best for my son, were able to value and enjoy him without wanting him to change in order that he fit into the current education system. From this perspective, it is first necessary to concentrate upon the value placed upon the life of a disabled child with learning difficulties in order to establish 'partnership'. It appears that a necessary precursor to valuing an individual's life is simply that of enjoying being with that individual. Such a starting point is hinted at by the following parent when she talks about her disabled son's new teacher:

> For a start she liked him, that was the main thing ... (cited in Todd & Higgins, 1998, p. 233.)

REFERENCES

ACE (1996) *Special Education Handbook—the law on children with special needs*, 7th edn (London, Advisory Centre For Education).
ARMSTRONG, D. (1995) *Power and Partnership in Education* (London, Routledge).
ASPIS, S. (forthcoming 2000) Inclusive Education—Disabled Children's Issues and Rights, in: P. MURRAY & J. PEYMAN (Eds) *Telling Our Own Stories – Reflections on Family Life in a Disabling World* (Sheffield, Parents with Attitude).
BARNES, C. (1991) *Disabled People in Britain and Discrimination—a case for anti-discrimination legislation* (London, Hurst & Co.).
BARRON, D. (1996) *A Price to be Born* (Huddersfield, Charlesworth).
BARTON, R. (1959) *Institutional Neuroses* (Bristol, Wright).
BASTIANI, J. (1987) From Compensation ... to Participation? A brief analysis of changing attitudes in the study and practice of home-school relations, in: J. BASTIANI (Ed.) *Parents and Teachers 1—perspectives on home–school relations* (Windsor, NFER-Nelson).
BLAMIRES, M. (1997) *Parent–Teacher Partnership* (London, David Fulton).
BOWLBY, J. (1989) *The Making and Breaking of Affectional Bonds* (London, Routledge).
BOWLBY, J. (1990) *Child Care and the Growth of Love* (London, Penguin).
BRANDON, D. (1997) *The Invisible Wall—Niki's fight to be included* (Hesketh Bank, Parents with Attitude).
CAMPBELL, J. & OLIVER, M. (1996) *Disability Politics: understanding our past, Changing our future* (London, Routledge).
COHEN, L. & MANION, L. (1980) *Research Methods in Education* (London, Croom Helm).
COURT TRANSCRIPT (1997) *Peter and Wendy Crane v. Lancashire County Council* (London, Smith Bernal Reporting Limited).

DEPARTMENT FOR EDUCATION AND EMPLOYMENT (DfEE) (1994) *Code of Practice on the Identification and Assessment of Special Educational Needs* (London, DfEE Publication, Centre).
DISABILITY NOW (August, 1999) News Review, p. 6.
DYER, B. (1996) *Seeming Parted* (Middlesex, New Millennium).
EVANS, K. (1996) Hannah, in: *Mencap: Lessons From Our Lives* (London, Beacon Press).
FEATHERSTONE, H. (1980) *A Difference in the Family—life with a disabled child* (New York, Basic Books Inc.).
FULCHER, G. (1999) *Disabling Policies?—a comparative approach to education policy and disability* (Sheffield, Philip Armstrong).
GOFFMAN, E. (1963) *Stigma—notes on the management of spoiled identity* (London, Penguin Books).
GOODEY, C. (1991) *Living in the Real World* (London, Twenty One Press).
HANNAM, C. (1988) *Parents and Mentally Handicapped Children* (Bristol, Bristol Classical Press).
HORWOOD, W. (1988) *Skallagrig* (London, Penguin).
JONES, C. (1998) Early intervention: the eternal triangle?—issues relating to parents, professionals and children, in: C. ROBINSON & K. STALKER (Eds) *Growing Up with Disability* (London, Jessica Kingsley).
JORDAN, L. & GOODEY, C. (1996) *Human Rights and School Change—The Newham Story* (Bristol, CSIE).
JUPP, S. (1992) *Making the Right Start* (Hyde, Opened Eye).
MASON, M. (1995) Breaking of relationships, *Present Time*, January, pp. 3–7.
MASON, M. (1998) *Forced Apart—the case for ending compulsory segregation* (London, Alliance for Inclusive Education).
MERRIAM, S. (1991) *Case Study Research in Education—a qualitative approach* (Oxford, Jossey-Bass).
MEYER, D.J. (Ed.) (1995) *Uncommon Fathers—reflections on raising a child with a disability* (Bethesda, MD, Woodbine House).
MITTLER, P. & MCCONACHIE, H. (1983) *Parents, Professionals and Mentally Handicapped People: approaches to partnership* (London, Croom Helm).
MORRIS, J. (1991) *Pride Against Prejudice: a personal politics of disability* (London, Women's Press).
MORRIS, J. (1995) *Gone Missing?—a research policy review of disabled children living away from their families* (London, The Who Cares? Trust).
MURRAY, P. & PENMAN, J. (Eds) (1996) *Let Our Children Be—a collection of stories* (Sheffield, Parents With Attitude).
NORRIS, C. & CLOSS, A. (1999) Child and parent relationships with teachers in schools responsible for the education of children with serious medical conditions, *British Journal of Special Education*, 26, pp. 29–33.
OLIVER, M. (1990) *The Politics of Disablement* (London, Macmillan).
OSWIN, M. (1984) *They Keep Going Away: a critical study of short-term residential care services for disabled children* (London, King Edward's Hospital Fund for London).
PLOWDEN REPORT (1967) *Children and their Primary Schools* (London, HMSO).
PUGH, A. (1995) *Old School Ties*, BBC TV, Channel 4.
PUGH, G., DE'ATH, E. & SMITH, C. (1994) *Confident Parents, Confident Children—policy and practice in parent education and support* (London, National Children's Bureau).
RIESER, R. (1990) Disabled history or a history of the disabled, in: M. MASON & R. RIESER (Eds) *Disability Equality in the Classroom: a human rights issue* (London, Disability Equality in Education).
ROSE, H. (1997) *Tom—a gift in disguise* (Findhorn, the Findhorn Press).
STAKE, R. (1998) Case studies, in: N. DENZIN & Y. LINCOLN (Eds) *Strategies of Qualitative Inquiry* (London, Sage).
TODD, E. & HIGGINS, S. (1998) Powerlessness in professional and parent partnerships, *British Journal of Sociology of Education*, 19, pp. 227–236.

WARNOCK, M. (1978) *Special Educational Needs—report of the Committee of Enquiry into the Education of Handicapped Children and Young People* (London, HMSO).
WARNOCK, M. (1985) *Teacher, teach thyself: a new professionalism for our schools*, The Richard Dimbleby Lecture (London, BBC).
WOLFENSBERGER, W. (1972) *The Principle of Normalisation in Human Services* (Toronto, Ont, National Institute on Mental Retardation).
YIN, R. (1984) *Case Study Research—design and methods* (London, Sage).

Where Are the Children's Experiences? Analysing Social and Cultural Exclusion in 'Special' and 'Mainstream' Schools

J. M. DAVIS[1] & N. WATSON[2]

[1]*RUHBC, University of Edinburgh Medical School, Teviot Place, Edinburgh EH8 9AG, UK and* [2]*Department of Nursing Studies, University of Edinburgh, Edinburgh EH8 9LL, UK*

ABSTRACT *In this paper we employ ethnographic data to illustrate that disabled children encounter discriminatory notions of 'normality' and 'difference' in both 'special' and 'mainstream' schools, and that these experiences relate to both the structural forces in schools, and the everyday individual and cultural practices of adults and children. In contrast to much of the literature in the field, this paper examines the everyday life experiences of adults and disabled children from their own perspective. We highlight disabled children's own criticisms of 'special' and 'mainstream' schools to illustrate the fluid nature of disabled children's lives within educational settings. We argue that schools will be prevented from becoming fully inclusive until adults who control schools take account of children's views of specific educational processes and until educational policy makers adopt a more nuanced multi-level approach to inclusion. Children should be enabled to challenge the structural, cultural and individual conditions which create disability.*

Introduction

There is general agreement that the experiences of disabled children in the UK have changed rapidly as a direct result of social transformation in the past two decades. For example, there are now more disabled children educated in mainstream schools than was the case in the past, disabled children are sitting public examinations, and moving on into further and higher education. They are, in the main, no longer locked away in isolated, residential settings. However, the integration and inclusion of disabled children is far from complete.

This process has encountered many barriers. The tendency within writing on 'special education' is to explain the creation of these barriers in relation to marketplace educational policy which essentialises difference (Slee, 1996a). For example, it is argued that integration in 'UK schools' [1] is being blocked because structural changes, such as devolved management and national league tables have created competition between administrators, teachers, parents and children (Clark *et al.*, 1997). Many writers have argued that notions of equity have been downplayed in the face of right-wing ideology (Riddell, 1996). This writing mirrors arguments in the 1980s, which highlighted the conflict in the UK between right-wing market-based reforms of education and left-wing support for comprehensive schooling (Ball, 1987; Dale, 1989; Hargreaves, 1989; Lawton 1989).

This stand off does not take us very far when examining issues of inclusion because discussions surrounding ideology tend to be privileged over a qualitative empirical understanding of disabled children's lives. It is rare to find work that examines the everyday processes through which those who implement educational policies alter them as they put them into practice (Bowe & Ball, 1992; Riddell, 1996). Moreover, it is even rarer to find work that approaches the subject from the perspective of the disabled child. [Two exceptions would be Fairbairn & Fairbairn (1992), Alderson & Goodey (1998)].

It appears to us that much of the literature homogenises the lives of adults and children in schools. They are characterised as only responding to structural influences within their life worlds. The literature concentrates on social policy issues at the expense of gaining insights into the diverse everyday perspectives and practices of teachers and children. In contrast, this paper examines the everyday life experiences of adults and children in 'special' and 'mainstream' schools from their own perspective. By cross-culturally comparing ethnographic data from a number of 'special' and 'mainstream' schools we are able to highlight a variety of issues which create exclusion (see Davis, 1998; Corker & Davis, 2000; Davis *et al.*, 2000 for a fuller outline of our research approach). We illustrate that disabled children encounter discriminatory notions of 'normality' and 'difference' in both 'special' and 'mainstream' schools, and that these experiences relate not simply to the structural forces that impinge on schools and teachers, but also to the everyday individual and cultural practices of adults and children. Further more, we present data which presents disabled children as critical social actors. Through this we are able to highlight disabled children's own criticisms of schools and to illustrate the fluid nature of disabled children's lives within educational settings.

Institutionalisation of Difference

As soon as we entered a school, all staff, head teachers, learning support teachers, classroom teachers, auxiliaries, occupational therapists, physiotherapists, music therapists and many others would begin to label the children for us. The idea of 'disabled' children being distinct from other children was made clear; so this teacher in a 'special' school told us:

Note 21/01/98:

Our children don't understand what an aeroplane is. They hear it but they don't know what size it is. Could be the shape of an elephant for all they know. For example, when I asked them what a potato looked like they described a packet, meaning smash potato, not a real potato. And it's this problem you've got to get over. It's a case of trying to fill in the gaps and especially in terms of social cues. A lot of our children just don't understand what the social rules are and we have to get that across to them.

Over a number of settings we encountered this type of explanation. We were constantly told how different the children were to 'us.' Often, as above, these differences were based on value judgements. For example, this teacher appeared to be unaware that the children's comments about potatoes may owe more to material/class issues than whether their impairment prevented them from knowing the difference between 'real' or packet potatoes. Many teachers fail to reflexively question their own assumptions (Davis et al., 2000) and the construction of knowledge within schools is subjective (Corker, 1999).

It is, however, important to point out that these subjective views reflect the views of society as a whole. The medical model perspective, which concentrates on children's impairments, is found in much of the writings and policy on the education of disabled children (Riddell, 1996). In the case of some children the imposition of medically defined and adult-imposed notions of difference and normality lead to their identity only being described in terms of labels derived from the field of educational psychology. For example, on our first visit to a unit within a 'mainstream' school we were introduced to Patrick:

Note 24/2/98

We were sitting down discussing the operation of the unit with Gill (the head of the unit) when a child entered the unit. The teacher called out to him.

Gill: Patrick, come over here and tell these people why you're in the unit,

Patrick (looks down and mutters under his breath.)

Gill: Come on Patrick, tell them.

Patrick: A've, A've, A've, A've A've got Tourettes Miss.

Gill: And what does that mean Patrick.

Patrick: It means A dinae behaved miss.

Patrick has his identity imposed on him in a way that not only tells him very clearly and in an authoritative manner what he is, but also what he must be. At the same time Gill is not interested in letting us as researchers come to our own conclusions concerning Patrick. The children are expected to comply with the definition, with the status imposed on them. They are told that they are different, to naturalise that difference and for that difference to become part of their lifeworld.

Thus, processes of labelling and differentiation mark disabled children as different in both 'special' and 'mainstream' settings.

The Institutionalisation of Normality

There is, however, a constant tension between the above notions of difference imposed by the staff (or in some cases parents) and their wish that children should act 'normal'. That is, the children were constantly reminded that they were essentially different from their non-disabled peers, but they were also compelled to conform to specified ways of speaking, ways of walking, table manners and so on.

> *Note 2/2/98*
>
> Mr Z tells Morag off for constantly fixing her hair and putting her hands in her eyes, and he also tells Dibly off for putting his hands in his eyes.
>
> *Mr Z (To Morag)*: If I said spend a minute in detention for every time you had your hand in your mouth Morag would you stop?
>
> *Andrew interrupts*: Probably not.

Often children's hands or bodies were physically restrained by staff in an attempt to demonstrate to them the 'correct' behaviour (Davis *et al.*, 2000). For example, we witnessed members of staff employ techniques of physical restraint as they attempted to control the children's bodily actions. The staff in a variety of schools were trained in these techniques for reasons of safety and protection, but they were often used to control non-confrontational mannerisms, such as body rocking and head shaking. Rowley (1992) has argued that such practices act as barriers to full integration. The child is forced to fit into already existing educational and social processes and practices, which afford little space for the investigation or understanding of difference. This process is not so surprising when considered in the context that most research with disabled children has been preoccupied with differentiating children on the basis of their impairments, 'measuring children's bodies and minds against physical and cognitive norms' (Priestley, 1998). That is, it is not surprising that adults in schools pathologise disabled children when their lives have also been homogenised in both social and medical research (Shakespeare & Watson, 1998). This research has, in the main, been dominated by ideas of dependence and exclusion. Emphasis has also been placed on providing advice for best practice for working with children with specific impairments. There has been little attention paid to the social or cultural barriers that disabled children face everyday or to challenging the perception that children with certain impairments are always better off in schools for children with these impairments:

> *Note 4/11/97*
>
> They [disabled children] try to cope in the mainstream, but they just can't. They can't fit in, in the end, they all come to us.

A view persisted that it was the role of teachers to correct disabled children's 'abnormalities' and at times the 'correct' behaviour was linked to a narrative of dependency on non-disabled people:

Field note 2/2/98:

Lydia: We teach the children that they should be polite to the public, that they should use the public for necessary information but always to be polite. The problem is if one blind child isn't polite to the public then you can give blind people a bad name and then they might not help other blind people.

Disabled children are taught a discourse of dependency and charity that defines them as reliant on others. Although these normalising discourses were more prevalent in 'special' schools we also found that the same cultural process occurred in 'mainstream' schools:

Note 20/11/98

Teacher: Becky, well we are not sure about Becky's behaviour, 'em like whether it's appropriate, if you know what a mean. She gets bullied but were not sure if it really is bullying because she seems to like getting attention, eh so she does things to the boys and they don't like it so they react so last week she got coke poured on her to calm her down.

Following this conversation we learned that Becky was now spending her morning break and lunch times in the learning support base so that she did not get bullied and was being given individualised training in conflict avoidance strategies, as suggested by an educational psychologist. When asked by the researcher how she would have resolved the situation, Becky suggested that she would like to go out in the playground if action was taken to control the boys:

Becky: The head teachers should go ti them and tell them ti stop it or if they don't they'd get excluded fur it.

Above, the teacher uses the term 'appropriate' to denote 'normal' behaviour, she pathologises Becky's behaviour taking little account of the role of the boys. In contrast, Becky puts forward her own suggesting as to how the teachers could resolve this 'inappropriate' interaction. Becky is able to resist her teacher's interpretation of her interaction with the boys. This suggests that we, as academics, should not think that children passively accept adult discourses concerning normality. Indeed, Andrew, in the quote above, reinforces this conclusion with his perception that Lucy is capable of ignoring Mr Z's threats. However, despite this ability, Becky is not asked how she would solve the problem or how she sees the problem. Instead, she is ignored, whilst the boy's behaviour is normalised and not seen as requiring attention. That is, not only did we find, as Adams *et al.* (2000, p. 239) have found, that adult discourses concerning 'normality' mean that 'Any fault lies within the child not the teacher', but we also found that any fault is often found in the child not the peer group.

Becky's experience reflects that of many of the children we met, their opportunities to be fully included in the same social spaces as other children were restricted because many learning support staff and educational psychologists did not take account of sub-cultural relationships between children. Whilst the staff articulated the rhetoric of inclusion, they only appeared to have strategies for changing individuals, rather than those which address group cultures. This meant that when Becky was on her own with other children she became a target for bullying. For example, she told us how she was continuously bullied at the bus stop, and on her way to and from school. This occurred because the other children did not see her as 'normal', and because the teachers, by defining the solution in terms of the need for Becky to change, reinforced the bullies' perspective.

By taking childrens' and adults' everyday practices and opinions as the starting point for our research we were able to demonstrate how people's individual and cultural perspectives concerning 'normality' and 'difference' led them to objectify disabled children. However, there are two issues worth remembering at this point; first, these beliefs cannot be separated from the structural issues at play within schools; secondly, nor should they be taken to demonstrate that disabled children and adults who work in schools are two distinct homogenous groupings.

Adult Beliefs and Structural Issues

Children in 'special' and 'mainstream' schools were not only differentiated in terms of their impairment and their ability to act 'normal', they were also segregated through streaming and the creation of 'units'. That is, as well as being differentiated because of their impairment and issues of 'normality' they were also, like other children, segregated on the basis of their perceived academic ability. Sometimes parents and children resisted the process of dividing children into streams.

> *Note 21/01/98:*
>
> *Teacher:* 'Egan's parents complained when I had decided that he shouldn't be in the classes doing standard grades. I had to explain to them that he wasn't up to the work. The parents still didn't believe me. So I kept sending homework home that Egan couldn't do until the parents realised that they had made a mistake. Eventually they got the message.

In contrast to rhetoric concerning parents and teachers rights, this teacher not only rejects out of hand the opinions of Egan and his parents, but also employs his structurally powerful position to force home his perspective. It became clear to us over time that the children who were placed in what the teacher termed 'the academic stream' were considered by him to be closer to his notion of normality. Our data suggests that, like Hargreaves (1967), Ball (1981) and Hargreaves (1989) before us, in regard to non-disabled children, an interplay between structural issues within schools (e.g. streaming, timetabling staff/child ratios and wider economic consideration) and teachers' attitudes acts to limit disabled children's educational opportunities. The structures encourage teachers and children to recognise and adopt ideas of rank and status, which, in turn, require parents and children to know their place. Very few adults recognise that this judgement often relates more to their own value system and prejudices than to objective academic criteria. That is, they appear unaware that their beliefs about the world may influence their perceptions of different children.

Our findings fit well with the belief that the shift to inclusive education encouraged by parts of the Warnock report (DES, 1978) has not necessarily been complimented by a shift in thinking in all 'UK schools'. Riddell (1996) has suggested that this may be because there are internal contradictions within the Warnock report. She argues that despite the change in emphasis in terms of the origins of SEN, other areas of the report (specifically, those which concentrate on children's impairments and 'special schools') reinforce essentialist medical model perspectives, which concentrate on the deficits of children.

We found that these pressures led to the informal exclusion of children from mainstream schools. Indeed, one head teacher from a mainstream school suggested that he could only have 15% of children with a learning difficulty in any year if he was to meet his national targets. Moreover, we also found that exclusion within mainstream schools, on the basis of academic and other criteria, led to disabled children being educated in separate 'learning support units' or 'impairment specific units'. Like Clark *et al.* (1997) we concluded that mainstream education is very often less segregated, rather than fully inclusive.

Our experiences also confirm the suggestion that a lack of a commitment to integrated schooling on the part of professionals and administrators stems from structural changes within the Scottish and English & Welsh education systems such as devolved management of schools, lower public spending, national testing, school league tables, etc. (Alan *et al.*, 1991; Armstrong & Galloway, 1994; Clark *et al.*, 1997; Riddell, 1996). Structural changes are understood to have put pressure on the resources 'mainstream' schools direct at 'special education' and to have led to resources being diverted away from improving the overall quality of teaching and learning to providing support to individual children (Clark *et al.*, 1997). These changes are also believed to discourage reflexive practice by teachers and to result in teachers and administrators needs being put before those of children during processes of assessment and labelling (Armstrong & Galloway, 1994). It is also suggested that as a consequence of this process of individualisation there has been a return to pre-Warnock forms of assessment which define disabled children in medical model terms and which concentrate on children's individual needs and deficits (Clark *et al.*, 1997).

This return to individualisation holds little benefits for disabled children because a statement or record of SEN often leads to children receiving the support the local authority or school can afford, rather than the services they have been assessed as requiring (Fairbairn & Fairbairn, 1992). These findings are mirrored in a number of countries by a number of authors who highlight similar reasons for what Booth (1996) calls the fragmented nature of inclusive education. For example, inclusion is believed to be restricted in New Zealand and Australia by tension between professionals and administrators (Loxley & Thomas, 1997); in Australia by the fact that schools were already dysfunctional pre-attempts at inclusion and that this status meant that inclusion became problematic (Slee, 1996b); in Norway by the structure and organisation of schools (Vislie & Langfeldt, 1996); in the USA and the UK by a lack of Key Adult stakeholders (Rouse & Florani 1996); and in China by the structure of schooling and teachers' methods (Chen, 1996).

These findings are very similar to those within educational sociology concerning the education system in the 1980s (e.g. Bain, 1990; Ball, 1981, 1987; Gatherer, 1989; Lawton, 1989; Hargreaves, 1989). Indeed, their arguments are strangely reminiscent of this work. In the 1980s it was argued that educational innovation was obstructed by a number of factors. These were:

- lack of resources for planning and training;
- a lack of parental involvement;
- teachers' resentment at having several changes imposed by central government;
- large classroom sizes;
- teacher autonomy in the classroom;
- poorly maintained school buildings;
- by teachers, especially senior staff, blocking change to protect their vested interests which, for example, in secondary schools relate to resource allocation between different subject departments and different subjects teaching traditions.

Though our own experiences confirm much of this work, what is lacking from these structural characterisations of Special Education are the voices of disabled children and a complex understanding of how teacher's cultural positions affect their working practices and enable them to resist specific structural pressures. It is not simply the case, as might be derived from a reading of most of the literature in Special Education, that these changes are the sole cause of differential treatment of disabled and non-disabled children by adults in 'mainstream' schools. Indeed, we found that adults and children do not respond in a uniform way to the structural issues outlined above.

Different Adults

Throughout the schools we visited we encountered a great diversity of adults. We found that many of the children differentiated between adults in terms of their everyday practices and that they could identify specific adults who were easier to work with. We came to refer to these adults as reflexive practitioners (see also Davis *et al.*, 2000). These were adults who questioned their own professional practices and cultural assumptions. We encountered these people in both mainstream and special schools, and we have chosen two, Paul and Mary to highlight here. Paul was very critical of a variety of practices in his special school:

Note 29/3/98

Paul: When I came here there wasn't even a reading scheme in place, and there were kids leaving here with nothing. It was a damn shame. It was a disgrace. The thing about the reading scheme and generally how you teach, its about giving the children enough opportunities to learn how to teach themselves, to work out their own strategy. A do a lot of exercises where they've got to guess what's coming next. This encourages them to think ahead and work it out for themselves. I think the children have really thrived on the fact that I can say I've made a mistake ...

... One of the other staff told me that one of the senior staff were complaining about me and saying. 'He just wants to be pals with the kids' (Long grunt). What's wrong in that eh? At least I try to build a relationship. If you can't do that, if you've got to always be in control, then you're just turning them off still. Their problem is that I have a different approach to theirs with the kids. I mean how are you gonna teach them the difficult subjects like maths and language if you haven't got a rapport with them? You know you've got to be a bit transient and fluid. I can see where I'm in a friendship role with them, but then I notice when the respect's starting to go, so they need a gentle reminder. So I have to play more of a teacher role. And they all look at me for me to play that role too ...

... It doesn't help when some of the other teachers intervene with these kids. You know you work really hard to build their confidence up about something, and then for example, Alex when he went to home ecci, he came back yesterday and said, 'The home ecci teacher told me to tell you to teach me joined up writing.' That really annoyed me. You know he's really come on. His writing's come on a lot, and OK he might not be doing joined up writing but at least he's getting somewhere now ...

Here, Paul is critical of the cultural (everyday teachers values, such as being able to admit mistakes), the material/structural (lack of resources for books, and policies on reading plans) and the philosophical (notions of empowerment) basis of his school. He explains how his practice is different to other staff and how this leads to him being labelled because he is different. Hence, we learn that adults are subjected to negative discourses in the school setting in just the same way as children. At the same time Paul does not link children's resistance to irrationality or 'not thinking like us', rather he perceives it to be an intelligent response to the circumstances they have encountered. Paul's perspective is similar to that of Mary in a mainstream school:

Note 29/10/98

Mary: I once observed a class with another teacher and in a 40-minute lesson there was something like 600 negative remarks and about 6 positive ones counted. Teachers by whatever. I don't know, maybe they're the kind of people that become teachers, or maybe it's part of teacher training, but they're much more likely to be negative. Don't do this, don't do that ...

JD: Some secondary school teachers have suggested that they don't want to accept children from primary schools who have so bad literacy problems they don't know where to start to help them.

Mary: Well that's, unprofessional. If any of my staff were to say that they'd be on training courses before their feet touched the ground. There are courses provided in this city. The training for learning support in this city is exceptional. It is highly skilled, highly professional, and if there is nothing available on the quality service provision, the authority will pay for learning support teachers to go to the university for training ... every time something new comes in, I organise in service training for the staff.

Mary and Paul found it easy to identify the problems within the systems they worked in and to put forward solutions to those problems. They possessed the personal and professional resources to respond to the structural and cultural barriers they encountered. Indeed, their comments reinforce the belief that children what ever the level of their impairment should be treated as competent social actors who can be included in the everyday process of schools if the necessary structural, cultural and individual issues are addressed (see also Samad & Fairbairn, 1992; Davis *et al.*, 2000).

However, not all teachers have the personal resources to use structures to their own benefit (like Mary) or fight against the structures they encounter (like Paul). Some adults differentiate themselves from their colleagues on the basis of power relationships, for example, a speech therapist in one school explained that she would like to give children more choice in relation to where and how they sat in her class:

John Note 4/2/98:

Heather: They have a completely different way of thinking about room than we do. Like if you were in a group, they might all sit with their backs to each other and we would expect them to sit in a circle and face each other. I mean I don't mind if they sit with their backs to each other. But I'm a bit worried that if somebody else, like the head, comes into the classroom they'll say, 'Hey what are you doing here? You're supposed to be teaching these children social rules?

Heather did not have enough confidence in her own position in the school to break the conventional method. She allowed her knowledge of the views of other staff to impinge on her classroom practices. Another type of pressure that teachers experience is a genuine fear of litigation. This fear underpinned much of the practice in the schools that we worked in:

Note 2/2/98:

Lydia: 'We're under a lot of pressure to teach them properly, we can't let them out of the school on their own if we're unhappy about their safety. There's a real fear of, there was a teacher at a school down south and she was sued because a child of hers was in an accident. She apparently hadn't taught the child how to cross the road properly. So that sort of thing is like a big axe hanging over you all the time.

The perceptions of Lydia and Heather suggest a culture of defensive practice has developed amongst some adults who work with disabled children and that disabled children's lives are controlled by those adults on the basis of whether the children are considered 'safe' or whether they are likely to get them into trouble. This suggested to us that though it was possible to identify adult discourses and practices which were not disabling, the processes through which beliefs are played out in practice is problematic and adults in schools, like many children, are subjected to labelling processes which create pressure for them to conform to other adults' expectations. Their everyday work experiences are fluid and involve constant interactive moments where they have to decide whether to act in a manner that is true to their selves or a manner that is best appropriate to the expectations of those they work with. There is no separation between individual action, culture and structure, all these factors are at play in any given moment. Moreover, as we shall see below, this social fluidity not only relates to adults' everyday experiences but also to those of children.

Children Negotiating Cultural and Structural Forces in Schools

So far we have mainly outlined the perceptions and experiences of different adults within schools. However, unlike many studies within the field of special education we are able to illustrate how children responded to the various beliefs and practices of adults within their schools.

It would be unwise to assume that all children experience and respond to these practices in the same way. We found that children's everyday life worlds were fluid. Adults often control educational discourses within schools, however pupils are able to resist these discourses (Davis & Watson, 1999; Corker, 1999).

For example, in the following illustration from a special school, disabled children were found to mark each other as different:

Note 17/3/98:

I learn that Karen and the other girls used to be in the same class as Andrew and Dibly. They got split up in S1.

Karen: It's because Andrew and Dibly weren't doing the work and Dibly was being really stupid.

John: What, to you?

Karen: Yes, not only to me but to Kes as well. So Kes went and told and then we stopped being in the same class as them.

(*Later same day*)

John: I hear Kes and Karen used to be in the same class as you?

Andrew: Aye they had like, learning difficulties, they were miiiles behind, So we just go wi' them for home ecci now.

These explanations are illuminating because the children draw from the adult discourses of differentiation, outlined earlier, to label each other. One group labels the other as 'stupid' and the other as 'miiiles behind'. One employs the 'doesn't know how to behave' criteria, the other the 'not academically able' criteria. Their interpretation of each other's abilities creates social distance between them. This cultural ascription of difference was rooted firmly in the structural imposition of physical space between them created by the school's policy of streaming. Even within the same stream we found that some children competed to highlight their own abilities over that of their classmates:

Note 24/3/98

Billy's describing to Nick about a meeting with a psychologist in which he was asked to describe what pasta's like. He says, 'I told him It's a bit like worms to me'. And Andrew says, 'No, to me it's brown and pink'. And he says it a couple of times to reinforce the fact, that he can see colours and Billy can't. And it's also the way that Billy says, 'To me it's like worms, as if he even knows before he even speaks that Andrew's going to contradict what he says'.

Andrew marks himself as different on the basis of visual rather than academic ability. The children can choose from the same diverse range of criteria as adults when differentiating between each other. However, it would be wrong to suggest that the children's behaviour was only determined by the structural organisation of schools or adult values. Indeed, some children in the mainstream setting utilised streaming to meet their own ends:

Note 20/11/98

Kyle and Alan are two boys in the lowest-streamed French class. This class is full of aggressive boys, no girls. Kyle and Alan are not as aggressive as the other boys and are here because they are dyslexic, the others seem to be here because they are 'badly behaved'. Also I've noticed over a number of visits that these two are not as 'stupid' as the teacher thinks and can do this work easily. When I ask them why they are in this class they both say its 'for a skive'—if they let on they could do the work they'd be put in a harder class.

Children can renegotiate the meaning of streaming. Kyle and Alan in a mainstream school see it as giving them the opportunity to opt out, Andrew in a special school sees it as meaning he doesn't go to the same classes as the 'miiiles behind' kids, and Karen sees it as meaning they don't have to be in the same class as 'stupid' boys. Hence, streaming has both positive and negative outcomes for these children in terms of their immediate everyday aspirations. In this case Kyle and Andrew's response to streaming acts to have the opposite effect to that which is hoped for by the senior staff in the schools. Rather than boosting their exam performances and improving the school's position on the league table it will result in them under-achieving in certain subjects.

The children we met were extremely aware of the practices of adults and were able both to utilise structural issues to meet their own ends and, as we shall see below, to critically reflect on inconsistencies in different adults' practices.

Note 24/03/98:

Dibly: The people here are too protected. I can do a lot more things than they give me credit for. For example, a few months ago I got a pass to go to the back shops and the access person and I agreed that I can go through there, that I've got the confidence to do it. But for the first few times they kept on checking up, following me, and they still check up. But I'm very confident about it. I can do it. I can't understand why they want to check up on me, but they do and they keep on doing it. You get this awful feeling, you're over protected. At home I negotiate my way round the local town OK. I'm capable of doing lots. My mother never had any quibbles about it. I just do what I can do, and I just wish here they wouldn't be so overprotective.

As we have seen, fear of litigation often led adults to overprotect children. This practice was recognised by some of the children and was often resented.

Dibly draws attention to the ways in which; staff in his school question his independence. He has a firm grasp of the different layers of structure that surround his everyday world and the differences between the home and school settings. Being over protected undermines his abilities. As Corker (1999) points out, disabled children are acutely aware of the dissabling nature of rules. Here, the rules seem to relate more to adult safety than child safety.

The issue of safety was also raised in mainstream schools and was used by some staff to justify segregation or exclusion from a particular class or subject. For example, we met Callum, a boy with a hearing impairment, who was denied access to Craft, Design and Technology on the grounds of safety. He felt that this was unfair and was discriminatory (see Corker & Davis, 2001). Kenworthy & Whittaker (2000, p. 220) describe many school rules as 'petty regulations'. They demonstrate how schools and local authorities utilise notions of 'appropriate behaviour' against disabled children. We feel that, as well as questioning the appropriateness of specific rules within schools, it is also important for us to question the fact that Dibly and Callum, or Becky earlier, were not consulted about these practices. Alderson & Goodey (1999) argue that special schools place most emphasis on children's failings and consequently their capabilities for independent thought are overlooked. We observed many similar examples of this in both 'special' and 'mainstream' schools. Central to this is that fact that some adults (in contrast to Peter earlier) feel they do not have to enter into dialogue with the children they work with. They do not find it necessary to explain or justify their actions to children. This raises cause for concern when considered within the context of legislation on children's rights. The UN Convention on the Rights of the Child, the *Education Act 1981* (as amended by the *Education Act, 1996*); the *Children Act, 1989* and the *Children (Scotland) Act 1995* all have sections which encourage those who work with disabled children to take account of their views. Unfortunately, this legislation, as yet, appears to have had little impact on everyday practices within schools (Corker & Davis, 2000). Indeed, there is much debate concerning the extent to which law ever protects disabled children (Morris, 1999; Davis & Watson, 2000).

Concluding Comments

These data have outlined the way in which adults in a number of different schools talk to and about disabled children. We have demonstrated that the discourses which disabled children encounter are interrelated with subjective notions of essential difference based on judgements of cognitive, physical and social ability. Once a child is considered to have a physical or sensory impairment other diagnosis of academic, cultural and social deficits are but a short step away. Judgements of ability are not value free because they are interlinked with the structural organisation of schools, and the beliefs and actions of different adults and children. Our data suggest that very few adults in schools question the processes and social contexts in which they construct notions of difference. Much emphasis on inclusion is placed on the removal of structural barriers. Whilst this is important, our findings suggest that personal and institutional cultural values also need to be addressed. Policies which aim to create positive outcomes for disabled children within the education system should not be based simply on structural issues, but should be based on a more nuanced multi-level approach which challenges the structural, cultural and individual conditions which create disability. Schools have to address the issues which lead to unreflexive adult practices. These include; poor resources and training, the unquestioning use of discourses of difference, and the privileging of teachers own cultural beliefs and hierarchical notions of ability. The practices that disempower children need to be challenged. Though we ourselves still believe that every child should have the right to attend a mainstream school in their local area, we also believe that a great deal of change is required within 'mainstream' schools before disabled children will actually experience inclusion.

Academic streaming, professional values, issues of safety, fear of litigation, concepts of normality, social class values, and ideas concerning a variety of criteria relating to physical and social skills can be employed by professionals to label children. As Armstrong & Galloway (1994) have pointed out, some adults labelled the children to suit their own interests. They allow the requirements of their structural role within the education process to govern their perceptions of the children. This process is combined with and reinforced by the tensions created by market place educational policy, as outlined by Riddell (1996), Armstrong & Galloway (1994) and Alan *et al.* (1991). One outcome of this is an unreflexive processes of diagnosis within special and mainstream schools, which can result in professionals silencing and excluding disabled children. The children's capacity to make choices is also overlooked.

Process and action cannot be separated from discourse. Corbett (1993) rightly asserts that there needs to be a change in language in 'special' education. Leicester (1992) outlines a checklist for appraising the content of books and other learning resources. These approaches do act to counter the discourses we have highlighted above. However, these approaches in themselves will not bring about inclusive schooling and genuine equity. As Fulcher (1996) indicates simply changing language practice can often let policy makers of the hook because it is easier to do this than to change the structural and cultural practices of an organisation. Slee (1996b) argues that in Australia it has enabled organisations steeped in the medical model to gain control of funds set aside to promote inclusive education simply through a change in rhetoric.

Our findings concur with those of Leicester (1992), which suggest that a lack of resources and the attitudes of adults and other children create difficulties for children and prevent full inclusion in 'mainstream' schools. We do not see this as evidence that policies of inclusion should be stopped. It is our belief that those who argue for the existence of special schools on the grounds that they prevent disabled children from being harmed by other children or adults are deluding themselves, because we have found that the same oppressive processes are to be found in both types of schooling.

We argue, following Ainscow (1992), that any improvements to the schooling of disabled children will also have important positive outcomes for all children. We do so because we find many similarities between our work and the work of other sociologists who have identified how education systems, processes of school organisation and adult values/expectations lead to discrimination against girls (Prendergast, 1994), working-class boys (Willis, 1977; Ball, 1981) and children from a variety of ethnic and religious backgrounds (Gill *et al.*, 1992; Figueroa, 1993; Connolly, 1998).

Support must be given to those reflexive adults who at present are isolated and attacked because their colleagues resist innovation, and attempt to safeguard their own practices and vested interests. Our experiences of good practice suggest that changing this process may not be as troublesome as some would make out. Indeed, the empowerment of teachers may not be that problematic when put into the context that they are not 'cultural dopes' (Evans, 1990), nor as we have shown (in contrast to, for example, Adams *et al.*, 2000) are they always agents of reproduction and control. We believe that the Disability Movement has many allies within the teaching profession. Unfortunately, this is overlooked by many who write about inclusive schooling. It is our contention that it is not good enough for writers to criticise schools and teachers en mass. Teachers like Paul and Mary require our support. We can support them by highlighting why their teaching practices are 'better' and by calling their colleagues to account.

Finally, in keeping with a multi-level approach to educational innovation, it is our belief that full inclusion is only likely to be achieved when policy decisions are built on disabled children's own lived experiences as articulated directly to policy makers or as collected within empirical studies. This process would be in sharp contrast to the Warnock Committee, which consisted of a few professionals with an interest in 'special educational need' (Kirp, 1982). If real change is to occur disabled children and their allies must gain a share of the power in educational institutions.

NOTE

[1] The Scottish education system is separate from that in England and Wales and there is no such concept as a 'UK school'. However, we would argue that the ideas highlighted in this paper are relevant to both systems.

REFERENCES

ADAMS, J., SWAIN, J. & CLARK, J. (2000) What's So Special? Teachers' Models and Their Realisation in Practice in Segragated Schools. *Disability & Society*, 15(2), pp. 233–246.

AINSCOW, M. (1992) Doing the right things: seeing special needs as a school improvement issue, in: G. FAIRBAIRN & S. FAIRBAIRN (Eds) *Integrating Special Children: some ethical issues* (Aldershot, Avebury).

ALDERSON, P. & GOODEY, C. (1999) *Enabling Education: experiences in special and ordinary schools* (London, Tufnell Press).

ALAN, S., BROWN, S. & MUNN, S. (1991) *Off the Record: 'mainstream' provision for pupils with non-recorded learning difficulties in primary and secondary schools* (Edinburgh, Scottish Council for Research in Education).

ARMSTRONG, D. & GALLOWAY, D. (1994) Special educational needs and problem behaviour; making policy in the classroom, in: S. RIDDELL & S. BROWN (Eds) *Special Educational Needs Policy in the 90's: Warnock in the market place* (London, Routledge).

BAIN, L. (1990) *A Critical Analysis of the Hidden Curriculum in Physical Education*, in: D. KIRK & R. TINNING (Eds) *Physical Education, Curriculum and Culture* (London, Falmer Press).

BALL, S. (1981) *Beachside Comprehensive* (Cambridge, Cambridge University Press).

BALL, S. (1987) *The Micropolitics of the School* (London, Routledge).

BOOTH, T.A. (1996) Perspective on inclusion in England, *Cambridge Journal of Education*, 26(1), pp. 87–100.

BOWE, R. & BALL, S. (1992) *Reforming Education and Changing Schools: case studies in policy sociology* (London, Routledge).

CHEN, Y. (1996) Making Special Education Compulsory and Inclusive in China, *Cambridge Journal of Education*, 26(1), pp. 47–58.

CLARK, C., DYSON, A., MILLWARD, A. & SKIDMORE, D. (1997) *New Directions in Special Needs Schooling: Innovations in mainstream schools* (London, Cassell).

CONNOLLY, P. (1998) *Racism, Gender Identities and Young Children: social relations in a multi-ethnic, inner city primary school* (London, Routledge).

CORBETT, J. (1993) Post-modernism and the 'special needs' metaphors, *Oxford Review of Education*, 19(4), pp. 547–553.

CORKER, M. (1999) *They Don't Know What They Don't Know—disability research as an 'emancipatory' site of learning*, Sites of Learning Conference, University of Hull, September.

CORKER, M. & DAVIS, J.M. (2000) Disabled children—invisible under the law, in: J. COOPER & S. VERNON (Eds) *Disability and the Law* (London, Jessica Kingsley).

CORKER, M. & DAVIS, J.M. (2001) Portrait of Callum: the disabling of a childhood, in: B. EDWARDS (Ed.) *Children, Home and School: autonomy, connection or regulation* (London, Falmer Press).

DALE, R. (1989) *The State and Education Policy* (Oxford: Oxford University Press).

DAVIS, J.M. (1998) Understanding the meanings of children: a reflexive process, *Children and Society* 12(5), pp. 325–335.

DAVIS, J.M. & WATSON, N. (1999) *Challenging the Stereotypes: disabled children and resistance*, Sites of Learning Conference, Centre for the Social Study of Childhood, University of Hull, 14–17 September.

DAVIS, J.M. & WATSON, N. (2000) Disabled Children's Rights in Everyday Life: problematising notions of competency and promoting self-empowerment, *International Journal of Children's Rights*, 8, pp. 211–228.

DAVIS, J.M., WATSON, N. & CUNNINGHAM-BURLEY, S. (2000) Learning the lives of disabled children: developing a reflexive approach, in: P. CHRISTIENSEN & A. JAMES (Eds) *Conducting Research with Children* (London, Falmer).

DEPARTMENT OF EDUCATION AND SCIENCE (1978) *Special Educational Needs: report of the Committee of Enquiry into the Education of Handicapped Children and Young People, the Warnock Report* (London, HMSO).

EVANS, J. (1990) Ability, Position and Privilege in School Physical Education, in: D. KIRK & P. TINNING (Eds) *Physical Education, Curriculum and Culture* (London, Falmer Press).

FAIRBAIRN, G. & FAIRBAIRN, S. (1992) Integration; an ethical issue?, in: G. FAIRBAIRN & S. FAIRBAIRN (Eds) *Integrating Special Children: some ethical issues* (Aldershot, Avebury).

FIGUEROA, P. (1993) Equality, multiculturalism, antiracism and physical education in the National Curriculum, in: J. EVANS & B. DAVIES (Eds) *Equality, Equity and Physical Education* (London, Falmer).

FULCHER, G. (1996) Beyond Normalisation but not Utopia, in: L. BARTON (Ed.) *Disability and Society: emerging issues and insights* (Harlow, Addison Wesley Longman).

GATHERER, W.A. (1989) *Curriculum Development in Scotland* (Edinburgh, Scottish Academic Press).

GILL, D., BLAIR, M. & MAYOR, B. (1992) *Racism & Education: structures and strategies* (Buckingham, Open University Press).

HARGREAVES, A. (1989) *Curriculum and Assessment Reform* (Oxford, Oxford University Press).

HARGREAVES, D.H. (1967) *Social Relations in a Secondary School* (London, Routledge Keegan Paul).

JAMES, A., JENKS, C. & PROUT, A. (1998) *Theorising Childhood* (London, Polity Press).

KENWORTHY, J. & WHITTAKER, J. (2000) Anything to declare? The struggle for inclusive education and children's rights, *Disability & Society*, 15(2), pp. 219–232.

KIRP, D. (1982) Professionalisation as a policy choice: British special education in a comparative perspective, *World Politics*, 34, pp. 137–174.

LAWTON, D. (1989) *Education, Culture and the National Curriculum* (London, Hodder & Stoughton).

LEICESTER, M. (1992) Integrating inequity: prejudice, power and special needs, in: G. FAIRBAIRN & S. FAIRBAIRN (Eds) *Integrating Special Children: some ethical issues* (Aldershot, Avebury).

LOXLEY, A. & THOMAS, G. (1997) From inclusive policy to the exclusive real world: an international review, *Disability & Society*, 12(2), pp. 273–291.

MORRIS, J. (1999) *Disabled Children and the Children Act* (London, The Who Cares Trust).

PRENDERGAST, S. (1994) The space of childhood: psyche, soma and social existence. Menstruation and embodiment at adolescence, in: J. BRANNEN & M. O'BRIEN (Eds) *Childhood and Parenthood* (London, Institute of Education University of London).

RIDDELL, S. (1996) Theorising special educational need in a changing political climate, in: L. BARTON (Ed.) *Disability and Society: emerging issues and insights* (Harlow, Addison Wesley Longman).

ROUSE, M. & FLORANI M. (1996) Effective inclusive schools a study of two countries, *Cambridge Journal of Education*, 26(1), pp. 71–86.

ROWLEY, D. (1992) Creating a desirable future for people with significant learning difficulties, in: G. FAIRBAIRN & S. FAIRBAIRN (Eds) *Integrating Special Children: some ethical issues* (Aldershot, Avebury).

SAMAD, K. & FAIRBAIRN, S. (1992) Equal opportunities and integration—a 'mainstream' perspective, in: G. FAIRBAIRN & S. FAIRBAIRN (Eds) *Integrating Special Children: some ethical issues* (Aldershot, Avebury).

SHAKESPEARE, T. & WATSON, N. (1998) Theoretical perspectives on research with disabled children, in: C. ROBINSON & K. STALKER (Eds) *Growing Up with Disability* (London, Jessica Kingsley).

SLEE, R. (1996a) Clauses on conditionality: the reasonable accommodation of language, in: L. BARTON, (Ed.) *Disability and Society: emerging issues and insights* (Harlow, Addison Wesley Longman).

SLEE, R. (1996b) Inclusive schooling in Australia? Not yet!, *Cambridge Journal of Education*, 26(1), pp. 9–32.

SCOTTISH EDUCATION DEPARTMENT (1978) *The Education of Pupils with Learning Difficulties in Primary and Secondary Schools in Scotland; a progress report* (Edinburgh, HMSO).

VISLIE, L. & LANGFELDT, G. (1996) Finance, policy making & the organisation of special education, *Cambridge Journal of Education*, 26(1), pp. 59–70.

WILLIS, P. (1977) *Learning to Labour* (Aldershot, Gower).

'I Value What You have to Say'. Seeking the Perspective of Children with a Disability, Not Just their Parents

BELINDA GARTH & ROSALIE ARONI

School of Public Health, Faculty of Health Sciences, La Trobe University, Bundoora, Victoria, Australia 3086

ABSTRACT *The UN Convention on the Rights of the Child acknowledges the right for children to express opinions about issues affecting them and the right to have these views heard (Davis, 1998). There has been an increase in the number of international studies including children as informants in research, but there is noticeably less published research including children as informants in Australia if they have a disability. Rather, there has been a reliance on parents/carers for insight into their child's experiences. In this article we present the results of a qualitative pilot study where we interviewed parents and their children who have cerebral palsy about their perceptions and experiences of communication in the medical consultation. We found that the views of children and parents were different, further reiterating the need to seek the perceptions of children as well as their parents.*

Introduction

In recent years there has been a growing body of literature that identifies the importance of including children as participants in research. Several authors have referred to the UN Convention on Rights of the Child, acknowledging that children hold the right to express their opinions about issues affecting them and the right to have these views heard (Morrow & Richards, 1996; Davis, 1998). Further to this, Article 2 states, 'all rights on the Convention must apply without discrimination of any kind irrespective of race, colour, language, religion, national, ethnic or social origin, disability or other status' (Lewis & Lindsay, 2000, p. 26).

Although there are relatively few studies that explore the perceptions of children with learning disabilities or communication difficulties (Mitchell & Sloper, 2001), researchers from the United Kingdom in particular have led the way with a number of informative studies, as well as investigating areas related to children's interaction with health care professionals (Minkes *et al.*, 1994; Beresford & Sloper, 2000; Watson *et al.*, 2000; Mitchell & Sloper, 2001). These studies have provided an understanding of the child's perspective, rather than relying solely on the parent or carer for insight into the child's experiences.

The Victorian Government in Australia has developed the State Disability Plan for advocating a more inclusive community by 2012, where everyone has the same rights and opportunities to participate in the life of the community (Department of Human Services, 2002). If inclusion as a philosophy is being advocated, then it would seem that children with disabilities should also not be excluded (whether intentionally or not) from participating in research. Recent Australian studies have included adults and young adults with disabilities as informants (Crisp, 2000; Lenney & Sercombe, 2002), and there has been a focus on issues surrounding the family when a child has a disability, such as financial strains (Bain, 1998), social isolation (Cant, 1992), and the perspective of parents, teachers and therapists regarding the social experiences of children (Baker & Donelly, 2001). Despite the hive of activity in the UK and the policy desire for an 'inclusive community' in Victoria, there has been insufficient Australian research designed to include children with disabilities as informants.

While the research into the perceptions and experiences of parents has been valuable, there has tended to be a reliance on the parent for insight into the child's experiences. In doing so, the child's right to express opinions about issues affecting him/her and having these views heard has been overlooked (Morrow & Richards, 1996; Davis, 1998).

In this article, we report the findings of our pilot study that explored the experiences and perceptions of Australian children with cerebral palsy (CP) and their parents about communication in the medical consultation. This study was undertaken to gain an understanding of the issues relevant to children with CP and their parents. The findings are being used in the development of a larger study that will also incorporate the perspectives of doctors.

The Medical Consultation

Many studies have examined doctor–patient communication (Street, 1992; Charles *et al.*, 2000; Ruusuvuori, 2001) and an increasing number of reports of studies have examined the doctor–parent–child triad in medical interactions over the last 30 years (Meeuwesen & Kaptein, 1996; Tates & Meeuwesen, 2001). This area of study has been recognised as important because communication forms a key component of all doctor–patient interactions and has a potential impact on patient health outcomes (Roter & Hall, 1993). Correlations have been found between effective communication and improved health outcomes in areas such as emotional health, resolution of symptoms, pain control and physiological measures such as blood pressure (Meryn, 1998). It is noteworthy that most research into doctor–patient communication has focused on adults as patients (Charles *et al.*, 2000; Ruusuvuori, 2001) and of the few studies that examine doctor–child communication (Pantell *et al.*, 1982), the children did not have an impairment or disability.

It has also been suggested that the development of a partnership between a doctor and patient can enhance health outcomes where an effective partnership includes:

- a shared vision;
- shared control, power and decision making;
- integrity;
- respect;
- open communication (Consumers' Health Forum, 1999).

Although the doctor–patient relationship is said to have changed during recent years with the doctor becoming less authoritarian and the patient more autonomous (Lagerløv *et al.*, 1998), empirical research indicates that partnership is often still lacking and paternalistic models of communication remain widespread (Law Reform Commission of Victoria, 1989; Case, 2000; Charles *et al.*, 2000). This is reflective of the 'expert model' of professional practice (Cunningham & Davis, 1985), where the doctor's expertise provides legitimation of the authority for control over decision-making and patients have typically not been included in that decision-making process. It would seem important to gain a better understanding of what enables communication which leads to effective, ongoing partnerships given that we know the way doctors communicate with patients can affect adherence to therapeutic regimens, satisfaction with medical care (Pantell *et al.*, 1982) and health outcomes.

Medical and Social Models

In Australia, the term 'person with a disability' is advocated (Scope, 2002). Therefore, we refer to 'children with disabilities', rather than 'disabled children' in this paper, as we also prefer to identify children as *children* first and having a disability second.

Notwithstanding the current controversies regarding how impairment and disability should be defined, we operate with the following understanding as the backdrop to our analyses. The medical model constructs disability as a deviation from physiological and neurological norms that directly result from disease or trauma (Bickenbach *et al.*, 1999). This construction of disability from the medical perspective is criticised as being partial and limited, as disability is portrayed as entirely a medical problem ignoring the sociological and psychological aspects (Brisenden, 1998). Looking through a sociological lens, disability is not solely 'the product of isolated individual pathologies' (Goodley, 2001, p. 225), but is also socially constructed with 'disabling barriers and social restrictions' created by institutionalised practices of society (Oliver, 1996; Crisp, 2000). According to Oliver (1996), 'it [the social model] does not deny the problem of disability but locates it squarely within society' (p. 32).

Although the recent reclassification of disability (World Health Organisation, 2001) incorporates aspects of both the medical and social models, research indicates that the world view inherent in the medical model still permeates the way in which health professionals treat people with disabilities (Bricher, 2000). According to those using the social model, the maintenance of the unintegrated medical model of professional practice contributes to the continuing oppression and marginalisation of people with disabilities (Bricher, 2000).

Parents' Perspective

However, it is important to note that skilfully delivered support by health professionals of families that have a child with a disability is said to make a significant contribution to the functioning of the child and family (Taanila et al., 1998), particularly via counselling (Donovan et al., 1989) and early intervention services (Reddihough et al., 1996). Despite this, it is clear from other research (Case, 2000) that some parents feel uninformed by doctors regarding the cause, diagnosis or potential outcome of the child's condition. Other issues examined in the literature include dissatisfaction with the way some doctors communicate the diagnosis of the child's disability (O'Sullivan et al., 1992; Quine & Rutter, 1994), inadequate information provision regarding the child's disability (Quine & Rutter, 1994; Case, 2000, 2001), and a lack of support of the family in terms of the impact of the disability on personal or family needs (O'Sullivan et al., 1992). In some instances, families believed that the only useful advice came from other parents that have a child with a disability, not the doctor (Case, 2000).

Researching the Child's Perspective

It has been suggested by Myerscough & Ford (1996) that, in some instances, a patient with a disability may be 'talked over' as comments are directed to a third party (such as parents in the case of children). Whether this actually happens to children with disabilities (or if children perceive this to happen) is not clearly stated in the literature. The published research on doctor–child communication has not paid specific attention to child patients with a disability, with the exception of Tannen & Wallat (1986, 1987) who focused on a single case involving a child with CP and her family. Even though they looked at how the paediatrician coped with conflicting demands during the consultation, both papers (1986 and 1987) were largely concerned with communication between the paediatrician and parents, not the child. However, their 1987 paper did reveal that the paediatrician 'joked around' more with the child and was 'more serious' with the parents.

While parents can provide insight into their child's situation (Case, 2000), children's understanding and experience of the world is different from their parents (Thomas & O'Kane, 1998) and children with disabilities are able to identify 'good practice' (Watson et al., 2000).

It has been suggested that research that includes children with disabilities as informants may be perceived as 'time-consuming and labour intensive' (Minkes et al., 1994; Case, 2001) and access to children may been seen as difficult. Nevertheless, to exclude children from being informants in research simply because it's 'too hard' is questionable, and suggests that their views are not important and not worthy of our time and energy. When research includes children with disabilities as informants, several issues require attention—access, informed consent, research design and communication tools. These are only briefly outlined in the methodology section as they have been discussed extensively elsewhere (see Lewis & Lindsay, 2000; see also Davis, 1998; Mauthner, 1997; Thomas & O'Kane, 1998, for issues related to including children as informants in research).

Methodology

Strauss and Corbin's model of grounded theory was the methodological approach used, hence our interpretations are based on the perspectives of the participants (Strauss & Corbin, 1994).

Participants and Sampling

We recruited our participants from a specialist school in Victoria, Australia, which operates in collaboration with an organisation providing therapy to students. The first author previously worked with this organisation, and had access to families and had experience in communicating with children who have a disability. We used volunteer and criteria sampling (Liamputtong Rice & Ezzy, 1999). Selection criteria were:

- the child was between 6 and 12 years of age;
- the child had CP;
- the child attended the specialist school;
- the parents were the natural birth parents;
- the family spoke fluent English;
- the child could communicate either verbally or non-verbally.

It was decided to focus on CP because it is the most common childhood physical disability in the country (Australian and New Zealand Perinatal Societies, 1995).

Four children with CP aged 12 (Marcus), 9 (Daniel), 6 (James) and 6 (Corey), and six mothers who each had a child with CP participated in our pilot study. To protect the privacy of participants we have allocated pseudonyms to the children and mothers have not been referred to by their names. While we asked for 'parents' during recruitment, only mothers responded. No fathers contacted us for an interview. It may be that because mothers are the major health care providers for their families (Braithwaite, 1986) that they assume responsibility for the main care-taking role of their child, and thus are more likely to respond and take part in research that involves their child. The families who participated in this study all had boys with CP; hence, no girls were interviewed (a recognised limitation of our study).

The ethics committees at La Trobe University and the Department of Education, Employment & Training approved our study. The role of parents and teachers as 'gatekeepers' (Zwiers & Morrissette, 1999) was another access issue we needed to consider. After consent was given from the school's Assistant Principal and the children's parents, children themselves were asked whether they wanted to participate. Children were also reminded that their participation was voluntary and that they could withdraw from participation at any time (Davis, 1998). Further to this, before each interview, mothers signed an Information and Consent Form, which included a statement that their child had been asked to participate and that their child also consented to an interview. Immediately prior to each interview all children were again asked if they still wanted to participate and if they wanted their mother to sit in on the interview. All children chose to have their mother present.

Interviews

We used in-depth, semi-structured interviews that lasted approximately 30–60 minutes (Minichiello *et al.*, 1995). All interviews were audiotaped and a brief interview schedule was used to begin the interview process. Our research design required the use of more creative methods of communication for non-verbal children. As well as engagement with and interpretation of the children's bodily orchestrations and vocalisations, their mothers were able to assist with interpreting some responses that were not clear. The children indicated if their mother's or the interviewer's interpretations were accurate by nodding or shaking their heads. Four mothers were interviewed with their child present, one was interviewed alone and one was interviewed with one of her other children present.

Two child participants were able to speak fluently and clearly enough for full verbal communication, and the other two communicated using vocalisations and body language. While it is suggested that to empower children with disabilities in the research process researchers should use tools that allow children to communicate (Detheridge, 2000), in our study James had not yet learned how to use a communication device and Daniel preferred not to use his.

Readers should note that we acknowledge there is more material presented about mothers' views compared to children's views, as mothers tended to talk more and for longer. Nevertheless, the views of the children are fully and accurately reflected in our report of the study. For us, as for other researchers, this reflects a key methodological issue about the reporting of less verbal responses.

Data Analysis

Interviews were transcribed and sent to participants who were asked to comment on the accuracy of the transcripts. Thematic analysis enabled us to identify *in vivo* or living themes in the transcribed text (Strauss & Corbin, 1998), which were examined for meaning (Minichiello *et al.*, 1995). Initially, open coding was used and then refined using axial coding, and further integrated and refined using selective coding (Strauss & Corbin, 1998).

Results and Discussion

Even with the small number of participants in our study, we believe the results to be important because they reflect the experiences and views of the medical consultation from the perspective of children, as well as parents, and provide a good starting point for a larger study.

Children's Perceptions and Experiences

Two main themes emerged from interviews with the children: the desire to be included in medical consultations and the desire to be informed. One child also expressed that there were other aspects of the hospital visit that were more important than the consultation itself. Although not all children expressed this, it was felt that it should be included because this was one of the dominant themes raised by that child.

Being included and informed. Children felt strongly about being included in the medical consultation and perceived that inclusion was important, even if they did not understand what was being said. Marcus, Daniel and James perceived that they were included in the consultation. Their concept of being included was characterised by direct communication with the doctor, the doctor asking them questions and the opportunity to ask questions of the doctor:

> BG: Do you like it when the doctor talks to mum?
> Daniel: ... [shakes head indicating 'no'].
> BG: No? Would you prefer the doctor to talk to you?
> Daniel: [nods].
> BG: When the doctor does talk to you can you understand some of the things that they're saying?
> Daniel: [shakes head indicating 'no'].
>
> BG: Does the doctor tend to ask you questions?
> James: [vocalises] Yeah.
> Mum: Mmm.
> BG: Yes?
> James: [vocalises] Yeah.
> BG: Do you like it when the doctor asks you questions?
> James: [vocalises strongly] Yeah!

While Marcus wanted to be included in the consultation, he preferred not to be told the details as they worried him. This was reiterated by Marcus' mother, who said that a doctor once explained to Marcus the details of a particular problem he was having and Marcus was 'very upset'. It is possible that because Marcus is older, doctors discuss treatments in greater detail with him compared to a younger child (Pantell *et al.*, 1982). One could suggest that doctors believe that an older child is more able to absorb and comprehend the discussion because of better language use, hence an assumed increase in maturity. While this information sharing includes the child, it has been found to carry consequences as identified in Marcus' comments. However, it is important to note that Marcus *did* want to be informed by the doctor of any tests or procedures immediately prior to their occurrence, and it 'annoyed' him if he wasn't told. For example, if the doctor was going to take his temperature, or take him out of his wheelchair and place him on an examination bed, he wanted the doctor to tell him what was going to happen, rather that just 'doing it' or telling his mother instead of him.

We ascertained from Marcus that there were some things he did not wish to know because the details worried him, but what about other children? Why is it that there are some things that some children do not wish to know and others might? A larger study could perhaps look at this important communication issue in greater detail:

> BG: So would you prefer the doctor talk more to mum and dad?
> Marcus: [nods].
> BG: You would?
> Mum: Can you speak?
> Marcus: Yes.
> BG: And why would you prefer the doctor to talk more to mum and dad?
> Marcus: ... So I don't put it in my head.

Being informed of the procedures performed by doctors was also important for most children. When asked whether the doctor informed them before performing a test Marcus, Daniel and James indicated that doctors usually tell them first, but not always. Only Corey reported that doctors did not directly inform him prior to conducting procedures, however, this did not bother him. Informing the child prior to clinical events appeared important to parents also, as mothers consistently commented that *they* would tell their child what was happening if the doctor did not.

The value placed on both being included and informed by the child participants in our study supports suggestions by Myerscough & Ford (1996) that it is important to include patients with a disability and it is not acceptable to communicate solely to a third party (such as the parent). However, despite the concerns of Myerscough & Ford (1996) children in our study reported that doctors generally do communicate directly to them, not just to their parents.

Children's perceptions of going to hospital regularly. Previous research (Inman, 1991) has identified that in some instances children perceived the medical consultation as less important than the other social aspects of visiting the hospital as an outpatient. This was the case for Corey—he looked forward to an 'outing' and perceived this as the most significant aspect of hospital visits, not the medical consultation:

> BG: Do you like going to the doctors?
> Corey: Yes ... we get to go to McDonalds ... [lines edited for brevity] ... No! I don't go there anymore ... I go to the cafe! ... to get a chocolate ... [lines edited for brevity].
> BG: So you like going to the doctors because you get to have McDonalds, is there anything else that's good about going to the doctors?
> Corey: I get the froth off Nana.
> Mum: He gets the froth off Nana's cappuccino.

Mothers' Perceptions and Experiences

While it is well stated in the available literature that some health professionals communicate quite insensitively with families (e.g. Quine & Pahl, 1986; Quine & Rutter, 1994), we felt it necessary to record that this remains the case. Even though mothers in our study stated several times that they were 'generally satisfied' with the communication between their child, their child's doctors and themselves, other comments indicated that frustration was still a predominant theme. For instance, frustration was linked with a delay in the child's diagnosis and poor communication in the delivery of that diagnosis.

Some parents perceived that the delay in diagnosis was deliberate due to the fear doctors had about misdiagnosis:

> ... it shouldn't be up to a doctor whether they tell them [the parents] now or ... later ... I feel that doctors still tend to keep it quiet until it gets to a point where it's too obvious ... before they're perfect and can turn around and say 'yes it is cerebral palsy'... it's like they're putting off actually ... telling you ... I'd rather know up front if I've got an instinct there's something wrong, tell me there's something wrong.

In addition, the overt comment (below) provides a clear example of the nature of the degree of difficulty in communication upon delivery of diagnosis:

> ... the first doctor I saw at the Children's Hospital, he's the one that told me [child's name] has cerebral palsy, he was ... not nice at all, yeah ... he doesn't talk nice, he talk to you like ... you're not human, and he talks about the child like he's an animal ... so I didn't like that doctor ... he describe him like he's a 'dead vegetable' ... and here's a paper, sign it ... we have to send him ... to a nursing home or whatever.

Lack of information for care management. Also associated with frustration was the perceived lack of information given to parents by their child's doctor. This confirms previous research (Quine & Rutter, 1994), which found that parents did not receive information regarding the child's future development, or advice on how to help and manage their child. Mothers in our study also perceived that information transfer required for care management was lacking, and they were left wondering how the disability would affect their child and the family. For example, one mother believed it was important for doctors to supply parents with information regarding the services available to help in everyday living, such as adjustments to the family home, funding available for wheelchairs and equipment, and where to go to get a parking permit for people with a disability:

> They should have something ... why don't they have leaflets on, on Melbourne City Mission? 'This is what this company does ... Yooralla, this is what they do'.

Lack of information for decision-making. Some doctors' communication skills were also perceived to hinder parental ability to make informed decisions regarding treatment options for their child. In some cases, it appeared that doctors did not provide sufficient information or options to parents regarding particular treatments or surgery for their child, and often became quite rude when the family questioned the need for or, in fact, sought a second opinion:

> ... he [the neurosurgeon] originally recommended doing a partial dorsal rhizotomy, which is cutting the nerves to the legs ... another doctor had suggested something else that wasn't quite as drastic and we said we'd like to try that first so he wasn't impressed ... and was quite ... short and blunt and everything about it ... but we just put it down to that hopefully he was having a bad day, he was an excellent surgeon ... but I think if you had doctors like that all the time it'd be pretty horrible going to.

The abrupt response of the neurosurgeon when the family decided not to go ahead with the recommended surgery is consistent with a doctor operating within the expert model (Cunningham & Davis, 1985), where doctors believe it is in the patients' best interests if the doctor alone, makes all the decisions. The neurosurgeon may have felt that his medical expertise was being undermined and that it was in the child's best interests if his recommendations were carried through. Contrary to this, parents want to be informed and involved in decision-making, particularly when surgery and subsequent rehabilitation are involved.

Development of assertiveness. In response to the frustration experienced by most mothers, and possibly as a result, some mothers perceived themselves as having developed a sense of assertiveness that they did not possess before having a child with CP:

> And I'll tell you what, after having [child's name] I've, I've become man, I've grown balls! I really have ... I have become so strong ... I take no crap, you tell me straight off, don't beat around the bush.

This mother suggested that, due to her increased assertiveness, she received more straightforward responses from doctors treating her child, and tests were performed promptly without waiting several days or even weeks. This is consistent with Street (1992) who found that parents who asked more questions, and expressed more concerns and frustrations received more information and directives from doctors.

Gender issues. Whether a doctor was male or female did not appear to be important to the mothers (or children) in our study. What was important was the perceived expertise of the doctor and that they were approachable:

> I don't mind [if the doctor is male or female], as long as they're nice and good!

However, a gender issue raised by one of the mothers was that communication is largely directed at the mother during consultations where both the child's mother and father are present:

> I definitely, definitely, um, can state that not everything's directed at the father, everything's always directed at the mother ... and my husband picked up on that from when [child's name] was first born ... and the eye contact is with the mother and everything's said to the mother, and the father's like, and he said to me 'well why did I even come?' it's like 'why am I here?' ... 'nothing's said to me' ... and that's always been a problem with dads ... always.

This raises questions about the way in which doctors perceive the role of fathers as carers. It may be further evidence of the gendered division of care in society (Braithwaite, 1986), whereby some doctors, like others in society, assume that the mother is the main caregiver of the child and thus communicates mostly with her during the consultation. This highlights the potential communication difficulties that might arise between fathers and their child's doctors, and needs to be further explored. It may also be one of the reasons why fathers were less inclined to participate in our research.

Support from other parents. A previous study (Case, 2000) identified that families believe the only useful advice comes from other parents who have a child with a disability, not a doctor. Similarly, some mothers in the present study reported that other parents who have a child with a disability are a great source of support and, because some doctors were perceived as providing parents with inadequate information, other parents were able to fulfill this need:

> ... CP is a physical disability, no one explained that to me, I learned that from other parents.

> ... if it wasn't for other parents I wouldn't have known anything [a little later on] ... first of all it was playgroup and I met up with [other mother 1] and [other mother 2] and we've become fairly close, I mean, now it's like '... I saw this thing on the internet, you've gotta see it, it's grouse! It does this it does that!'. You know, and like, if it wasn't for them two I wouldn't have known anything.

Continuity of care as a means of developing partnership. Continuity of care, as opposed to short-term involvement, was found to be important for all mothers in our study. They perceived it as enhancing communication during the medical consultation, and enabling their child to be more relaxed and comfortable:

> ... you know [child's name] loves going to see [his paediatrician] ... loves going to see [his other paediatrician], it's like you know, 'oh great!' ... they're more like friends and you know that most general appointments aren't going to be that way.

Mothers identified that doctors treated and communicated 'normally' with their child. For example, talking and focusing on the child, informing the child when performing tests, using humour to enhance communication, viewing the child's misbehaviour as normal 'child' behaviour and communicating in a non-patronising manner. The relationships between these children and their long-term doctors (who were often paediatricians) is consistent with the findings of Tates & Meeuwesen (2001), yet in other ways dissimilar. They found that when the doctor interacts with the child he/she was largely restricted to social behaviour and joking to stop the doctor feeling uncomfortable, yet the relationships between children and their doctors in our study were quite different. As one mother stated (below), humour is used by the doctor as a means of relating to the child, rather than as a response to the doctor feeling uncomfortable. Mothers also perceived that continuity of care provided the doctor with a more holistic view of their child, which in turn led to an understanding of the child's overall personality, not just the impairment. This they perceived as leading to better communication and better health outcomes:

> So it's not only knowing his medical history she knows his behaviour, his stubbornness, his idiosyncrasies so she takes all that into account with things as well ... I think because she's got a bit of a wicked sense of humour, [child's name] even when he's being mischievous she doesn't sort of um, pussy foot around she says 'have you got your devil horns of again [child's name]?!' ... I think, I think he just likes that she sort of talks to him and relates to him that, but in a straight way too, if he's messing around or if he's been playing up being silly she's on it, she doesn't just go ... soft and ... gushy.

> Even though ... he [the child] mightn't understand it all but she [the general practitioner] still makes an effort by not talking in baby talk but by talking to him at the level she thinks that he will understand.

Continuity of care not only appears to benefit children in terms of communication, but also provides support for parents. We found that parents perceived a sense of partnership with their child's doctor when communication was open and they felt respected (Consumers' Health Forum, 1999).

While research (O'Sullivan *et al.*, 1992) has indicated that some paediatricians are not helpful with information relating to the effect of the disability on personal or family needs, our study (although comparatively small) found that a number of mothers reported a great deal of support from their child's paediatrician. This included paediatricians being approachable and easy to talk to, as well as responding appropriately to questions and returning phone calls in a timely fashion. In some cases, support from the paediatrician was provided for the family as a whole, not just the child. This confirms suggestions by Taanila *et al.* (1998) that skilful support by doctors makes a significant contribution to the functioning of the child and family:

> ... they [his two paediatricians] don't just sort of advise just for [child's name] but looking at the whole picture as a whole family and how things will affect us and how [child's name] will cope with things and you know, long term pictures ... I think the doctors, the two main doctors that we have, have always gone out of their way to support and work as a whole affect on everything.

Although much research reports that the pattern of doctor–parent communication that operates is still the paternalistic one (Law Reform Commission of Victoria, 1989; Davis & Fallowfield, 1991; Case, 2000; Charles et al., 2000) and that the partnership model is often lacking, it appears in our study, that when there is continuity of care the doctor is less authoritarian and parents are more autonomous.

Different Perceptions of Children and Mothers

While the children and mothers in our study had similar views about the importance of communication, there were obvious differences in what was perceived to be important. As previous research has suggested, children and adults have a different understanding and experience of the world (Thomas & O'Kane, 1998), and this was shown to be the case for the children and mothers in our pilot study. This further reiterates the importance of gaining the child's perspective (Morrow & Richards, 1996; Davis, 1998) when conducting exploratory research into their experiences, not just the parent's.

Concluding Comments

Our pilot study provides valuable information and insight into how children with a disability and their parents perceive the way in which doctors communicate with them in the medical consultation. The results support the findings of previous research examining parental perspectives and further highlights the importance of encouraging continuity of care as a means of developing a sense of partnership. Given that the concerns voiced about doctor–patient communication are centred on issues of understanding, our study clarifies the need for doctors to ascertain (from both children and parents) the degree to which their child patients wish to be included in the consultation. In addition, as researchers, by including children with disabilities as informants we not only enabled them to voice their opinions, but we in turn were empowered in providing a more accurate evidence base for informing improvements in policy and clinical practice.

What remains to be done in future research is to further explore some of the issues raised by the participants in our study. This includes an examination of the perceived lack of interaction between doctors and fathers in the consultation, and an examination into the reasons why some children prefer not to know the details of their medical condition from their doctor and others might. It also includes engaging with doctors as participants who can inform us about their perceptions of communicating with children who have a disability and their parents in the consultation—this would enable us to gain a more holistic view of communication in the medical consultation from the perspective of all involved—the doctor, the parent and the child.

REFERENCES

AUSTRALIAN AND NEW ZEALAND PERINATAL SOCIETIES (1995) The origins of cerebral palsy—a consensus statement, *Medical Journal of Australia*, 162, pp. 85–90.

BAIN, K. (1998) Children with severe disabilities: options for residential care, *Medical Journal of Australia*, 169, pp. 598–600.
BAKER, K. & DONELLY, M. (2001) The social experiences of children with disability and the influence of environment: a framework for intervention, *Disability & Society*, 16, pp. 71–85.
BERESFORD, B. & SLOPER, P. (2000) *Information Needs of Disabled Young People* (York, Social Policy Research Unit, University of York).
BICKENBACH, J.E., CHATTERJI, S., BADLEY, E.M. & ÜSTUN, T.B. (1999) Models of disablement, universalism and the international classification of impairments, disabilities and handicaps, *Social Science & Medicine*, 48, pp. 1173–1187.
BRAITHWAITE, V.A. (1986) The burden of home care: how is it shared? *Community Health Studies*, 10(Suppl.), pp. 7–11.
BRICHER, G. (2000) Disabled people, health professionals and the social model of disability: can there be a research relationship? *Disability & Society*, 15, pp. 781–793.
BRISENDEN, S. (1998) Independent living and the medical model of disability, in: T. SHAKESPEARE (Ed.) *The Disability Reader: social science perspectives*, pp. 20–27 (London, Cassell).
CANT, R. (1992) Friendship, neighbouring and the isolated family: the case of families with disabled children, *International Journal of Sociology of the Family*, 22, pp. 31–50.
CASE, S.P. (2000) Refocusing on the parent: what are the social issues of concern for parents of disabled children? *Disability & Society*, 15, pp. 271–292.
CASE, S.P. (2001) Learning to partner, disabling conflict: early indicators of an improving relationship between parents and professionals with regard to service provision for children with learning disabilities, *Disability & Society*, 16, pp. 837–854.
CHARLES, C., GAFNI, A. & WHELAN, T. (2000) How to improve communication between doctors and patients. Learning more about the decision making context is important, *British Medical Journal*, 320, pp. 1220–1221.
CONSUMERS' HEALTH FORUM (1999) Building partnerships in general practice, *Australian Health Consumer*, 3, pp. 20–22.
CRISP, R. (2000) A qualitative study of the perceptions of individuals with disabilities concerning health and rehabilitation professionals, *Disability & Society*, 15, pp. 355–367.
CUNNINGHAM, C. & DAVIS, H. (1985) *Working with Parents: frameworks for collaboration* (Buckingham, Open University Press).
DAVIS, H. & FALLOWFIELD, L. (1991) *Counselling and Communication in Health Care* (Chichester, John Wiley & Sons).
DAVIS, J. (1998) Understanding the meanings of children: a reflexive process, *Children & Society*, 12, pp. 325–335.
DEPARTMENT OF HUMAN SERVICES (2002) *Victorian State Disability Plan 2002–2012: a summary* (Melbourne, Victorian Government Department of Human Services).
DETHERIDGE, T. (2000) Research involving children with severe learning difficulties, in: A. LEWIS & G. LINDSAY (Eds) *Researching Children's Perspectives*, pp. 112–121 (Buckingham, Open University Press).
DONOVAN, T.J., REDDIHOUGH, D.S., COURT, J.M. & DOYLE, L.W. (1989) Health literature for parents of children with cerebral palsy, *Developmental Medicine & Child Neurology*, 31, pp. 489–493.
GOODLEY, D. (2001) 'Learning difficulties', the social model of disability and impairment: challenging epistemologies, *Disability & Society*, 16, pp. 207–231.
INMAN, C.E. (1991) Analysed interaction in a children's oncology clinic: the child's view and parent's opinion of the effect of medical encounters, *Journal of Advanced Nursing*, 16, pp. 782–793.
LAGERLØV, P., LESETH, A. & MATHESON, I. (1998) The doctor–patient relationship and the management of asthma, *Social Science & Medicine*, 47, pp. 85–91.
LAW REFORM COMMISSION OF VICTORIA. (1989) *Informed Decisions about Medical Procedures—Doctor and Patient Studies* (Melbourne, LRCV).
LENNEY, M. & SERCOMBE, H. (2002) 'Did you see that guy in the wheelchair down the pub?' Interactions across difference in a public place, *Disability & Society*, 17, pp. 5–18.

Lewis, A. & Lindsay, G. (Eds) (2000) *Researching Children's Perspectives* (Buckingham, Open University Press).
Liamputtong Rice, P. & Ezzy, D. (1999) *Qualitative Research Methods: a health focus* (Melbourne, Oxford University Press).
Mauthner, M. (1997) Methodological aspects of collecting data from children: lessons from three research projects, *Children & Society*, 11, pp. 16–28.
Meeuwesen, L. & Kaptein, M. (1996) Changing interactions in doctor–parent–child communication, *Psychology & Health*, 11, pp. 787–795.
Meryn, S. (1998) Improving doctor–patient communication. Not an option, but a necessity, *British Medical Journal*, 316, p. 1922.
Minichiello, V., Aroni, R., Timewell, E. & Alexander, L. (1995) *In-depth Interviewing: principles, techniques, analysis*, 2nd edn (Melbourne, Longman Australia).
Minkes, J., Robinson, C. & Weston, C. (1994) Consulting the children: interviews with children using residential respite care services, *Disability & Society*, 9, pp. 47–57.
Mitchell, W. & Sloper, P. (2001) Quality in services for disabled children and their families: what can theory, policy and research on childrens' and parents' views tell us? *Children & Society*, 15, pp. 237–252.
Morrow, V. & Richards, M. (1996) The ethics of social research with children: an overview, *Children & Society*, 10, pp. 90–105.
Myerscough, P. & Ford, M. (1996) *Talking with Patients—Keys to Good Communication*, 3rd edn (New York, Oxford University Press).
Oliver, M. (1996) *Understanding Disability: from theory to practice* (London, Macmillan).
O'Sullivan, P., Mahoney, G. & Robinson, C. (1992) Perceptions of pediatricians' helpfulness: a national study of mothers of young disabled children, *Developmental Medicine & Child Neurology*, 34, pp. 1064–1071.
Pantell, R.H., Stewart, T.J., Dias, J.K., Wells, P. & Ross, A.W. (1982) Physician communication with children and parents, *Pediatrics*, 70, pp. 396–402.
Quine, L. & Pahl, J. (1986) First diagnosis of mental handicap: characteristics of unsatisfactory encounters between doctors and parents, *Social Science & Medicine*, 22, pp. 53–62.
Quine, L. & Rutter, D.R. (1994) First diagnosis of severe mental and physical disability: a study of doctor–parent communication, *Journal of Child Psychology & Psychiatry & Allied Disciplines*, 35, pp. 1273–1287.
Reddihough, D.S., Tinworth, S., Moore, T.G. & Ihsen, E. (1996) Early intervention: professional views and referral practices of Australian paediatricians, *Journal of Paediatrics & Child Health*, 32, pp. 246–250.
Roter, D. & Hall, J. (1993) *Doctors Talking with Patients/Patients Talking with Doctors—Improving Communication in Medical Visits* (Connecticut, Auburn House).
Ruusuvuori, J. (2001) Looking means listening: coordinating displays of engagement in doctor–patient interaction, *Social Science & Medicine*, 52, pp. 1093–1108.
SCOPE (2002) *Disability Speak: communicating and interacting with people who have a disability* (Melbourne, St Kilda).
Strauss, A. & Corbin, J. (1994) Grounded theory methodology: an overview, in: N. Denzin & Y. Lincoln (Eds) *Handbook of Qualitative Research*, pp. 273–285 (London, Sage).
Strauss, A. & Corbin, J. (1998) *Basics of Qualitative Research: techniques and procedures for developing grounded theory*, 2nd edn (London, Sage).
Street, R. (1992) Communication styles and adaptations in physician-parent consultations, *Social Science & Medicine*, 34, pp. 1155–1163.
Taanila, A., Jarvelin, M. & Kokkonen, J. (1998) Parental guidance and counselling by doctors and nursing staff: parents' views of initial information and advice for families with disabled children, *Journal of Clinical Nursing*, 7, pp. 505–511.
Tannen, D. & Wallat, C. (1986) Medical professionals and parents: a linguistic analysis of communication across contexts, *Language in Society*, 15, pp. 295–311.

TANNEN, D. & WALLAT, C. (1987) Interactive frames and knowledge schemas in interaction: examples from a medical examination/interview, *Social Psychology Quarterly*, 50, pp. 205–216.

TATES, K. & MEEUWESEN, L. (2001) Doctor–parent–child communication. A (re)view of the literature, *Social Science & Medicine*, 52, pp. 839–851.

THOMAS, N. & O'KANE, C. (1998) The ethics of participatory research with children, *Children & Society*, 12, pp. 336–348.

WATSON, N., SHAKESPEARE, T., CUNNINGHAM-BURLEY, S., BARNES, C., CORKER, M., DAVIS, J. & PRIESTLEY, M. (2000) *Life as a Disabled Child: a qualitative study of young people's experiences and perspectives*, final report to the ESRC (Edinburgh, Department of Nursing Studies, University of Edinburgh).

WORLD HEALTH ORGANISATION (2001) *International Classification of Functioning, Disability and Health: final draft*. Available at: http://www.who.int/icidh (accessed August 8, 2001).

ZWIERS, M. & MORRISSETTE, P. (1999) *Effective Interviewing of Children: a comprehensive guide for counselors and human service workers* (Philadelphia, Accelerated Development).

Nothing to be had 'off the peg': consumption, identity and the immobilization of young disabled people

Bill Hughes, Rachel Russell and Kevin Paterson
Glasgow Caledonian University, UK

Contemporary sociology makes the case that the concepts of society and social structure are past their sell-by dates. Our world is marked by impermanence and social life is characterised by mobilities. Even self-identity has become liquid. Social actors use consumption artefacts and services to re-design themselves in ways that are commensurate with their deepest desires. However, we argue that disabled people are unlikely to recognise themselves in these debates. Young disabled people, in their quest for identity and consumer citizenship, meet with ubiquitous barriers and closed markets. In their experience choice and mobility are rhetorical. They encounter immobilization and exclusion from the kinds of consumer lifestyles that their non-disabled peers take for granted. Furthermore, we argue, that at the heart of consumer culture is an aesthetic of youthfulness that is profoundly alien to 'the anomaly'. The signifiers of 'youth' and disability are in profound tension. Cultures of consumption are constituted in ways that mark young disabled people off as outsiders who need not apply for entry.

Introduction

Apparently, the pace of change in the contemporary world is such that structure is all but moribund. Newtonian time is dead. Long live the post-Newtonian world of plasticity, impermanence, flux and flow. Scholars of the natural world describe it as a place of chaos and complexity and some advise that sociology would be wise to reflect on this new post-Newtonian epistemological naturalism in order to renew its own—dated—methodological 'rules' (Urry, 2000a,b). This is not merely another obituary for Emile Durkheim. It is a postmodernist, soul-searching, millennialism in which the declaration of 'ends' is 'à la mode', if not compulsory. Keen observers of the sociological obituary columns will note that among the fatalities are society, the social and sociological theory (Seidman, 1991). Such concepts are in decline because they conjure up a picture of stasis and imply relative permanence and durability. They misrepresent the social world. They have become epistemologically inept and outdated because the world in which we live is about impermanence, flux, flow, plasticity, networks and mobilities. John Urry's view is that if sociology itself is to avoid the obituary column—to which many of its key categories are condemned—then it must embrace the temporal pace and indeterminacy that reflect the world it seeks to explain.

This should make interesting reading for sociologists interested in disability studies, particularly those in the UK who have been strong proponents of the social model. A sociology that has mobility rather than structure as its epistemological mantra does not sit well with the claim that disability is a form of social oppression or with a research paradigm that embodies an emancipatory imperative (Oliver, 1997; Barnes, 2001; Mercer 2002). Advocates of structure assume a 'relatively' stable society that supports and re-produces the indignities of oppression, legitimates emancipatory reseach and keeps alive the social divisions that make the world a place commensurate with the needs and values of non-disabled people.

Interestingly, the virtues of post-Newtonian science—from which it is proposed that mobile sociology acquires its epistemological template—seem to be eminently commensurate with sociological constructionism and consonant with much that can be traced to the impact of postmodern and poststructuralist thought on contemporary sociology. Proponents of the social model are, by contrast, much less sanguine about the value of the postmodern, social constructionist agenda (Barnes, 2003). The irony is that sociological admirers of chaos and complexity like Urry (2000a,b), Castells (1996) and Barbara Adam (1998) seem to be proposing a return to methodological naturalism, albeit primarily at a metaphorical level. Durkheim's methodological naturalism reflected the high point of sociological modernism and its re-birth, it seems, will signal the sociological good riddance to all the outdated modernist baggage. What chaos and complexity theorists hate above all else is reductionism and the way in which science has assumed that the link between explanation and prediction is unproblematic (Gleick, 1998; McLennan, 2003). Yet this sounds very familiar. There are many social scientists, mostly from the long and distinguished anti-positivist tradition, including those who contribute to the emancipatory agenda of Disability Studies, that have shared these same pet hates. This leaves one wondering if the message of 'mobile sociology' is as new as it claims. However, in this paper, we want to make the case that mobile sociology and its epistemological imperatives constitute a narrative that does not make much sense to disabled people. In particular, by drawing on empirical material and theoretical arguments that are derived from the emancipatory tradition in disability studies, we will argue that the contemporary sociological idea that self-identity and embodiment are mobile or liquid may be relevant to those non-disabled consumers who relate to the market place from a perspective of economic advantage but that the experience of young disabled people who may be trying to relate to the marketplace as a space of unlimited freedom and choice are, in fact, most likely to end up consuming segregated leisure in segregated spaces or relate to and engage with the 'mainstream' market in ways that are mediated by impairment or more importantly by material barriers to their participation in cultures of consumption.

Furthermore, the processes that exclude disabled people from consumer lifestyles and narrow their choices of projects of self-identity should also be understood at a politico-aesthetic level. The representation of consumer goods and services is based on the projection of an image, by way of advertising media, in which symbolic or ersatz value counts as much—or in Baudrillard's (1998; Featherstone, 1982) view displaces— use value. An object sells as something that embodies youth, vigour, beauty and so on. On the other hand the physical, social and cultural capital associated with the disabled body is measured in negative terms relative to the aesthetic criteria that dominate judgements about bodies in consumer culture (Hughes, 1999, 2000). There is, therefore, an exclusionary mechanism built into the semiotic fabric of the consumer good or service. It is 'designed' as an object that is alien to the carnal constitution of disabled people and young disabled people in particular. Objects of consumption tend to be sold by mobilising the signifiers of youth and perfection. The signifiers of disability do not appeal to advertisers who wish to market a product or service. The 'psychic' properties of disability are inimical to the desired image of the product. The 'anomaly' challenges cultures of consumption in ways that go the utopianism at its core and it de-stabilises the desire that is, assumed to be, at its heart.

Mobile or liquid identities

Identity in the contemporary world is mediated by consumption and consumer choice is regarded as the key variable in transforming identity from a 'solid' to a 'liquid' condition, from one in which work and class are the main determinants to one in which identity is 'nomadic' and can be expressed through a diverse range of 'tribal' affiliations. Identity in industrial societies was regarded as relatively stable and based on relatively permanent social class hierarchies. In post-industrial or post-modern societies, identity is regarded as multiple, fragmented, contingent and uncertain.

Contemporary divisions in social identity arise out of the expansion of retail capital, the growth of mass markets and the increasing commodification of experience. Within these divisions the distinction between social and personal identity is less evident. The realm of the personal has become not only politicised but increasingly a site for establishing social identity (Gilleard & Higgs, 2000, p. 29).

Identity has been transformed from the singular to the plural. It has become a 'project' (Giddens, 1991; Shilling, 2003) rather than an attribute heavily influenced, if not determined, by one's social and economic circumstances. Consumer choice is regarded as the key resource in the making and perhaps un-making of such projects and consumer goods are used by individuals to shape their life histories. Globalisation disentangles identity from its 'traditional' association with the nation state and transforms civil society into a world arena in which all manner of new forms of group membership and identification—real and hyper-real—are possible (Urry, 2000b). Relationships have become much less dependent on proximity as technologies like the Internet and the mobile phone foster new networks and solidarities (Castells, 1996).

Social relations become fragmented, broken up by the media of modernity and reconstituted across global vistas of space and time. Interaction is no longer confined to human co-presence in a shared time and physical space, becoming disembedded from such contexts and reconstituted on a global level. Furthermore, the mirror through which individuals identify themselves is no longer that of a purely local community, but is instead a global one where humanity as a whole has become a 'we' against which personal identity as an 'I' is constituted (Burkitt 1999, p. 138).

Contemporary social theory suggests that self or identity, therefore, is mobile, plastic and malleable. Sociologists are not so naive as to assume that identity is entirely a matter of choice, but much of the rhetoric around identity assumes that there is a cornucopia of opportunities to form affiliations that will make projects of self-identity exciting and varied and that the satisfaction of desire is merely a purchase away. These arguments recognise the importance of surface and appearance in the making of contemporary identities and assume that 'we now have the means to exert an unprecedented degree of control over our bodies' (Shilling, 2003, p. 2):

> The body appears to provide a firm foundation on which to reconstruct a reliable sense of self in the modern world. Indeed, the increasingly reflexive ways in which people are relating to their bodies can be seen as one of the defining features of high-modernity. (Shilling, 2003, pp. 2–3)

Yet how much choice do disabled people have in relation to their bodies or over their affiliations and relationships, and what are the barriers for young disabled people who might wish to develop a project of identity by adopting a particular consumer lifestyle? It is these questions that this paper seeks to address. The affirmation of liquid identities by many sociologists and the transformation of mobility into a project for the renewal of sociology (Urry, 2000a,b) seem to ignore the view that for some people identity may be beyond the control of the individual and may in fact be re-enforced and even predicated upon forms of social and spatial organisation. Such processes can be difficult, if not impossible to escape if one wishes to do so and they may, at the very least, circumscribe one's project of self-identity. If a consumer society delivers or is supposed to deliver freedom, choice and 'liquidity' in relation to embodiment and self-identity, then it is not at all clear that it does so with equanimity.

Indeed, contemporary forms of social and spatial organisation are constitutive of disability (Oliver, 1990). A personal project of self-identity might help a disabled person to multiply their identities but such a project would be spitting in the wind with respect to social organisation. Contemporary social organisation 'invalidates'

(Hughes, 1999) or immobilises people with impairments. One should not read this claim as vindication of the disablist view that disabled people are short on agency but rather that young disabled people, in particular, are produced as 'docile subjects' through 'specialised' recreational and leisure services (Fullager & Owler, 1998). On the contrary, disabled people have been very active in challenging discrimination and exclusion but they are a long way from achieving enabling and inclusive social institutions (Barton, 2001). The 'liquidity' and 'mobility' that seems to mark non-disabled people's lives is not so apparent in the lives of disabled people. The 'othering' of disabled people, the process by which they are constituted as strangers in the contemporary world, means that the enterprise of identity formation among disabled people is regularly immobilised (Hughes, 2002). The growth of disability pride suggests that disabled people do not want to be other than they are. They are not rejecting disability as an identity or trying to escape the biological realities of impairment (Swain & French, 2000). They are, however, exasperated by the exclusionary processes that blight desire and curtail their opportunities to participate in contemporary cultures of consumption. Young disabled people seem to be very aware of the identity dynamics that reinforce their exclusion (Morris, 2002; Murray, 2002) and the ways in which their difference, far from being celebrated as diversity, is used to stereotype them as tragic figures. The Disabled People's Movement demands rights instead of charity but in everyday life disabled people are treated as if they are charity cases and related to as something other than fully-fledged persons. Constraints upon the development of identity are myriad and markets of desire that offer the important trinkets of identity are not always open or easily accessible to disabled people.

We should also note that the liquid life comes at a price. A mobile identity depends on consumption and it is important to note that 'in terms of the acquisition of valued consumer goods, disabled people, who usually have lower that average incomes tend to lose out' (Barnes & Mercer, 2003, p. 52). Many disabled people are poor. They have become part of that social group which Bauman (1997, p. 93) calls the 'new poor', those who have a deficit of economic capital and, therefore, are categorised as 'flawed consumers'. However, it is not only economic constraints that make the search for identity among young disabled people a frustrating experience.

The debate about identity in mainstream youth literature has been influenced by the metaphor of liquidity or mobility. This is hardly surprising, given that youth is widely regarded the most important period of identity formation and that it is often conceived as a period of 'storm and stress' (Du Bois-Reymond, 1997; Rattansi & Pheonix, 1997). Griffin (1997a,b) notes that young disabled people have a 'separate' status in this debate because the notion of flexible identity is largely confined to the triad of gender, ethnicity and class with sexuality bringing up the rear. The assumption seems to be that the proper place to discuss disabled identity is in the therapeutic literature. Mainstream youth studies still relates to disability as a 'natural' category which not only confuses disability with the concept of impairment but, also, assumes that the biological status of a disabled person is an obdurate barrier to identity experimentation. The next section will be devoted to an analysis of the barriers that young disabled people face as they try to develop projects of self-identity through participation in contemporary cultures of consumption.

Consuming segregation or the immobilisation of young disabled people's identity projects

Statutory and policy initiatives, such as the Disability Discrimination Act 1995; the Human Rights Act 1998; the Quality Protects Programme (England); Children First (Wales) and the Framework for Social Justice (Scotland), assume as a matter of principle that young disabled people have the right to be included in mainstream social and cultural activities. However, young disabled people are frustrated by the gap between the official rhetoric and their ubiquitous experience of being denied access to public transport, the built environment and the public spaces of production and consumption which non-disabled people take for granted. Young disabled people claim that their lives are not valued and that this is reflected in failures of public policy (Murray, 2002). Young disabled people don't have the same choices as their non-disabled peers. They experience diminished access to cultural and consumption activities (Cavet, 1998; Hirst & Baldwin, 1994). In a culture where consumer lifestyle is central to identity, particularly amongst young people (Miles, 2000), the curtailment of leisure and consumption opportunities is a major social disadvantage.

Segregated schooling can mean loneliness and exclusion when it comes to life beyond the school gates (Morris, 1999, 2002; Watson *et al.*, 1999; Abbott *et al.*, 2001). Young disabled people want to participate in mainstream leisure activities and describe their interests as being no different to young people in general: music, bowling, clubbing, hanging out, going to the shops, the pictures, the pub, out for meals or on holiday are the priorities (Murray, 2002). However, these interests and activities are not always organised in inclusive ways. Stalker (2002) argues that young disabled people in Scotland, like most of their non-disabled peers, want to have fun, experiment and learn from their mistakes (see also Children in Scotland, 2002). The forms of exclusion that young disabled people experience as they try to embrace mainstream cultures of consumption are many and varied. For example, Murray (2002) noted that her young respondents with visual impairments felt much aggrieved by the fact that Braille or large print editions of popular books—like the Harry Potter series—were not published until well after the standard edition. This, they argued, with some conviction, left them with little 'street credibility' and had a detrimental effect on their relationships with non-disabled peers. Watson *et al.* (1999) found that, although disabled children wanted to locate themselves within the mainstream consumer activities of their peers, there were a plethora of physical, attitudinal and communication barriers that, effectively, smothered such ambitions.

Morris (1999) argues that some young disabled people are, in effect 'warehoused' in residential institutions. They have few opportunities to make friends, be involved in their local community, or do anything meaningful day or night. Scope for any personal development is conspicuous by its absence. Some of the young people placed in residential establishments have little or no continuing contact with their social services department. This includes young people like Jennifer. Her extramural excursions are twice weekly either to a day centre or to visit her parents (Morris, 1999). Her life is dominated by choices made by others. Many young disabled people—who are not institutionalised—have little choice but to spend a lot of their leisure time with their parents, family or paid carers (Stalker, 2002; Children in Scotland (SHS), 2002). Such a high degree of 'adult surveillance' means that young disabled people have little experience of an independent social life (Morris, 1999, 2002). Parental dependency isolates them from the majority of their non-disabled peers (Murray, 2002), from experimentation and 'risk taking' (Cavet, 1998) and from the distinctive consumer lifestyles that characterise youth identity. You can't go clubbing or 'hang out' with your Mum and Dad. Youth culture depends on freedom from adult control but disabled kids—particularly girls—just don't get it (Thomas, 1998).

The geographical and corporeal mobility that is a marker of contemporary living is not reflected in the lives of young disabled people. They are less likely to play in the street, much more likely to pass time in their own home or garden than their non-disabled counterparts (Howard, 1996). Disabled children and young people also claim poor access to fast-food outlets and other child-centred spaces (Watson *et al.*, 1999) as well as shops, theatres, cinemas, pubs, clubs and banks (Hirst & Baldwin, 1994: Scottish Consumer Council, 1996). Access to leisure and consumer goods and activities is problematic for all young disabled people but the form that the problem takes varies with the kind of impairment. Young people with physical impairments voice most discontent about the infrastructure of consumer space and refer to reliance on family and friends for assistance because of the inaccessible design of urban centres and the transport networks that feed them. Young people with visual impairments also critique the organisation of space but tend to focus on the need to improve the ways in which goods and services are presented. Clarity with labelling and sign-posting and more audio messaging would make the experience of consumption much more inclusive for young people with visual impairments. Young people with hearing impairment are concerned primarily with communication barriers. They require more visual information, a much more disability-aware customer service orientation and appropriate deployment of apposite technology to alleviate the problems of exclusion associated with the ubiquitous use of the telephone. Young people with learning difficulties experience exclusion and discrimination that is largely a product of attitudinal and temporal barriers. Their lives as consumers could be much improved by exchange relationships that embody the virtue of 'patience' (Scottish Consumer Council, 1996). Research into the experience of young disabled people as consumers looks like a testimonial to the existence of multiple forms of immobilisation and a multiplicity of disempowering barriers. Disability business is big business but the customer—in this particular case—is not king:

> Disability is the focus of a multi-million dollar business comprised of diverse stakeholders in a capitalistic market place, where helping disabled people and making money are important goals. The stakeholder group include health care and medical professions;

hospitals, therapy businesses and home care agencies; assisted care living facilities; the pharmaceutical, medical supply and technology industries and insurance companies; architects, law practices, banks and accounting firms specializing in disability; government and lobby groups; politicians; and last, the consumer. In this environment, the consumer/disabled person is the stakeholder with the least power (Albrecht, 2002, p. 32)

Disabled people have mobilised themselves into a social movement in order to resist segregation and exclusion (Oliver, 1990). One should not assume that they are passive consumers but the markets in which they are positioned are not marked by responsiveness. So far we have focused on problems of access in relation to 'mainstream' consumption activities and the open market but disabled people also engage with a social market and a niche market in rehabilitation goods.

It should be noted that the non-disabled stakeholders who dominate both the social market and the specialist market in rehabilitation goods, tend to assume that a disabled identity is determined by a specific diagnostic category and by the tragedy and poor quality of life that is consequent upon it. These are not markets that encourage mobility or offer goods and services that might allow disabled people to engage with diverse, mainstream consumer lifestyles. The market in rehabilitation goods offers many useful prosthetic technologies which can and do enhance the lives and mobility of disabled people but it is driven by biological rather than social imperatives and while it may offer some excellent aids and state of the art wheelchairs, it is, in some senses, dependent for its survival on the inaccessibility of the 'major urban consumption items such as housing, education, transport and finance' (Gleeson, 1999, p. 138).

In the social market, disabled people tend to be 'captive customers' (Riddell *et al.*, 1999). The metaphor is diametrically opposed to the notion of the mobile citizen with a liquid identity. In fact Riddell *et al.* (1999) argue that the social market in for example, post-school education, training and community care, particularly for young people with learning difficulties, is one dominated by 'restriction'. Care managers and professionals make choices about what services young disabled people will get and what establishments that they will visit. The 'customers' might choose—from a pretty inflexible set of options—what activities they will participate in when they consume the service or participate in their designated establishment but the big decisions are the prerogative of the professionals. Cavet (1998) notes that young disabled people tend to be corralled into what she calls 'organised' as opposed to 'casual' leisure where the former suggests play or other activities that are managed and controlled by adults. As non-disabled children become teenagers, they tend to drift away from 'organised leisure' and find much more personal satisfaction in the casual culture of the street or the bedroom. For young disabled people, confined to the social market with its specialist, segregated forms of provision, there are few opportunities to escape from 'organised' activities. Fullagar and Owler (1998) show how the identity of people with learning difficulties has been produced through a narrative of 'lack' and 'incapacity' and that 'organised' leisure activities reflect this narrative. For people with learning difficulties, leisure has been framed in therapeutic and quantitative terms, but the emphasis is on 'filling-in time'. Leisure is equivalent to a rationalisation of time and space, a set of activities that keep disabled people occupied and supervised. In this context, the management of 'undesirable' behaviour is paramount. Activities are benign and despite the putative therapeutic intentions, they do not seem to support the development and formation of identity. In fact, leisure provision is driven by the economics of respite programmes, and therefore the needs of non-disabled carers. Disabled people's needs are secondary to carers who do paid work, or who need a break from unpaid work. Disabled service users are offered a conventional menu of events. If they are challenged by stakeholders because they are repetitive in nature, the standard response is that they are 'what people want'. 'Organised' social market leisure provision tends to produce individuals with poor leisure planning skills and little or no desire to make their own plans. Activities are repetitious and reproduce the routine of the (Fordist) workplace. They tend to inculcate a sense of fixed identity and produce 'docile subjects' (Fullager & Owler, 1998).

Clearly, the markets that have most significance for young disabled people are not particularly responsive to their projects of self-identity. Access to the mainstream open, market—despite contemporary projects like shopmobility and motobility—is still limited and problematic and entry into it can sometimes be heavily policed by an unwanted but practically necessary adult presence. The social market, therefore, is the segregated, unsatisfactory alternative to which some young people feel compelled to turn. Other young disabled people, particularly those with learning difficulties or severe physical impairments will have little experience of the spontaneous, casual leisure that develops organically from peer group affiliations. They will be used to consuming 'organized' leisure in segregated spaces. However, these forms of everyday immobilisation that young disabled people face as they are growing up should be contextualised. In the next section, we will make the case that young disabled people are constituted as 'flawed' consumers by the core aesthetic assumptions that underpin consumerism and by the ways in which objects of consumption are highly consonant with the meanings associated with youth but, largely, irreconcilable with anomaly.

Flawed consumers

The ancient Greeks were uncomfortable with imperfection and impairment. Such aesthetic sensibilities led to the exclusion of disabled people, to the banishment of the anomaly. Furthermore, infanticide has been a response to the birth of disabled children in a significant range of cultures. Modernity treated impairment as a pathology and disabled people—conceived through the prism of medical discourse—have been incarcerated in medical and educational institutions in which custodial rather than therapeutic values have dominated (Goffman, 1968; Braddock & Parish, 2001). Excluded from work on the grounds of 'impaired' labour power, disabled people, throughout modernity, have been constituted as 'flawed producers', as a group who burden the public purse or are dependent on the philanthropic instincts of well-intentioned (non-disabled) citizens. The notion that disabled people are 'flawed' or 'in deficit' and, therefore, living 'tragic' lives is writ large in the modern history of disabled people (see Humphries & Gordon, 1992). Eugenics as a response to disability was an early twentieth century social movement in which disabled bodies became the target of sterilisation and—in a totalitarian context—extermination (Kerr & Shakespeare, 2002). The 'othering' of disabled people and particularly disabled children has taken many forms including elimination, de-sexualisation, and incarceration. All of these practices are examples of extreme forms of 'immobilisation' or what Urry (2002b) has called 'coerced immobility'.

The immobilisation of young disabled people in their capacity as consumers is not only related to the exclusionary public policies described in the last paragraph or to the forms of market closure and constraint described in the preceding section but also to the aesthetics and semiotics of consumption and identity. Shilling (2003, p. 2–3) argues that 'it is the exterior territories, or surfaces of the body that symbolize the self at a time when unprecedented value is placed on the youthful, trim and sexual body'. Consumer culture positions youth at its heart. Youthfulness is an embodied quality that we are encouraged to consume and because consumer goods and services are represented as embodying the virtues that signify youthfulness (Featherstone, 1982). The qualities associated with disability and impairment symbolise negative value and deficit with respect to physical, cultural and social capital. Such qualities are not consistent with consumer desire but with practices of correction. 'The word orthopaedics', as Shakespeare and Watson note (1998, p. 20) derives from the Greek for 'child correction'. In a disablist society, youth slips easily into a discourse of desire, disability into a discourse of waste.

Youth signifies beauty, hope, potency, vigour, and strength. These 'ideal-typical' traits suggest that youth as a concept embodies everything that is not anomalous as well as everything that one might desire to represent one's identity. In fact, the category of youth, as a desired attribute of identity, implies the erasure or transcendence of anomaly. Disability is a signifier of ugliness, tragedy, asexuality, invalidity and frailty. These are the very qualities that signify the anomalous and the pathological and symbolise what Goffman (1963) once called 'spoiled identity'. Youth and disability, as signifiers, in a culture of consumption in which the 'external territories' of the body are paramount, are opposite and incompatible.

YOUTH	DISABILITY
beauty	ugliness
hope	tragedy
potency	asexuality
vigour	invalidity
strength	frailty

These binaries position youth and disability as 'categorically' incompatible. There is no way in which one can square the difference because the opposites repel rather than attract. Disability and youth are in profound tension and the logocentric imaginary is unable to bring them into harmonious relationship. In this meeting of mismatched signifiers disability has no hope of modifying the utopian narcissism of youth nor can it intrude in the happy harmony between youth and consumption. The concept 'disabled youth' is uncomfortable, continuously slipping into the liminal, because the former introduces the anomalous into the latter and deconstructs the possibility of aesthetic grandeur. One is compelled to conclude that youth and disability constitute two very distinct and incompatible 'tribes', identities that clash and recoil from one another. The way in which disability is expelled from youth is not simply a question of metaphorical or semiotic repulsion. It arises from the social processes that construct the aesthetic as unequivocally non-disabled (Silvers, 2002) and disability as sub-human. The voice of the mother of a young disabled person makes this point with striking clarity:

> People think of our children as something separate—when they think of them at all. They're not even in the same category as those who've had a dramatic accident and become paralysed ... because you see, they were once 'real' people and that's what makes the difference. If you were never 'real' then you are best left forgotten. (Quoted in Read, 2000, p. 99)

One notes that the meaning of impairment is transformed from an attribute of a person to a master status that makes it absolutely equivalent to the anomaly. This process preserves the integrity of the 'normal' but objectifies, dehumanises and invalidates disability. The status of consumer and citizen is stripped away. Meanwhile, as the biographies of disabled people are naturalised so that they become nothing more than the fossilised imprints of their (so-called) mental and physical abnormalities, objects of consumption acquire social meaning. Appadurai (1986, p. 3) notes that because commodities circulate in regimes of value, they have 'like persons, social lives'. Economic and social relations create material cultures of consumption and a symbolic world of value in which fetish objects are enlivened. In this world of value the signifiers of youth—beauty, hope, potency, vigour and strength—and the meanings attributed to objects of consumption are at one with each other. They embrace in happy partnership and on terms that signal the banishment of the anomaly and its guilt by association with the anti-aesthetic, namely, the ugly, the tragic, the asexual, the invalid and the frail. Youth and its signifiers will sell, disability will not! When we write the 'life stories' of consumer goods—at least in the hagiographic forms that they are likely to acquire through the efforts of promotional expertise—they are forever young, always gorgeous and sexy and steeped in an aura of optimism, vigour and strength.

The synergy between (non-disabled) youth and consumption means that non-disabled youth can 'travel' with ease through the regimes of value that mark contemporary cultures of consumption and the objects that constitute them. Young disabled people find it much more difficult to gain entry to the same symbolic territory. As a consequence they can become trapped in an identity that is over-determined by the multiple forms of aesthetic discrimination that young disabled people meet as they try to 'get a life'.

Conclusions

It is quite clear that contemporary sociology has been seduced by metaphors of mobility. The language of fluids and flows, networks and liquid relationships, surfing and scapes is central to sociological discourse (Castells, 1996; Urry, 2000a,b,c; Bauman, 2000). The characters that people sociological texts are all on the move. The *flaneur* was iconic with respect to modern culture. 'He' represented itinerancy, life as a stroll through the metropolis. 'His' postmodern equivalents (not so gendered) have no geographical boundaries and move much more quickly, sometimes in ways that re-draw the meaning of temporality. For contemporary sociology the mobile world is dominated by 'vagabonds', 'nomads' and 'tourists' (See, for example, Urry, 1990; Bauman, 1993). Itinerancy is the norm. I do not wish to labour the point that this describes the world of the elite who inhabit the cultures of the north Atlantic rim. It is, with respect to this critique, more apposite to note that disabled people do not recognise themselves in the metaphors and figures that dominate contemporary sociological discourse. The 'travellings' and the liquid identities of people who live a 'de-territorialised', nomadic life (Deleuze & Guattari, 1986) will seem strange to disabled people with mobility and some sensory and communication impairments. They experience 'territory' and travel in terms of multiple barriers and are alien to young disabled people who have little or no option but to consume segregated leisure in segregated places. The metaphors of disability studies – barriers, exclusion, inaccessibility and segregation—describe a curtailed relationship to space/time which is not relieved by opportunities to consume a lifestyle of ones choice or to take a new self-identity 'off the peg'. Indeed, opportunities to liquidise identity are much curtailed by a relationship to markets that is marked more by necessity than freedom, and which makes it very difficult to assume an identity other than the one that is 'conferred' by impairment.

Disabled people in general and young disabled people in particular do not have sufficient opportunities to 'go with the flow'. In fact 'the flow' is a source of their immobilisation. If being mobile is synonymous with the good life, then disabled people are not getting their share. John Urry (2002b) is fully aware that contemporary mobilities embody powerful exclusionary mechanisms and he argues that 'a good society would minimise coerced immobility'. However, this claim is developed only as a caveat. The nature and extent of 'coerced immobility' and how it impacts on particular social groups is not developed in any meaningful way and has no roots in the tradition of emancipatory disability research. Some sociologists may feel relieved from the burdens associated with the concept of structure and feel that this gives license for the development of new rules of sociological method based on the imperatives associated with the cosmic 'realities' of chaos and complexity. But many disabled people feel structure as oppression and this is manifest in the myriad places that they cannot go or are refused entry to. It is no doubt that in the contemporary world the analysis of dynamics is much more important the analysis of stasis but this does not necessarily mean that sociology requires some kind of epistemological revolution. This is most certainly the case if—as John Urry himself argues—sociology should develop in companionship with New Social Movements (2000b). The disability movement is in the business of challenging forms of 'immobilization' and cannot afford to ignore the fact that the discourse of mobilities is a discourse of non-disabled people and that such a discourse reflects the carnal priorities and projects of non-disabled people. Sociology has a history of leaving disabled people behind. One hopes that the new accent on (and calls for epistemological renewal around) the mobilities of contemporary life is not going to turn out to be another example of another sociological journey that leaves some potential travellers at the point of embarkation.

References

Abbott, D., Morris, J. & Ward, L. (2001) *Residential schools and disabled children: decision-making and experiences* (York, Joseph Rowntree Foundation).

Adam, B. (1998) *Timescapes of modernity: the environment and invisible hazards* (London, Routledge).

Albrecht, G. (2002) American pragmatism, sociology and the development of disability studies, in: C. Barnes, M. Oliver & L. Barton (Eds) *Disability studies today* (Cambridge, Polity Press).

Appadurai, A. (Ed) (1986) *The social life of things* (Cambridge, Cambridge University Press).

Barnes, C. (2001) *Emancipatory' disability research: project or process*. Available online at: www.leeds.ac.uk/archive/index (accessed 2 August 2003).

Barnes, C. (2003) *Disability studies: what's the point*. Available online at: www.leeds.ac.uk/archive/index (accessed 4 August 2003).

Barnes, C. & Mercer, G. (2003) *Disability* (Cambridge, Polity Press).

Barton, L. (Ed.) (2001) *Disability, politics and the struggle for change* (Sheffield, David Fulton Publications).

Baudrillard, J. (1998) *The consumer society* (London, Sage).

Bauman, Z. (1993) *Postmodern ethics* (London, Routledge).

Bauman, Z. (1997) *Postmodernity and its discontents* (Cambridge, Polity).

Bauman, Z. (2000) *Liquid modernity* (Cambridge, Polity).

Burkitt, I. (1999) *Bodies of thought: embodiment, identity and modernity* (London, Sage).

Braddock, D. & Parish, S. (2001) An institutional history of disability, in: G. Albrecht, K. Seelman & M. Bury (Eds) *Handbook of disability studies* (London, Sage).

Castells, M. (1996) *The rise of the network society* (Oxford, Blackwell).

Cavet, J. (1998) Leisure and friendship, in: C. Robinson & K. Stalker (Eds) *Growing up with disability* (London, Jessica Kingsley Publications).

Children in Scotland (2002) *What matters to me* (Edinburgh, Children in Scotland).

Deleuze, G. & Guattari, F. (1986) *Nomadology* (New York, Semiotext(e)).

Featherstone, M. (1982) The body in consumer culture, *Theory, Culture & Society*, 1, 18–33.

Du Bois-Reymond, M. (1997) Rethinking youth identities: new challenges, in: J. Brynner *et al.* (Eds) *Youth citizenship and social change, in a European context* (Aldershot, Ashgate).

Fullager, S. & Owler, K. (1998) Narratives of leisure: recreating the Self, *Disability & Society*, 13(3), 441–450.

Giddens, A. (1991) *Modernity and self-identity* (Cambridge, Polity Press).

Gilleard, C. & Higgs, P. (2000) *Cultures of ageing: self, citizen and the body* (Harlow, Prentice Hall).

Gleeson, B. (1999) *Geographies of disability* (London, Routledge).

Gleick, J. (1998) *Chaos: the amazing science of the unpredictable* (London, Vintage).

Goffman, E. (1963) *Stigma: notes on the management of spoiled identity* (Harmondsworth, Penguin).

Goffman, E. (1968) *Asylums* (Harmondswort, Penguin).

Griffin, C. (1997a) Representations of the young, in: J. Roche & S. Tucker (Eds) *Youth in contemporary society: theory, policy and practice* (London, Sage/Open University Press).

Griffin, C. (1997b) Youth research and identities; same as it ever was, in: J. Brynner *et al.* (Eds) *Youth citizenship and social change in a European context* (Aldershot, Ashgate).

Hirst, M. & Baldwin, S. (1994) *Unequal opportunities: growing up disabled* (HMSO, London).

Howard, L. (1996) A comparison of leisure time activities between able bodied children and children with physical disabilities, *British Journal of Occupational Therapy*, 59, 570–574.

Hughes, B. (1999) The constitution of impairment: modernity and the aesthetic of oppression, *Disability & Society*, 14(2), 155–172.

Hughes, B. (2000) Medicine and the aesthetic invalidation of disabled people, *Disability & Society*, 15(3), 555–568.

Hughes, B. (2002) Invalidated strangers: impairment and the cultures of modernity and postmodernity, *Disability & Society*, 17(5), 571–584.

Humphries, S. & Gordon, P. (1992) *Out of sight: the experience of disability 1900–1950* (Plymouth, Northcote House).

Kerr, A. & Shakespeare, T. (2002) *Genetic politics: from eugenics to genome* (Cheltenham, New Clarion Press).

McLennan, G. (2003) Sociology's complexity, *Sociology*, 37(3), 547–564.

Mercer, G. (2002) Emancipatory disability research, in: C. Barnes, M. Oliver & L. Barton (Eds) *Disability studies today* (Cambridge, Polity Press).

Miles, S. (2000) *Youth lifestyles in a changing world* (Buckingham, Open University Press).

Morris, J. (1999) *Transition to adulthood for young disabled people with complex health and support needs* (York, Joseph Rowntree Foundation).

Morris, J. (2002) *Moving into adulthood* (York, Joseph Rowntree Foundation).

Murray, P. (2002) *Disabled teenagers' experiences of access to inclusive leisure* (York, Joseph Rowntree Foundation).

Oliver, M. (1990) *The politics of disablement* (Basingstoke, Macmillan).

Oliver, M. (1997) Emancipatory research: realistic goal or impossible dream?, in: C. Barnes & G. Mercer (Eds) *Doing disability research* (Leeds, Disability Press).

Rattansi, A. & Pheonix, A. (1997) Rethinking youth identities: modernist and postmodernist frameworks, in: J. Brynner L. Chisholm & A. Furlong (Eds) *Youth citizenship and social change in a European context* (Aldershot, Ashgate).

Read, J. (2000) *Disability, the family and society* (Milton Keynes, Open University Press).

Riddell, S., Wilson, A. & Baron, S. (1999) Captive customers: people with learning difficulties in the social market, *British Educational Research Journal*, 25(4), 445–461.

Scottish Consumer Council (1996) *Change in store: the experience of young disabled people as consumers in Scotland* (Edinburgh, SCC).

Segal, L. (1999) *Why feminism?* (Cambridge, Polity Press).

Seidman, S. (1991) The end of sociological theory: the postmodern hope, *Sociological Theory*, 9(2), 131–146.

Silvers, A. (2002) The crooked timber of humanity: disability, ideology and the aesthetic, in: M. Corker & T. Shakespeare (Eds) *Disability/postmodernity* (London, Continuum).

Shakespeare, T. & Watson, N. (1998) Theoretical perspectives on research with disabled children, in: C. Robinson & K. Stalker (Eds) *Growing up with disability* (London, Jessica Kingsley Publishers).

Shilling, C. (2003) *The body and social theory* (2nd edn) (London, Sage).

Stalker, K. (2002) *Young disabled people moving into adulthood in Scotland* (York, Joseph Rowntree Foundation).

Swain, J. & French, S. (2000) Towards an affirmation model of disability, *Disability & Society*, 15(4), 569–582.

Thomas, C. (1998) Parents and families: disabled women's stories about their childhood, in: C. Robinson & K. Stalker (Eds) *Growing up with disability* (London, Jessica Kingsley Publications).

Urry, J. (1990) *The tourist gaze* (London, Sage).

Urry, J. (2000a) Mobile sociology, *British Journal of Sociology*, 51(1), 185–203.
Urry, J. (2000b) *Beyond societies: mobilities for the twenty-first century* (London, Routledge).
Urry, J. (2000c) Mobility and proximity, *Sociology*, 36(2), 255–274.
Watson, N., Shakespeare, T., Cunningham-Burley, S., Barnes, C., Corker, M., Davis, J. & Priestley, M. (1999) *Life as a disabled child: a qualitative study of young people's experiences and perspectives* (University of Edinburgh, ESRC Research Report).

'Chocolate ... makes you autism': impairment, disability and childhood identities

Berni Kelly
Donald Beasley Institute, New Zealand

This paper discusses perceptions and experiences of impairment and disability from the perspectives of learning disabled children, their parents and their social workers. The author reports on findings from her doctoral study that adults often fail to take into account the views and experiences of learning disabled children. As a result, these children developed their own interpretations of impairment and disability based on their experiences and interactions with others. Whilst this indicates that they are active social interpreters, it also suggests that adults should make greater efforts to inform and consult learning disabled children. The author concludes by reflecting on the relevance of these findings to contemporary theories of disability and childhood.

Introduction

In recent years there have been major developments in the sociology of childhood and disability theory. Developments in the sociology of childhood have challenged traditional views of children as passive, predictable and immature (Piaget, 1969) and recognised their role in society as skilful social actors with their own perspectives and experiences of the social world (James *et al.*, 1998). Disability theory has progressed from traditional medical perspectives that focused negatively on individual limitations of impairment to the social model of disability that emphasises the disabling impact of oppressive barriers in society on the lives of disabled individuals (Campbell & Oliver, 1997; Dowling & Dolan, 2001). In this way, disability is viewed as a socially created experience of discrimination, inequality and segregation.

Indeed, authors have begun to extend theoretical understanding of disability at two key levels. Firstly, it has been argued that more attention should be given to the multi-dimensional identities of disabled people across gender, age, class, ethnicity and sexuality (Morris, 1996, 1998, 2003; Thomas, 1998, 1999). Secondly, authors have increasingly acknowledged the need to consider the real experience of impairment in the lives of disabled people (Morris, 1996; Shakespeare & Watson, 1998; Thomas, 1999, 2003). These authors have suggested that it would be helpful to develop the social model to consider personal experiences of impairment alongside political and public experiences of disability. Thomas (1999) has argued that the personal impact of impairment and disability on disabled people's self-identity and self-esteem is just as important as addressing disabling barriers in society.

This emerging discourse is particularly relevant to the lives of disabled children (Middleton, 1996; Thomas, 1998; Cocks, 2003; Connors, 2003). It is suggested that connecting these theoretical developments within the social model of disability and the sociology of childhood may contribute to our understanding of the lives of disabled children, including their dual experiences as children and as disabled individuals (Cocks, 2003; Connors, 2003). This could create opportunities to explore their experiences and interpretations of disability and impairment alongside recognition of their abilities as competent social actors.

For the purpose of this paper, the terms 'disabled children' or 'learning disabled children' are employed instead of 'children with learning disabilities' or 'children with disabilities'. This is in recognition of the understanding that disability is a form of social oppression rather than belonging to the child. All of the children involved in this study had been diagnosed as having a 'learning disability' at various levels from mild to severe. This included children who were labelled as having autism, attention deficit and hyperactivity disorder, Down's syndrome and global developmental delay. In this context, the term 'learning disability' encompasses the terms 'cognitive impairment' and 'intellectual impairment' that are commonly employed in international contexts. Many children involved in this study also had other diagnoses relating to physical or sensory impairment (such as cerebal palsy) and medical conditions (such as epilepsy). The term 'impairment' is commonly employed to label socio-medical conditions that disabled children experience. Thus, the term impairment will be used in this paper when discussing children's perceptions of such experiences. Although the term impairment can be viewed as oppressive as it links with the notion of being impaired or deviant, unfortunately alternative, more empowering terms of description have yet to be adopted. It is acknowledged that these labels and diagnoses are applied to individuals based on social and cultural constructions of norms and difference and are open to change (Bogdan & Taylor, 1992; Thomas, 2003). Indeed, findings from this study highlight the negative consequences for disabled children of being labelled as having an impairment.

Disability, childhood and identity

A growing number of qualitative researchers have begun to seek the views of learning disabled children (Marchant *et al.*, 1999; Kelly *et al.*, 2000; Kelly, 2002a, b, 2003; Watson *et al.*, 2000; Davis & Watson, 2001; Morris, 2003). Such studies have highlighted the impact of dominant discourses and personal experience on the formation of self-identity for disabled children. On the one hand, negative dominant discourses impose categorical identities on disabled children. On the other hand, disabled children are seen as competent social actors who resist dominant discourses and create their own discursive spaces based on their own analyses and experiences.

Davies and Jenkins (1997) examined the impact of dominant discourses on the lives of 60 young people 'with learning difficulties' who were making transitions to adult life. The authors argued that the label of 'learning difficulties' often became a master status as experiential and power relationships promoted the incorporation of that categorical identity into self-identity. Davies and Jenkins (1997) recommended more careful consideration and debate about the ways in which categorical identity is included in discursive relations with disabled people. The authors stated:

> This is not to suggest that people should be 'told', but rather to recognise that the partial or inaccurate understandings with which those who have pursued the subject often have to work do not in fact protect them from incorporating this categorical identity into their self-identity via experiential relationships. In addition, these inadequate understandings derived from discourse can only further emphasise their disempowerment in their everyday social interactions in ordinary settings. (p. 108)

Young people involved in this study were dependent on their parents or carers to develop their understanding of 'learning difficulty' labels. However, most parents or carers avoided discussing learning difficulties with their children, assuming it would be unkind or their children would not understand their explanations. Indeed, some sought to conceal the particular label ascribed to their children. Interestingly, the authors found that young people who had received explanations from their parents did understand it in the way it was presented to them and accurately repeated those explanations in discussions about themselves. However, young people who had been given limited or partial information were more likely to develop idiosyncratic explanations.

Several researchers have begun to recognise the capacity of disabled children to resist dominant adult or professional discourse and become active agents in the construction and re-construction of their own identity. A study entitled 'Life as a Disabled Child' involved participant observations and discussions with children aged between eleven and sixteen years (Priestley et al., 1999; Watson et al., 2000; Davis & Watson, 2001). Researchers involved in this project emphasised that disabled children's everyday life worlds are fluid and children are able to resist adult control. Priestley (1999) stated:

> They [disabled children] are also social actors, responding to discursive practices, resisting and reconstructing them to fit their own experiences and priorities. (pp. 93–94)

Disabled children involved in this study were acutely aware of adult practice and often resented how adults over-protected them. Children viewed disability in different ways, and impairment or disability was more important to them in some situations than in others. In some cases, impairment became a normal, insignificant part of disabled children's everyday experiences.

However, researchers have also found that disabled children are often restricted from opportunities to freely negotiate their self-identity through relationships of power, disabling environments and discriminatory institutional structures (Priestley, 1999). For example, researchers have found that adults rarely consult disabled children or involve them in decision-making processes (Morris, 1998; Thomas, 1998; Burke & Cigno, 2000). Davis and Watson (2001) reported that few adults question the construction of difference within professional discourses and suggested that such unreflexive practices disempowers and excludes disabled children.

Such research draws attention to the need to further explore the impact of dominant adult discourse over the lives of learning disabled children and how these children interpret these influences in their construction of their own identities. Davis and Watson (2001) suggested that adults should make more efforts to communicate with children they work with, explain their actions and consult disabled children in everyday practice. Indeed, in recognition of the impact of disabling barriers on the development of self-identity, Cheston (1994) recommended that disabled children should be given information about their personal background and have access to social and psychological support.

Disabled children are surrounded by negative attitudes directed towards their impairment ranging from surgical treatment to 'fix' disabled children to negative media images or rejection from extended family and friends. Middleton (1996) stated:

> All these efforts to make a child normal by stimulating brain waves, hanging them upside down, pushing, pulling and cajoling, mean that the child receives the very clear message that there is something about them that nobody likes. Chances are that they will learn not to like it either. Since it is likely to be something about which, realistically, they can do little or nothing, this over emphasis is likely to only create a sense of failure or even self-hate. (p. 37)

Thomas' (1998) study revealed that parental interpretation of the meaning of impairment was crucial to the development of their child's identity. Parents who sought to challenge negative assumptions about impairment and barriers to inclusion encouraged more positive self-perceptions for their children than those who emphasised their child's limitations. Thomas (1998) found that for the child this either meant positive self-esteem and acceptance or self-hatred and embarrassment. Parents who ignored their child's impairment sometimes over-emphasised the importance of treating their disabled child as a normal member of the family. This research underlines the importance of positively embracing impairment as an integral part of the child's self-identity.

The study

The findings discussed in this paper are part of a larger study which examined the provision of family support services for learning disabled children (aged between two and sixteen years) and their families completed in 2002 (Kelly *et al.*, 2000; Kelly, 2002a, 2003). All of these children were selected from active social work caseloads from four Health and Social Services Trusts in Northern Ireland that provide support services for learning disabled children and their families. Semi-structured interviews were used to ascertain the views of 32 learning disabled children, their parents (n=32) and social workers (n=16). Interviews with each child were completed over a minimum of three visits and a range of communicative aids were employed to facilitate interviews, including projective techniques, play, sentence completion exercises, drawing and feelings cards. All of the children involved in this study consented to participate in interviews with the researcher and, towards the end of the study, findings were disseminated to children using pictorial bookmarks and booklets, including opportunities for children to provide feedback to the researcher in varied formats.

The findings from this study add to extant literature by exploring discourse and identity from the perspectives and experiences of learning disabled children and adults (parents and professionals). Interviews with parents and social workers provided information on how adults interpreted the meaning of disability and impairment for learning disabled children and how assumptions about impairment-related limitations impacted on children's daily experiences. This contributes to knowledge about the influence of adult discourse on the lives of these children, children's resistance to these dominant discourses and efforts children make to build self-identity on the basis of their own experiences and perceptions. The following section of the paper will explore adult discourses from the perspectives of parents and professionals. Then, the author will discuss how children interpreted their experiences of these adult discourses and how they resisted and reconstructed these experiences as competent social actors. In order to clearly illustrate key findings, quotations from interviews will be included throughout this paper using fictitious names.

Dominant adult discourses: disability, childhood and identity

Parents expressed different opinions about the impact of impairment on their child's life and their family life. Some parents commented on beneficial aspects of caring for their child, emphasising their reciprocal relationships. This included their disabled child's positive influence on family attitudes and increasing parental advocacy skills. However, other parents presented more negative experiences, including descriptions of their child as being 'a bit of a pest' and caring for their child as 'a very hard struggle'. These parents described being heartbroken by the tragedy of impairment and emphasised the negative effect this had on their lives. Joanne's mother related having a disabled child to feelings of pain and loss:

> ... the pain of a tragic death is not as extreme as the pain of constantly living with and caring for a child who has a learning disability. When parents lose a child they can come to terms with it quicker but parents of a child who has a learning disability find it harder to come to terms with it. In fact I haven't come to terms with it, especially asking for your child to be treated as normal ... The other ones [siblings] lead very full lives and fulfilling lives and she hasn't. (Parent of Joanne: 12 year old)

Parents discussed concerns they had about their children that were directly related to impairment and disability. Many parents expressed particular concern about their inability to understand their child's efforts to communicate. Almost two-thirds of parents were worried about the risk of harm to their child because of their lack of awareness of danger and inability to tell someone if an abusive incident occurred. In addition, many parents were worried about the impact of bullying experiences on their child at school and in the local community. For these reasons parents believed their disabled child had to be constantly supervised in order to protect themselves and others. However, this usually restricted opportunities for their child to participate in spontaneous or independent activities:

> He is very vulnerable with everyone and that's part of the reason we keep him in from outside. (Parent of Brendan: 9 year old)

Parents and children also discussed being treated differently by family members and the general public because of impairment. Family members were more lenient, pitiful and loving toward their disabled child and strangers in public often stared, criticised or ignored them. Generally, parents felt their children were excluded from many social opportunities and bullied because of negative social attitudes and ignorance about impairment. They felt angry, hurt and sad about their child being treated differently. Parents also acknowledged that, as a result of being treated differently and negatively, their child had developed particular behaviours. These ranged from threatening other children who teased them to being unresponsive to authority at home due to being spoiled by others outside the home.

It is important to emphasise that most parents felt that the positive aspects of their child outweighed any negative experiences of impairment or disability. However, the clear differences in parental experiences and feelings towards the impact of impairment and disability on their children's lives suggest a need to consider the impact of different parental perceptions on their children's developing self-identity.

Only 5 out of the 32 parents interviewed had discussed impairment or disability with their child. Some parents suggested their child was too young. Several parents believed their child understood without being given a specific explanation due to the impact of impairment on their daily life such as, pain or fatigue. Two parents had decided not to explain impairment or disability to their child to prevent them having negative feelings about themselves or becoming worried. Another two parents pointed out that their child believed they did not have an impairment:

> I try to explain. I think he knows the difference but ... according to him he is fine it is everybody else that needs to change. On the odd occasion I think the cub has a point. (Parent of Peter: 4 year old)

Five parents had explained impairment to their other children even though they had not addressed the topic with their disabled child. This reluctance to discuss disability or impairment with their disabled child is particularly interesting since parents were often aware that their child had learnt words, such as 'mongol face,' 'handicapped' and 'autism'.

> She called me mongol face ... She doesn't understand what it is. She just said, 'There's mongol face'. Somebody must have said it to her. I've asked her who said that to her but she didn't say. (Parent of Pauline: 13 year old)

> He said the word a few times but I think he has heard it in school. I don't think he is aware that there's anything wrong. He asked one time why he's not at his brother's school and

we just said that was because he had to go to a special school because he was a special boy. But he doesn't think any further you know ... but he was looking for chocolate one day and I said, 'No you're not getting any' and he said, 'Oh it makes you hyper—it makes you autism'. (Parent of Christopher: 10 year old)

It seems that although most parents had not discussed impairment or disability with their disabled child, these children were beginning to gather information from a range of other sources in an effort to describe and understand impairment and disability.

Professional discourse

Throughout this study, it was also clear that there were many times when professionals failed to provide adequate information or explanations to disabled children. Although reviews of services should offer opportunities for children to actively participate in the delivery and monitoring of services they use, none of the children had been to a review. Social workers usually excluded learning disabled children because of assumptions that they could not communicate and did not have sufficient understanding to form opinions about their needs. Indeed, three-quarters of all the social workers admitted that children were not genuine participants in decision-making processes or the development of services. Their comments revealed that parents were viewed as key informants and decision-makers rather than children. Only one social worker expressed concerns about parental and professional assumptions about children's inability to understand or communicate. This social worker suggested that more efforts were now being made to involve learning disabled children as active participants but described this as 'a long uphill struggle'.

Communication was an issue that more than half of the social workers interviewed found particularly difficult, especially in relation to feeling unsure if they were accurately representing disabled children's views. Almost all social workers emphasised their lack of knowledge about sign systems and the need to develop their skills for communicating with disabled children. One social worker stated:

> I'm not very good at working with severe learning disabled. I don't have enough experience and there is a tendency then to work with the family and not the child ... You feel that if you could use different ways to communicate with them maybe you could provide a better service for them and find out what they feel their needs are.

Some social workers suggested these communication difficulties could be overcome by providing appropriate training, having more contact with specialised staff and more time to develop closer working relationships with children. However, others suggested that, even if they did access further training, it would still be more appropriate to communicate with parents and specialist professionals (such as speech therapists) rather than directly communicating with learning disabled children. This reveals a clear reliance on adults to act as proxy communicators and translators for these children. In contrast, researchers have found that reliance on parental views is often inappropriate because parental self-determination can be undermined by the dominance of professional opinion and because parents and children often have very different views (Burke & Cigno, 2000; McConkey & Smyth, 2000). In addition, while parents are usually recognised as children's advocates and protectors, research has shown they can also sometimes have a lasting negative impact on their child's identity (Thomas, 1998; Burke & Cigno, 2000).

Parents involved in this study often supported professional decisions to exclude their child from reviews. Almost all of the parents interviewed believed their child's absence was appropriate due to concerns that their behaviour would disrupt the process and beliefs that their child would not understand information discussed. This collusion with professionals that their child should not be consulted effectively silenced children's voices. Only five parents expressed a desire for their child to participate in reviews. These parents felt that others underestimated their child's ability to understand information and that it was important for everyone at reviews to at least meet their child. They believed their child had relevant opinions and feelings that should be presented at reviews.

Children's experiential discourse of disability and identity

Despite the lack of information about impairment and disability from adults and exclusion from reviews of services, learning disabled children involved in this study could articulate their experiences of impairment and disability. Children discussed feeling different and being treated differently as an experience of impairment and disability. Some children suggested they were different from other children because they looked or acted differently from other children. Several comments these children made are equally applicable to non-disabled children. For example, one child explained she was different because she did not have her ears pierced and another felt he was different 'because people call me fat'. However, other children talked specifically about how they felt different or were treated differently on the basis of impairment or disability. Children discussed these differences at two levels: (a) difference as a result of disabling barriers (disability), and (b) difference related to the experience of impairment (impairment). Children who felt different as a result of exclusionary and discriminatory barriers in their social worlds described being excluded from play activities and being teased or bullied. They felt sad and angry about being treated differently. Children who discussed feeling different as a result of their experience of impairment explained how some things are more difficult for them, such as concentrating or not being able to do a particular activity.

One child, Laura, recognised her experience of both impairment and disability. At one level, she described how restrictive environments meant she could not participate in the same play activities her siblings. On the other hand, she talked about wanting to be able to walk and feeling that she could not tell her mother about desiring to be able to walk:

> My life is different when I can't go sit on the beach and play with my sisters on the sand ... Well when I was tiny I wanted to be able to walk and then I can't. And then I haven't been able to tell Mum I wanted to walk. (Laura: 12 year old)

Children who highlighted how difficulties related to their experience of impairment impacted on their lives had often devised effective strategies to counteract these difficulties. Brendan explained that, although his brain made things harder for him, he was able to divert his brother's attention away from these difficulties by confusing him:

> My brain. But I just know what to say. My brother says, 'What?' I say, 'J [brother] what's what?' And he says, 'What?' I say, 'What's what?' And then he says, 'I don't know'. (Brendan: 9 year old)

Such comments illustrate the ability of these children to articulate the experience of impairment and disability in their daily lives. Adults in Laura's life did not provide any information for her about impairment or create opportunities for her to discuss experiences of impairment. Despite this lack of information, Laura had formed her own opinion of what it means to be disabled and also developed awareness of the barriers that exist in her relations with her family. These children's comments support the view of learning disabled children as active social interpreters and 'experiencers' of disability and impairment in their lives.

Children also discussed aspects of impairment and disability when they described their roles within the family home. Both children and their parents identified activities they were *not able* to do, such as cooking, using a computer mouse, making beds or doing puzzles. Interestingly, parents and disabled children also identified activities they were *not allowed* to do even though their siblings (and often younger siblings) were, such as baking or visiting a friend's house. Parents explained that their disabled child was not allowed to do these activities because of issues relating to risk, behaviour or social exclusion. Comments disabled children made demonstrate that they were acutely aware of these restrictions and high levels of adult supervision:

> I'm not allowed to do household jobs by myself—mummy always has to do them with me. (Laura: 12 year old)

> I'm not able to cook dinner—I'd like to when I'm trusted. (Joanne: 12 year old)

Indeed, children often rebelled against adult-imposed restrictions. For example, children moved into play areas they were not allowed to enter so they could interact with peers. Whilst this caused much anxiety for parents, it demonstrates how these children were able to re-interpret the boundaries of their home life and resist barriers to their social and recreational activities.

Indeed when children were invited to make two 'magic wand wishes', only Laura mentioned the effects of impairment by wishing to be able to walk. Other children wished for a wide range of things including parties, money, toys, animals and boyfriends. Most of these wishes are common desires expected from children in general which reinforces that fact that learning disabled children are children first who do not view their impairment as the most important thing in their lives.

Disabled children as social actors

Although adults often assumed learning disabled children could not understand or communicate, children involved in this study became active participants in the research process and often made independent decisions about how each research visit would progress. For example, children added new items to the range of picture cards already provided and independently designed games to play with the researcher. Children repeatedly provided evidence that they were able to interpret their experiences and articulate their views on complex issues, such as feelings, needs and sources of support. For example, although children were excluded from reviews of respite care services, they were able to tell the researcher about their experiences of these services. Children were often upset because they missed their family when they stayed at respite care. However, their views were rarely considered when parents and professionals made decisions about their respite care placement. Three children had told their parents they did not like going to respite care but still continued to attend the same respite facility. These children had learnt to accept that telling an adult they did not want to go to respite care made no difference. Indeed, many of these children felt that adults pressurised them to go to respite care and social workers admitted that the needs of parents often overrode the wishes and feelings of the child.

Children and their parents also discussed the range of professionals they met regularly and preferred professionals who spent time with them, participated in activities with them or took them on social outings. Children explained that professionals who listened to them made them feel 'liked', 'important' and 'happy.' Some children indicated that meeting professionals made them feel nervous or scared and that professionals usually prioritised meeting their parents over meeting them:

> Laura: P [social worker] never speaks to me. He listens more to Mummy ...
> Int: How does that make you feel?
> Laura: Really sad. P [social worker] doesn't like me that much I don't think.
> (Laura: 12 year old)

Children were often dissatisfied when professionals focused solely on service-related priorities and ignored other important aspects of their lives. Laura explained she did not like her social worker because he was only interested in discussing respite care services and came to visit her at school:

> I didn't like him coming out ... I want him to stop hassling me. He goes on about respite all the time ... He came to my school and he questioned me about respite and I was going to cry in front of everybody. He talked to me in front of my school friends. I was really really cross when I got home because I thought I had to tell my Mum. I don't want him to do that ever again. I could've told my Mummy. (Laura: 12 year old)

This emphasises the importance of respecting children's right to decide where, when and how they are consulted about services. Children's perspectives highlight the need for professionals to take time to develop rapport with children, clarify professional roles and offer children opportunities to discuss issues they deem to be important rather than service-led priorities.

Theoretical reflections on disability, childhood and identity

Few researchers and theorists have connected developments in the sociology of childhood and disability theory with regard to the lives of disabled children (Cocks, 2003;

Connors, 2003). Disabled childhood seems to enter an abyss between: (a) theoretical understanding of childhood because of disability; and (b) disability theory because of childhood. However, findings from this study highlight the possibility for dialogue between theoretical understanding of childhood and disability. The sociology of childhood can be further developed to acknowledge the diversity of childhood, including the experiences of disabled children. Similarly, disability theory can be advanced to allow further consideration of the fluid and diverse experiences of disabled children.

A social model of disability that focuses on oppressive barriers in society does not fully account for the experiences of children involved in this study. Findings reveal their experiences and feelings about impairment. Impairment and disability were particularly significant experiences for some children and not so important for others. For some children, experiences of impairment (such as not being able to understand or desiring to be able to walk) were just as important as disabling structures in society. For others, experience of disabling barriers in society (such as adult surveillance or exclusion from social opportunities) was more salient than their experience of impairment. The information children provided during the 'magic wand wishes' activity revealed that most children's aspirations were less concerned with issues related to impairment or disability and more concerned with issues that impacted on other aspects of their identity, such as having money or a boyfriend.

Although children involved in this study were aware of disabling barriers and had unique experiences of impairment, embracing this experience as part of their self-identity was inhibited by the absence of opportunities to discuss and explore impairment and disability with their parents and professionals. As evident from Laura's perspective, this can sometimes lead to a silence between disabled children and adults about an aspect of their life that is important to them. Indeed, Thomas' (1998) study of disabled women's experiences of childhood found that this denial could lead to embarrassment and self-hatred. This failure to create opportunities to explore experiences of impairment and disability means that learning disabled children can only develop their understanding of these experiences based on their relationships with others in different social contexts where impairment is often likely to be either ignored or criticised. Whilst this may develop their understanding of disability as they experience discrimination in a range of contexts, it does not provide an environment to support exploration of their experiences of impairment from a positive perspective. Therefore, there is a need for adults to create space for disabled children to communicate about their views and experiences of impairment and disability *if they want to*. This communicative space should be a supportive opportunity for children to explore impairment and disability as part of their everyday life experience, rather than as a personal tragedy.

Professional and parental attitudes can promote the medical view of impairment as a tragedy or perceive impairment as an everyday part of their child's identity and work towards countering disabling barriers they experience. Professionals have a significant role to play in supporting parents to develop their confidence, challenge negative attitudes they encounter and recognise their child's abilities and strengths

(Dobson *et al.*, 2001). Professionals can reflect on the messages about impairment or disability they portray to families and support parents to understand the role of impairment in children's identity. By doing so, significant adults in disabled children's lives can encourage them to develop a strong, positive self-identity that embraces impairment as one element of their fluid and complex identity (Thomas, 1998; Galvin, 2003). It is important that efforts to discuss impairment and disability with disabled children do not promote the view that impairment determines who they are or that impairment must be the most important aspect of their lives (Watson, 2002; Galvin, 2003). In contrast, as children in this study repeatedly emphasised, experience of impairment or disability is only one aspect of their lives that may be more important to some children than to others and, as a fluid concept, can be deconstructed and reconstructed beyond ascribed categories or stereotypes (Watson, 2002).

Involving children throughout this research process underlines their competency as active 'experiencers' and highlights the relevance of the sociology of childhood to the experiences of disabled children. Findings suggest that learning disabled children are not passive incompetent individuals. Instead, these children demonstrated their ability to articulate their views and, to participate in, and influence, the research process. These findings indicate that adults should be more careful not to underestimate the abilities of learning disabled children (Hughes & Patterson, 1997). In many cases it seems that both professionals and parents over-emphasise individual limitations of impairment which denies children's real experiences and contradicts evidence from research that disabled children can provide valuable information about how best to support their needs (Marchant *et al.*, 1999; Kelly, 2000, 2003; Watson *et al.*, 2000; Kelly & Monteith, 2003; Morris, 2003). This draws attention to deeper inequality based on negative professional discourses of impairment that justifies the reluctance to consult and listen to the views of disabled children (Priestley, 1998; Davis & Watson, 2001). Such practice takes little account of human rights, independence or empowerment. This is in stark contradiction to current policy, such as, the Children (NI) Order 1995 (Department of Health and Social Services [DHSS], 1995) and the United Nations Convention on the Rights of the Child 1989 (Russell, 2003). Each of these policies specify a need to address inequality, consult disabled children and take their views into account when making decisions that affect their lives.

Professionals need to consider alternatives to the negativity of current discursive professional practice that focuses on limitations of impairment. They should reflect on their assumptions, prejudices and attitudes towards impairment and consider the powerful impact of their view of disabled childhood on their daily practice (Priestley, 1998). Professionals should also reflect on power relations between adults and children, create a space for the active participation of children who use varied communication styles and encourage parents to recognise their child's ability and right to become active participants (Morris, 1998; Kelly, 2003; Kelly & Monteith, 2003). Such reflexive practice promotes the position of disabled children as citizens who have important roles in making decisions and improving services as active service users (Middleton, 1996; Morris, 1998; Dowling & Dolan, 2001). This places an onus on professionals to carefully consider the methods of communication that best suit individual children's abilities. Service providers need to consider how they ask children questions, methods for communication and take time to consult disabled children without the presence of other adults (Morris, 1998; Burke & Cigno, 2000; Kelly & Monteith, 2003).

Conclusion

Based on the perspectives of learning disabled children, their parents and social workers, this research has clear messages for service providers and researchers. This study has found that learning disabled children do develop understanding of impairment and disability in the context of their own lives and are able to articulate their own experiences and perceptions, despite the absence of discussion with their parents or professionals.

The experiences and views of children involved in this study underline the relevance of the sociology of childhood and disability theory to their life worlds. Intertwining disability theory with the sociology of childhood can allow more eclectic consideration of the varied and complex nature of disabled childhood (Cocks, 2003; Connors, 2003). This would more holistically acknowledge disabled children's public and personal experiences of impairment and disability, but also recognise their competency as equal and active citizens. This urges professionals to develop reflexive practice that acknowledges and challenges the effects of discrimination and oppression that learning disabled children experience. Within this approach, there is a clear need for professionals and researchers to consult learning disabled children and provide opportunities for them to fully participate in the planning and delivery of support services.

References

Bogdan, R. & Taylor, S. (1992) The social construction of humanness: relationships with severely disabled people, in: P. Ferguson & S. Taylor (Eds) *Interpreting disability: a qualitative reader* (New York, Teachers College Press), 275–294.

Burke, P. & Cigno, K. (2000) *Learning disabilities in children* (Oxford, Blackwell Science).

Campbell, J. & Oliver, M. (1997) *Disability politics* (London, Routledge).

Cheston, R. (1994) The accounts of special education leavers, *Disability and Society*, 9(1), 59–69.

Cocks, A. (2003) Interweaving theory: disability studies and childhood sociology, paper presented at the conference *Disability Studies: Theory, Policy and Practice*, Lancaster, 4–6 September.

Connors, C. (2003) Barriers to 'being': the psycho-emotional dimension of disability in the lives of disabled children, paper presented at the conference *Disability Studies: Theory, Policy and Practice*, Lancaster, 4–6 September.

Davies, C. & Jenkins, R. (1997) 'She has different fits to me': how people with learning difficulties see themselves, *Disability & Society*, 12(1), 95–109.

Davis, J. & Watson, N. (2001) Where are the children's experiences? Analysing social and cultural exclusion in 'special' and 'mainstream' schools, *Disability & Society*, 16(5), 671–687.

Department of Health and Social Services (DHSS) (NI) (1995) *Children (NI) order 1995* (Belfast, DHSS).

Dobson, B., Middleton, S. & Beardsworth, A. (2001) *The impact of childhood disability on family life: findings* (York, Joseph Rowntree Foundation).

Dowling, M. & Dolan, L. (2001) Families with children with disabilities: inequalities and the social model, *Disability & Society*, 16(1), 21–35.

Galvin, R. (2003) The paradox of disability culture: the need to combine versus the imperative to let go, *Disability & Society*, 18(5), 675–690.

Hughes, B. & Patterson, K. (1997) The social model of disability and the disappearing body: towards a sociology of impairment, *Disability & Society*, 12, 325–340.

James, A., Jenks, C. & Prout, A. (1998) *Theorising childhood* (Cambridge, Polity Press & Blackwell Publishers).

Kelly, B. (2002a) *The provision of family support services for children who have learning disabilities and their families in the context of current social policy and legislation*. Unpublished PhD thesis, University of Ulster at Magee.

Kelly, B. (2002b) Disabled children as active citizens, *Child Care in Practice*, 8(3), 220–222.

Kelly, B. (2003) Working together to support children who have intellectual disabilities and their families, *Childrenz Issues*, 7(2), 50–55.

Kelly, B., McColgan, M. & Scally, M. (2000) A chance to say: involving children who have learning disabilities in a pilot study on family support services, *Journal of Learning Disabilities*, 4(2), 115–127.

Kelly, B. & Monteith, M. (2003) *Supporting disabled children and their families in Northern Ireland: a research and policy review* (London, National Children's Bureau).

Marchant, R., Jones, M., Julyan, A. & Giles, A. (1999) *Listening on all channels: consulting with disabled children and young people* (Brighton, Triangle).

McConkey, R. & Smyth, M. (2000) *Not so different? The experiences and views of parents and school-leavers with severe learning difficulties* (Belfast, University of Ulster and Eastern Health and Social Services Board).

Middleton, L. (1996) *Making a difference: social work with disabled children* (Birmingham, Venture Press).

Morris, J. (Ed.) (1996) *Encounters with strangers* (London, The Women's Press).

Morris, J. (1998) *Don't leave us out: involving disabled children and young people with communication impairments* (York, Joseph Rowntree Foundation).

Morris, J. (2003) Including all children: finding out about the experiences of children with communication and/or cognitive impairments, *Children and Society*, 17, 337–348.

Piaget, J. (1969) *The psychology of the child* (London, Routledge).

Priestley, M. (1998) Childhood disability and disabled childhoods: agendas for research, *Childhood*, 5(2), 207–223.

Priestley, M. (1999) Discourse and identity: disabled children in mainstream high schools, in: M. Corker & S. French (Eds) *Disability discourse* (Buckingham, Open University Press).

Priestley, M., Corker, M. & Watson, N. (1999) Unfinished business: disabled children and disability identity, *Disability Studies Quarterly*, 9(2), 90–97.

Russell, P. (2003) 'Access and achievement or social exclusion?' Are the government's policies working for disabled children and their families? *Children and Society*, 17, 215–225.

Shakespeare, T. & Watson, N. (1998) Theoretical perspectives on research with disabled children, in: C. Robinson & K. Stalker (Eds) *Growing up with disability* (London, Jessica Kingsley).

Thomas, C. (1998) Parents and family: disabled women's stories about their childhood experiences, in: C. Robinson & K. Stalker (Eds) *Growing up with disability* (London, Jessica Kingsley).

Thomas, C. (1999) *Female forms: experiencing and understanding disability* (Buckingham, Open University Press).

Thomas, C. (2003) Defining a theoretical agenda for disability studies, paper presented at the conference *Disability Studies: Theory, Policy and Practice*, Lancaster, 4–6 September.

Watson, N., Shakespeare, T., Cunningham-Burley, S., Barnes, C., Corker, M., Davis, J. & Priestley, M. (2000) Life as a disabled child: a qualitative study of young people's experiences and perspectives, unpublished report, Department of Nursing Studies, University of Edinburgh. Available online at: http://www.hull.ac.uk/children5to16programme/briefings.htm (accessed 24 February 2005).

Watson, N. (2002) Well, I know this is going to sounds very strange to you, but I don't see myself as a disabled person: identity and disability, *Disability & Society*, 17(5), 509–527.

Children's experiences of disability: pointers to a social model of childhood disability

Clare Connors and Kirsten Stalker
[a]*Durham University, UK;* [b]*Strathclyde University, UK*

The social model of disability has paid little attention to disabled children, with few attempts to explore how far it provides an adequate explanatory framework for their experiences. This paper reports findings from a two-year study exploring the lived experiences of 26 disabled children aged 7–15. They experienced disability in four ways—in terms of impairment, difference, other people's behaviour towards them, and material barriers. Most young people presented themselves as similar to non-disabled children: it is suggested they may have lacked a positive language with which to discuss difference. It is further argued that Thomas's (1999) social relational model of disability can help inform understandings of children's experiences, with 'barriers to being' having particular significance.

Introduction

Disabled children have received little attention within the social model of disability: the extent to which it provides an adequate explanatory framework for their experiences has been little explored. Many studies about disabled children make reference to the social model, often in relation to identifying social or material barriers or in formulating recommendations for better services (Morris, 1998a; Dowling & Dolan, 2001; Murray, 2002; Townsley *et al.*, 2004; Rabiee *et al.*, 2005). Few have focused specifically on children's perceptions and experiences of impairment and disability or explored the implications of these for theorizing childhood disability. Watson *et al.* (2000) and Kelly (2005), following Connors and Stalker (2003a), are notable exceptions. Ali *et al.* (2001), in a critical review of the literature relating to black disabled children, concluded that the disability movement in Britain has neglected children's experiences.

The research reported in this paper was a two year study conducted in the Social Work Research Centre at the University of Stirling, funded by the Scottish Executive. A full account can be found in Connors and Stalker (2003b). The paper begins by outlining the study's theoretical framework, which drew on insights from disability studies and the sociology of childhood. The study's aims and methods are outlined and some key findings presented. We conclude by speculating why most of the children focused on 'sameness' rather than difference in their accounts and the implications of the findings for developing a social model of childhood disability.

Theoretical framework

The sociology of childhood, the new social studies of childhood

Until the early 1990s research on childhood was largely concerned with children's psychological, physical and social development. Children were usually prescribed a passive role in this process and were seen through adult eyes (Waksler, 1991; Shakespeare & Watson, 1998)—they were adults in training. The idea that childhood, unlike biological immaturity, might be a social construction influenced by factors such as class, gender and ethnicity emerged through the 'sociology of childhood'. Here, children are recognized as having a unique perspective and actively shaping their own lives (James, 1993; James & Prout, 1997; Mayall, 2002). Listening to children's accounts of their experiences has encouraged recognition that their lives are not homogeneous and need to be studied in all their diversity (Brannen & O'Brien, 1995). In order to understand general themes in children's lives it is necessary to pay attention to their narratives and personal experiences. Shakespeare and Watson (1998) pointed to the potential for drawing on insights from both the social model of disability and the sociology of childhood to explore disabled children's experiences.

Reliance on personal experience, which constitutes much of the research with children, has been a contested area within disability studies. Finkelstein (1996) questioned its relevance, believing that attempts on the part of disabled people to describe the detail of their lives is a route back to viewing disability as a tragic event which 'happens' to some individuals. Several disabled feminists (Morris, 1993; Crow, 1996; Thomas, 1999) have suggested that not to do so is to ignore lessons from the feminist movement:

> In opposition to Finkelstein's view that a focus on individual lives and experiences fails to enable us to understand (and thus to challenge) the socio-structural, I would agree with those who see life history accounts ... as evidence that 'the micro' is constitutive of 'the macro'. Experiential narratives offer a route to understanding the 'socio-structural'. (Thomas, 1999, p. 78)

The social relational model of disability

Thomas' work (1999) was particularly important to our study because she has developed definitions of disability which relate directly to people's lived experience. She views disability as being rooted in an unequal social relationship. It follows a similar course to racism and sexism and results in 'the social imposition of restrictions of activity on impaired people' by non-impaired people, either through 'barriers to doing' or 'barriers to being'. The former refers to physical, economic and material barriers, such as inaccessible buildings or transport, which restrict or prevent people from undertaking certain activities; the latter refers to hurtful, hostile or inappropriate behaviour which has a negative effect on an individual's sense of self, affecting what they feel they can be or become. Thomas calls this process 'psycho-emotional disablism'. Barriers to being are not confined to the personal, one-to-one level: exclusionary institutional policies and practices can have the same effect.

Thomas also identified impairment effects, i.e. restrictions of activity which result from living with an impairment. This could include the fatigue or discomfort associated with some conditions or the inability to do certain things. Historically, disability studies has avoided acknowledging the limitations which can be associated with impairment (Crow, 1996). Shakespeare and Watson (2002) saw this as a great weakness in social model theory, arguing that impairment is 'experientially ... salient to many'. Thomas (2001) suggested that acknowledging personal experiences of living with impairment and disability is politically unifying because it enables a full range of disability experiences to be recognized and this inclusivity will better represent all disabled people in society (Reeve, 2002).

Difference

The idea of difference is another debate within disability studies relevant to our research. One view is that difference does not exist, but rather individuals' bodies are constructed and then maintained as disabled by social opinions and barriers (Price & Shildrick, 1998). An alternative view is that disabled people are 'essentially' different from non-disabled people (Thomas, 1999), so that difference is part of the 'essence' of a disabled person. For Morris (1991) having an impairment makes a person fundamentally different from someone who does not have one. This difference exists beyond the socially constructed effects of disablism, making the presence of impairment the key difference between disabled and non-disabled people. Scott-Hill (2004) suggested that difference has been neglected because its acknowledgement poses a threat to the disabled people's movement and its political message: she calls for more 'dialogue across difference'.

The fusion of ideas from disability studies and the sociology of childhood is at an early stage and while there are reasons to be cautious, there are indications that it could be a very fruitful relationship (Watson *et al.*, 2000) as we seek a framework within which to understand and describe the richness and diversity of disabled children's everyday lives.

Study aims and methods

The aims of the study were:

- to explore disabled children's understandings of disability;

- to examine the ways in which they negotiate the experience of disability in their daily lives;
- to examine the children's perceptions of their relationships with professionals and their views of service provision;
- to examine siblings' perceptions of the effects on them of having a disabled brother or sister.

In this paper we focus on the first of these aims.

At the beginning of the study, when the research proposal was being written, we recruited two 'research advisors', aged 11 and 12, through a voluntary organization for disabled people. The children gave us valuable advice about the design of information and consent leaflets for different age groups, the wording of questions and the suitability of interview materials.

Families were recruited to the study through schools and voluntary organizations, which were asked to pass on letters to parents and information leaflets and 'agreement forms' to children. We were not aiming to recruit a representative sample, but rather to include children and young people from a range of age groups, with a variety of impairments, attending different types of school, and so on. Twenty five families, who had 26 disabled children in total, agreed to take part.

Before formal data collection commenced, an initial visit was made to each family to discuss the implications of participating in the research. This provided an opportunity for researcher and family members to begin to get to know one another, agree ground rules, ensure that everyone understood what the study entailed and had an opportunity to ask questions or raise concerns. This meeting enabled the researchers to identify each child's accustomed communication method and to some extent assess their cognitive ability, thus enabling us to use an appropriate approach in the interviews.

One-to-one guided conversations were conducted with the young disabled people in their own homes, spread over two or three visits. With younger children a semi-structured interview schedule was used, supplemented by a range of activities and communications aids, such as 'spidergrams', word choice exercises and picture cards, to engage the child's interest and facilitate communication. This approach was also used with all the youngsters who had learning disabilities: piloting showed that the more structured format of this questionnaire was more accessible to this group than the topic guide (covering the same subjects) designed for older children.

We asked the children to tell us about 'a typical day' at school and at the weekend, relationships with family and friends, their local neighbourhood, experiences at school, pastimes and interests, use of services and future aspirations. While open-ended questions were enough to launch some children on a blow-by-blow account of, for example, everything they had done the previous day, other youngsters, notably those with learning disabilities, needed the question broken up into more manageable chunks, such as: 'what time do you usually get up?; what do you like for breakfast?' We did not include direct questions about impairment in the children's interview schedules, nor did we think it appropriate to ask the children, in so many words, how they 'understood disability'. Rather, we preferred to wait and see what they had to say on these topics while telling us about their daily lives generally and in response to specific questions such as the following.

- Are there some things you are quite good at?
- Are there any things you find difficult to do?
- What's the best thing about school?
- What's the worst thing?
- Have you ever been bullied at school?
- Are there any things you need help to do?
- If you had a magic wand and you could wish for something to happen, what would you wish?

If individual children made little or no reference to impairment as the interview proceeded we raised the subject in follow-up questions, e.g. after the 'magic wand' question we might ask: 'what about your disability?; would you change anything about that?' This was easier with those who had physical or sensory impairments than those with learning disabilities (see Stalker & Connors, 2005, for an account of these children's views and experiences).

Over the last decade an increasing number of publications have offered guidance on seeking the views of disabled children for consultation or research (see, for example, Ward, 1997; Morris, 1998b, 2003; Potter & Whittaker, 2001; Stone, 2001). In our experience talking to disabled children is often no different from talking to any child: it is important to see every child as a child first and with an impairment second. However, one of the authors (Connors), who conducted most of the fieldwork, is fluent in British Sign Language and Makaton: the ability to draw on these methods was essential to avoid excluding four children from the study. A fifth child used facilitated communication: his mother went through some of the questions with him and passed on the responses to us. Two children had profound multiple impairment and here we interviewed their parents, although being careful not to treat their views as 'proxy' data.

Ethical issues are heightened in research with children. Consent was treated as an ongoing process. Thus we asked the children at the start of each session if they felt okay about talking to us again, checked that we could tape record what they said, reminded them they could stop at any time or 'pass' on any question they did not wish to answer and that nothing they said would be reported to their parents, unless it indicated the children were at risk of harm. One child decided not to proceed with a second interview, which (despite losing potentially valuable data!) reassured us that he did not feel under pressure to participate.

The children, 15 boys and 11 girls, were aged between 7 and 15. There was one black child, reflecting the relatively low population of black and minority ethnic families in Scotland, and all had English as their first language. We deliberately avoided using medical diagnoses to recruit children and did not 'measure' severity of impairment, but simply recorded any conditions or diagnoses which parents or schools gave us. Broadly, 13 children were described as having learning disabilities, five sensory impairments and six physical impairments. As noted above, two had profound/multiple impairment. The youngsters attended a variety of schools: 'special' (segregated), mainstream (inclusive) and 'integrated' (segregated units within mainstream schools). All lived in central or southern Scotland.

Twenty-four siblings and 38 parents also took part in one interview each. Semistructured schedules were used to explore their views and experiences, but these are not reported in detail here (see Stalker & Connors, 2004, with respect to siblings' views about impairment, disablism and difference).

Data recorded on audio or video tape (interviews conducted in British Sign Language) were transcribed in full. The transcripts were read through carefully several times, a sample being read and discussed by both authors. Emerging patterns, common themes and key points were identified and these, together with additional material taken from field notes and pen profiles of the families, were used to distil the findings.

Full details of the methodology can be found in Stalker and Connors (2003).

Findings

The findings suggest that children experienced disability in four ways, in terms of impairment, difference, other people's reactions and material barriers.

Impairment

Much of what children talked about as 'disability' was impairment and the effects of impairment on their day-to-day living (although none used the word 'impairment'). The children's main source of information about the cause of their impairments was their parents. Parents told us they tended to use one of three explanations: the child was 'special', impairment was part of God's plan for the family or there had been an accident or illness around the time of birth. Several parents commented on their dread at being asked for explanations and it was notable that disabled children seemed to ask once and then let the subject drop; perhaps they were aware of the distress felt by parents. Generally, there seemed not to be much discussion within families about impairment. A number of children had never talked to their parents about it and in some families there was avoidance and/or silence about the subject. One sibling, a 13-year-old boy, reported that his mother had forbidden him to tell other people about his sister's impairment but rather to 'keep it in between the family'.

The disabled children tended to see impairment in medical terms—not surprisingly, given that most had a high level of contact with health services. Most had experienced multiple hospital admissions, operations and regular outpatient appointments, all of which might lead them to conclude that having an impairment linked them directly to healthcare professionals. A few had cheerful memories of being in hospital; for example one said she would give her doctor '20 out of 10' points for helping her, while another said his consultant was 'brilliant'. A 10-year-old boy with learning disabilities recalled an eye operation he had undergone aged 5 or 6:

Researcher:	What happened? Did you go into hospital on your own?
Child:	My mum wasn't allowed to come in with me.
Researcher:	Was she not?
Child:	Into the theatre.
Researcher:	Into the theatre. Was she allowed to be with you in the ward?
Child:	Yes. Uh-huh.
Researcher:	Good.
Child:	What made me scared most was, there were these tongs, they were like that … with big bridges with lights on them, you know, and 'oh, oh, what are they for? What are they for?'
Researcher:	Hmm. Hmm.
Child:	And there were things all in my mouth.
Researcher:	Hmm. Hmm.
Child:	Then everybody was there.
Researcher:	Ah ha.
Child:	Then I went 'Mum!'
Researcher:	Hmm. So it's quite scary. Did it help?
Child:	Yeah.

However, none of the children appeared to view impairment as a 'tragedy', despite the close ties between the 'medical' and 'tragedy' models of disability (Hevey, 1993). They made no reference to feeling loss or having a sense of being hard done by.

Indeed, for some children it seemed that having an impairment was not a 'big deal' in their lives. When offered a 'magic wand' and asked if they would like to change anything about themselves or their lives, only three referred to their impairment: two said they would like to be able to walk and one wanted better vision. One girl with mobility difficulties compared herself favourably with other children: 'When I see people as they two are, I think "gosh" and I'm like glad I can walk and people see me and I walk like this'. When a boy aged 9 was asked if he ever wished he didn't have to use a wheelchair, the reply was: 'That's it, I'm in a wheelchair so just get on with it … just get on with what you're doing'.

The children did tell us about what Thomas (1999) called 'impairment effects' (restrictions of activity which result from living with impairment, as opposed to restrictions caused by social or material barriers). They talked about repeated chest infections, tiring easily, being in pain, having difficulty completing schoolwork. At the same time, most seemed to have learned to manage, or at least put up with, these things. Most children appeared to have a practical, pragmatic attitude to their impairment. The majority appeared happy with themselves and were not looking for a 'cure'. However, there were some indications that a few of the younger children thought they would outgrow their impairment. The mother of a 9-year-old Deaf boy said he thought he would grow into a hearing adult. (This child had no contact with Deaf adults.) Only one younger child thought she would need support when she grew up, in contrast to most of the older ones, who recognized they would need support in some form or other.

Difference

Parents usually thought their children were aware of themselves as different from other children, but most of the children did not mention it. Instead, the majority focused on the ways their lives were similar to or the same as those of their peers. Most said they felt happy 'most of the time', had a sense of achievement through school or sports and saw themselves as good friends and helpful classmates. They were active beings with opportunities to mould at least some aspects of their lives. Most felt they had enough say in their lives, although some teenagers, like many youngsters of that age, were struggling with their parents about being allowed more independence. One girl said of her mother:

> She's got to understand that she can't rule my life any more .... I just want to make up my own mind now because she's always deciding for me, like what's best for me and sometimes I get angry. She just doesn't realize that I'm grown up now but soon I'm going to be 14 and I won't be a wee girl any more.

When asked what they would be doing at their parents' age the children revealed very similar aspirations to those of other youngsters, for example becoming a builder, soldier, fireman, vet, nurse or 'singer and dancer'.

Most problems the children identified were in the here and now: it was striking that on this subject their responses differed from their parents' accounts. Most parents were able to tell us about occasions where their child had been discriminated against, treated badly or faced some difficulty, but the children themselves painted a different picture of the issues which concerned them. Some, particularly in the older group, reported a high level of boredom; many of these young people attended special schools and so had few, if any, friends in their local communities. One teenager explained:

> It's like weird because people at my [segregated] school, they are not as much my friends as people here 'cos I don't know them that much. My friends past the years, they come to my house but not them. They've never even seen my house.

As Cavet (1998) pointed out, at this age leisure and friendship 'happen' either in young people's homes or venues like sporting facilities or shopping centres, neither of which may be accessible to some disabled adolescents and teenagers.

Fifteen children in the sample had some degree of learning disabilities. These youngsters made very few references to their impairment, with only one mentioning her diagnosis. This 13-year-old girl had written a story about herself for the researcher, with whom she had this exchange as they read it together:

> Researcher: What's that? My name is ....
> Child: Pat Brownlie, I have De Soto syndrome.
> Researcher: Right. Tell me what De Soto syndrome is.
> Child: Em ... eh .... What is it again?
> Researcher: How does it make you feel? ....
> Child: Different.

It was interesting that, unlike Pat, most of the children focused on 'sameness'—in many cases it would be hard to avoid or minimize their difference. Our evidence suggests that it was the way difference was responded to and managed which was crucial.

Some schools with 'inclusive' policies seemed to take the view that difference should not even be acknowledged. We were not allowed to make contact with families through some schools because our research was about disabled children and they were not to be singled out (despite the fact that all the interviews were to take place in the family home). One danger of treating all children 'the same' is that rules and procedures designed for the majority do not always fit the minority. In an example from a mainstream school one mother told us that her 14-year-old son, a wheelchair user, had been left alone in the school during fire drill:

> He was telling me the other day how they did the fire alarm and everybody was screaming out in the playground. Richard was still in the school and everybody was outside. He was saying 'Mum, I was really, really worried about what happens if there's a real fire.' No one came to his assistance at all.

Where difference was badly managed children could feel hurt and excluded, resulting in the 'barriers to being' that Thomas (1999) identified. One boy who attended an integrated unit within a mainstream school asked his mother what he had done 'wrong' to be placed in a 'special' class. Lack of information and explanation had led him to equate difference with badness or naughtiness.

Some special schools seemed to focus on difference in an unhelpful way, defining the children in terms of their impairment. At one school teachers apparently referred to pupils as 'wheelchairs' and 'walkers'. A wheelchair user at this school commented: 'It's sad because we're just the same. We just can't walk, that's all the difference'. Another pupil at this school told us: 'I'm happy being a cerebral palsy'. Despite her stated 'happiness', it seems unlikely that being publicly labelled in this way, and then apparently internalizing the definition, would help children develop a rounded sense of self. At the same time, a couple of children believed that needs relating to their impairment were better met in a special school than they would be in a mainstream school, with one boy commenting that a deaf girl preferred to be:

Child:	Where there's signing, where everyone signs, all the teachers, all the children.
Researcher:	Why is that better than going to a school with hearing children?
Child:	Hearing children, no one signs. I don't understand them and they don't understand me.

Echoing findings made elsewhere (Davis & Watson, 2001; Skar & Tamm, 2001), there were several reports of children in mainstream schools feeling unhappy with their special needs assistants (SNAs), whose role is to facilitate inclusion. One older girl was very annoyed that at break times her SNA regularly took her to the younger children's playground when, understandably, she wanted to mix with young people of her own age. In another case a SNA always took a pupil into the nursery class at lunch times, because she (the SNA) was friendly with the nursery staff!

On the other hand, some schools responded to difference in a positive way. Many children had extra aids and equipment at school or were taken out of their classes for one-to-one tuition. Much of this support seemed to be well embedded in daily routines and not made into an issue. The mother of a boy attending mainstream school recounted:

> There was that time, remember, when. ... they'd asked a question in the big hall ... . It was 'does anybody in here think they are special?' and he put his hand up and said 'I am because I have cerebral palsy' and ... he went out to the front and spoke about his disability to everybody.

It could be argued that encouraging children to see themselves as 'special' because they have an impairment is not a positive way forward. As indicated earlier in this paper in relation to different types of school, the word 'special' can be a euphemism (or justification) for segregated facilities. 'Special' might also be seen as a somewhat mawkish or sentimental way of portraying disabled children. However, some parents used this word to emphasize that their children were unique and valued individuals. Most worked hard to give the children the message that they were just as good as their brothers and sisters and any other children, that it was possible to be different but equal.

Reactions of other people

Nevertheless, children could be made to feel different and of lesser value by the unhelpful and sometimes hostile words and actions of others, whether people they knew or complete strangers. These are another example of what Thomas (1999) referred to as 'barriers to being', relating to the psycho-emotional dimension of disability. We were told of incidents where people unknown to the child had acted insensitively, for example:

- staring;
- talking down, as if addressing a young child;
- inappropriate comments;
- inappropriate behaviour;
- overt sympathy.

Children who used wheelchairs seemed to be a particular target for the public at large. An older boy who had difficulty eating disliked going out to restaurants because he was stared at. He used a wheelchair and got annoyed when people bent down to talk to him as if he was 'small' or 'stupid': 'I don't mind if it's wee boys or wee girls that look at me but if it's adults ... they should know. It's as if they've never seen a wheelchair before and they have, eh?' A 13-year-old girl with learning disabilities described the harassment which she and her single mother had experienced from neighbours, including:

> The man next door came to our door and rattled the letter box and shouted 'come out you cows or I will get you'. So we called the police and then they did not believe us because I was a special needs.

Other children could also be cruel: almost half the disabled children had experienced bullying, either at school or in their local neighbourhood. One boy reported that he was 'made fun of' at school 'about nearly every day'. His mother reported he had once had a good day in school because no-one had called him 'blindie'. Although the children were very hurt by this kind of behaviour, a few took active steps to deal with it, reporting the bullying to parents or teachers. One girl faced up to the bullies herself and was not bothered by them again. A few were not above giving as good as they got, as this boy's response shows: 'No, I just bully them back. Or if they started kicking us, I'd kick them back'.

Material barriers

Thomas (1999) described 'barriers to doing' as restrictions of activity arising from social or physical factors. These caused significant difficulties in the children's lives. They included:

- lack of access to leisure facilities and clubs, especially for teenagers;
- transport difficulties;
- paucity of after-school activities;
- lack of support with communication.

One boy reported he had been unable to go to a mainstream high school with friends from primary school because parts of the building were not accessible to him. A 13-year-old boy who wanted to go shopping with his friends at the weekend found that his local Shopmobility scheme had no children's wheelchairs. A 14-year-old who wanted to attend an evening youth club at school was told it was not possible to arrange accessible transport at that time. It was suggested he remain in school after afternoon lessons ended until the club began. Understandably, he was not willing to wait around in school by himself for four hours, nor to attend the youth club wearing his school uniform.

There was less evidence of material barriers in the accounts given by children with learning disabilities. Some complained of boredom at weekends and during school holidays, sometimes linked to the fact that they attended a school outside their neighbourhood and lacked friends locally. Alternatively, they may have been less affected by, or aware of, the physical barriers affecting some of the children with physical and sensory impairments.

Discussion

So, children experienced disability in terms of impairment, difference, other people's behaviour and material barriers. Some had negative experiences of the way difference was handled at school, many encountered hurtful or hostile reactions from other people and many also came up against physical barriers which restricted their day-to-day lives. Despite all this, most of the children presented themselves as much the same as others, young people with fairly ordinary lives. They focused on sameness. Why?

There could be a number of explanations. First, it may be that some of the children felt they had to minimize or deny their difference. Youth culture and consumerism exert heavy pressures on young people to follow the crowd, keep up with others, not to stand out. Disabled youngsters are by no means immune to such pressures, albeit, as Hughes *et al.* (2005) argued, they may find themselves excluded from 'going with the flow'. The concept and practice of 'passing' as 'normal' was first identified by Edgerton (1967) in his longitudinal study of people with learning disabilities in the USA. More recently, Watson *et al.* (2000) reported that some children with invisible impairments exclude themselves from the 'disability' category. A significant number of children in our study were not encouraged to talk about impairment and disability at home or at school. These attitudes—or pressures—would tend to discourage children from talking about difference. It is notable that children at special schools tended to talk more openly about their impairments, although the schools themselves still seemed to be operating out of a medical model of disability.

Secondly, and taking a different tack, we could argue that the children in this study are self-directing agents, choosing to manage their day-to-day lives and experiences of disability in a matter of fact way. It is important to stress here that the children's (mostly positive) accounts of their lives differ significantly from earlier research findings about disabled children based on parents' or professionals' views, which tend to be considerably more negative (see Baldwin & Carlisle, 1994). Some of the older children were also active in responding to the hostile responses of other people, although there was less they could do about the structural barriers they came up against. They were also developing frameworks within which to understand the behaviours shown to them and, as active agents, chose not to be categorized by these responses. Impairment, and the resulting disability, was not seen as a defining feature of their identities. This concurs with the findings of Priestley *et al.* (1999), who noted that although children could identify the disabling barriers they encountered, they were still keen to be seen as 'normal', if different, and resisted being defined as disabled. However, there were exceptions, like the girl who described herself as 'a cerebral palsy'.

However, we lean towards a third explanation. Perhaps the children were neither 'in denial' nor fully in command of resisting the various barriers they face. It may be that they did not have a language with which to discuss difference. We have already noted that they lacked contact with disabled adults—they did not have positive role models of disabled people nor opportunities to share stories about their lives with other disabled children. Without this framework it could be that children strove to be, or appear, the same as their non-disabled peers. If so, then there is a need for disabled children to have contact with organizations of disabled people and access to information and ideas about social models of disability. A counter-narrative is a critique of dominant public narratives constructed by people excluded from mainstream society to tell their own story (Thomas, 1999). The social model of disability is a counter-narrative (which has had considerable impact), but up to now children's narratives have played little part in its construction. Thus, there is a need for the social model to take children's experiences on board. How can it do this?

Our findings show that Thomas' social relational model of disability, which was developed from women's accounts of disability, can also inform our understandings of disabled children's experiences. First, despite the fact that the majority had relatively little information about the cause and, in some cases, nature of their impairments, impairment was a significant part of their daily experience. They reported various 'impairment effects'. In addition, our analysis showed some significant differences in the experiences and perceptions of those with learning disabilities compared with those with physical and sensory impairment. Secondly, there was evidence of 'barriers to doing' in the children's accounts, particularly those with physical or sensory impairments. They identified various material, structural and institutional barriers which restricted their activities.

Thirdly, the young people told us about their experiences of being excluded or made to feel inferior by the comments and behaviour of others, sometimes thoughtless, sometimes deliberately hurtful. Some parents strove to give their disabled children positive messages about their value and worth and fought for them to have an ordinary life, for example to attend mainstream schools or be included in local activities, and some children received good support from teachers or other professionals. Nevertheless, they could be brought up against their difference, so to speak, in a negative way by other people's reactions, at both a personal and institutional level. In the children's accounts it was these incidents which upset them most, albeit some showed active resistance to, or rejection of, the labels or restrictions others sought to impose on them. Thus, in thinking about disabled childhoods, 'impairment effects', 'barriers to doing' and 'barriers to being' all seem to have a place. Our findings suggest that the last of these may have particular significance during the childhood years, when young people are going through important stages of identity formation which may lay the foundations of self-confidence and self-worth for years to come.

It is early days and these ideas are no more than a potential starting point. There is a need for a two-way process in which disabled children have access to ideas and information about social models of disability, and social models of disability take account of their experiences and understandings. To facilitate this process we need to open up more space for conversations between disabled children, disability activists and researchers and their allies.

References

Ali, Z., Qulsom, F., Bywaters P., Wallace, L. & Singh, G. (2001) Disability, ethnicity and childhood: a critical review of research, *Disability & Society*, 16(7), 949–968.

Baldwin, S. & Carlisle, J. (1994) *Social support for disabled children and their families: a review of the literature* (Edinburgh, HMSO).

Brannen, J. & O'Brien, M. (1995) Childhood and the sociological gaze: paradigms and paradoxes, *Sociology*, 29(4), 729–737.

Cavet, J. (1998) Leisure and friendship, in: C. Robinson & K. Stalker (Eds) *Growing up with disability* (London, Jessica Kingsley).

Connors, C. & Stalker, K. (2003a) Barriers to 'being'; the psycho-emotional dimension of disability in the lives of disabled children, paper presented at the conference *Disability Studies: Theory, Policy and Practice*, University of Lancaster, 4–6 September.

Connors, C. & Stalker, K (2003b) *The views and experiences of disabled children and their siblings: a positive outlook* (London, Jessica Kingsley).

Crow, L. (1996) Including all of our lives: renewing the social model of disability, in: C. Barnes & G. Mercer (Eds) *Exploring the divide: illness and disability* (Leeds, UK, The Disability Press).
Davis, J. & Watson, N. (2001) Where are the children's experiences? Analysing social and cultural exclusion in 'special' and 'mainstream' schools, *Disability & Society*, 16(5), 671–687.
Dowling, M. & Dolan, L. (2001) Disabilities—inequalities and the social model, *Disability & Society*, 16(1), 21–36.
Edgerton, R. B. (1967) *The cloak of competence: stigma in the lives of the mentally retarded* (San Francisco, CA, University of California Press).
Finkelstein, V. (1996) Outside, inside out, *Coalition*, 1996(April), 30–36.
Hevey, D. (1993) The tragedy principle: strategies for change in the representation of disabled people, in: J. Swain, V. Finkelstein, S. French & M. Oliver (Eds) *Disabling barriers—enabling environment* (London, Sage).
Hughes, B., Russell, R. & Paterson, K. (2005) Nothing to be had 'off the peg': consumption, identity and the immobilization of young disabled people, *Disability & Society*, 20(1), 3–18.
James, A. (1993) *Childhood identities: self and social relationships in the experience of the child* (Edinburgh, Edinburgh University Press).
James, A. & Prout, A. (Eds) (1997) *Constructing and reconstructing childhood: contemporary issues in the sociological study of childhood* (London, Falmer).
Kelly, B. (2005) 'Chocolate ... makes you autism': impairment, disability and childhood identities, *Disability & Society*, 20(3) 261–276.
Mayall, B. (2002) *Towards a sociology for childhood* (Maidenhead, UK, Open University Press).
Morris, J. (1991) *Pride against prejudice: transforming attitudes to disability* (London, The Women's Press).
Morris, J. (1993) Gender and disability, in: J. Swain, V. Finkelstein, S. French & M. Oliver (Eds) *Disabling barriers—enabling environments* (London, Sage).
Morris, J. (1998a) *Still missing? Disabled children and the Children Act* (London, Who Cares? Trust).
Morris, J. (1998b) *Don't leave us out: involving disabled children and young people with communication impairments* (York, UK, Joseph Rowntree Foundation).
Morris, J. (2003) Including all children: finding out about the experiences of children with communication and/or cognitive impairments, *Children & Society*, 17(5), 337–348.
Murray, P. (2002) *Hello! Are you listening? Disabled teenagers' experiences of access to inclusive leisure* (York, UK, York Publishing Services).
Potter, C. & Whittaker, C. (2001) *Enabling communication in children with autism* (London, Jessica Kingsley).
Price, J. & Shildrick, M. (1998) Uncertain thoughts on the disabled body, in: M. Shildrick & J. Price (Eds) *Vital signs: feminist reconstructions of the biological body* (Edinburgh, UK, Edinburgh University Press).
Priestley, M., Corker, M. & Watson, N. (1999) Unfinished business: disabled children and disability identity, *Disability Studies Quarterly*, 19(2), 90–97.
Rabiee, P., Sloper, P. & Beresford, B (2005) Doing research with children and young people who do not use speech to communicate, *Children and Society*, 19(5), 385–396.
Reeve, D. (2002) Negotiating psycho-emotional dimensions of disability and their influence on identity construction, *Disability & Society*, 17(5) 493–508.
Scott-Hill, M (2004) Impairment, difference and identity, in: J. Swain, S. French, C. Barnes & C. Thomas (Eds) *Disabling barriers—enabling environment* (London, Sage).
Shakespeare, T. & Watson, N. (1998) Theoretical perspectives on research with disabled children, in: C. Robinson & K. Stalker (Eds) *Growing up with disability* (London, Jessica Kingsley).
Shakespeare, T. & Watson, N. (2002) The social model of disability: an outdated ideology?, *Research in Social Science and Disability*, 2, 9–28.

Skar, L. & Tamm, M. (2001) My assistant and I: disabled children's and adolescents' roles and relationships to their assistants, *Disability & Society*, 16(7) 917–931.

Stalker, K. & Connors, C. (2003) Communicating with disabled children, *Adoption & Fostering*, 27(1) 26–35.

Stalker, K. & Connors, C. (2004) Children's perceptions of their disabled siblings: "she's different but it's normal for us", *Children & Society*, 18, 218–230.

Stalker, K. & Connors, C. (2005) Children with learning disabilities talking about their everyday lives, in: G. Grant, P. Goward, M. Richardson & P. Ramcharan (Eds) *Learning disability: a life cycle approach to valuing people* (Maidenhead, UK, Open University Press).

Stone, E. (2001) Consulting with disabled children and young people, *Findings, 741* (York, UK, Joseph Rowntree Foundation).

Thomas, C. (1999) *Female forms: experiencing and understanding disability* (Buckingham, UK, Open University Press).

Thomas, C. (2001) Feminism and disability: the theoretical and political significance of the personal and the experiential, in: L. Barton (Ed.) *Disability, politics and the struggle for change* (London, David Fulton).

Townsley, R., Abbott, D. & Watson, D. (2004) *Making a difference? Exploring the impact of multi-agency working on disabled children with complex needs, their families and the professionals who support them* (Bristol, UK, Policy Press).

Waksler, F. (Ed.) (1991) *Studying the social world of children: sociological readings* (London, Falmer).

Ward, L. (1997) *Seen and heard: involving disabled children and young people in research and development projects* (York, UK, Joseph Rowntree Foundation).

Watson, N., Shakespeare, T., Cunningham-Burley, S., Barnes, C., Corker, M., Davis, J. & Priestley, M. (2000) *Life as a disabled child: a qualitative study of young people's experiences and perspectives: final report to the ESRC* (Edinburgh, University of Edinburgh Department of Nursing Studies).

Notions of self: lived realities of children with disabilities

Vanessa Singh[a,b] and Anita Ghai[b]

[a]*Graduate School of Neural and Behavioural Sciences, International Max Planck Research School, Tübingen, Germany;* [b]*Department of Psychology, Jesus and Mary College, University of Delhi, India*

> To research children's notions of self, semi-structured interviews, drawings and focused group discussions were used with 14 children with mobility 'impairments' aged 11–16 years. The objective was to capture children's 'lived realities'. Findings illuminated immense variation and fluidity in children's understanding of 'disability'. Children desired to appear similar to 'non-disabled' children. Most attributed 'disability' to existential causes. Parents' ambivalent attitudes and societal reactions to 'disabled' children are discussed. The study points out the unremitting hope and potential of these children, which is often silenced by the overarching 'negativism' that surrounds 'disability'.

Introduction – 'disability' in India

Within the Indian subcontinent awareness of the issues and concerns of lives touched with disability is a fairly recent phenomenon. It was only in the forty-ninth year of independence from colonial oppression that the first legislation advocating equal rights for disabled people became a living reality. The Persons with Disabilities (Equal Opportunities, Protection of Rights and Full Participation) Act was passed in 1995. This is important legislation that provides guidelines for education, employment, vocational training, reservation quotas, research and human resource development, the creation of a barrier-free environment and inclusion and independent living. This is supplemented by the Rehabilitation Council of India Act 1992, which is responsible for standardizing and monitoring training courses for rehabilitation professionals, granting recognition to institutions running courses and maintaining a Central Rehabilitation Register of rehabilitation professionals. The Rehabilitation Council of India (RCI) Act was amended in 2000 to give the RCI the additional responsibility of promoting research in rehabilitation and special education. To substantiate the earlier legislation, the National Trust Act 1999 aimed to provide for the welfare of people with autism, cerebral palsy, 'mental retardation' and multiple disabilities. The Act mandates promotion of measures for the care and protection of persons with these disabilities in the event of the death of their parents, procedures for appointment of guardians and trustees for persons in need of such protection and support for registered organizations to provide needs-based services in times of crisis to the families of the disabled. While there has been this legislation, a will to translate them into action is not clearly evident. The recommendations given do, however, give an idea that there is awareness of the necessity of going beyond medical definitions and moving towards an analysis of social and political factors.

The social and cultural construction of childhood and 'disability' evinces the commonalities considered between them. Children are considered 'disabled' if they have an identifiable level of 'deficit' when formally measured or compared with a social/cultural norm of learning, physical abilities, etc. Like 'disabled', children too are denied attributions of agency, competence and civil rights. Burns (1992) and Brown (1994) argued that society, fearing the consequences in terms of procreation, wishes to keep people with 'disability' in a state of 'suspended childhood'. Influenced by such perspectives, one finds in the research that even when children have been included, childhood experiences have been homogenized. What is needed is an attempt to elucidate children's own experiences, definitions and constructions of their daily lives. With this thought in mind, the present study was conceptualized to understand the experiential realities of 'disabled' children. A prerequisite of this venture is to first understand 'disability' as a category within the Indian context.

The comprehension and meaning of 'disability' in India needs to be negotiated as embedded in multiple cultural discourses, with subtle nuances (Ghai 2002a, 2002b). Within India and elsewhere (Braathen and Ingstad 2006) 'disability' has been understood as a retribution for past 'karma' or sins and the disabled stoically accept their fate (Dalal and Pandey 1999; Ghai 2003). Disability is attributed to god's will, without signifying external factors such as poverty, poor health facilities violence/accidents as responsible for causing disability. The implication is that the consequences of past deeds have to be borne, thereby not placing enough weight on efforts to improve life conditions. The predominant responses to the predicament of 'disability' remain charity and philanthropy. In fact, philanthropy also has its roots in one's dharmic (religious) duty toward the needy rather than a concern for the 'disabled' (Ghai 2002a, 2002b).

On the one hand is the assumption that 'disability' implies a 'lack' or 'flaw' leading to significantly diminished capability. This assumption is rooted in the dominant Hindu mythology in which the two most popular epics, the Mahabharata and Ramayana, contain negative images associated with disability. In the former king Dhritrashtra is deprived of the throne because of his visual impairment. Another set of images associates disability with evil and as something to fear with an expectation of submissiveness. Within the Mahabharata the central turning point is intervention by an orthopaedically impaired man, Shakuni, while in the Ramayana it is intervention by a female dwarf, Manthra, both being presented as evil. The narratives generally depict disabled people as suffering the wrath of God, being punished for misdeeds that either they or their families had committed. Yet another strand conceives of disability as eternal childhood, where survival is contingent upon constant care and protection. Here the emphasis is on images of dependency, thereby reinforcing the charity/pity model. This list, although not exhaustive, illustrates the underpinnings of a negative cultural identity. Historically there are also narratives containing instances where disabled people are considered the children of God. This positioning provided spaces, in the spheres of religion and knowledge, in which the ability to transcend the body was a distinct possibility. Even though the implicit meaning of such possibilities may be disturbing within our present understanding of disability, it does indicate a dignified negotiation of difference. Thus, the renowned scholar Ashtvakra, who had eight deformities, and the great poet Surdas, who was visually impaired, are illustrations of strength and the ability to fight oppression. However, within these constructions disability is something that can be overcome. All the same, the predominant cultural construction of disability is largely negative. While there are different strands in the historical rendering of 'disability', the associations that are conveyed construct the 'disabled' as objects of pity and charity, coupled with images of deviance, treachery, evil behaviour and villainy. Another set of images portray the 'disabled' as capable of heroic efforts that result in overcoming the 'disability', setting an exemplary standard for others to follow. Needless to add, the objective of all these images is to posit 'disability' as an oppositional category to 'normality' (Ghai 2002b; Dalal 2001).

Birth of a 'disabled' child in the family has a profound effect on the family's structure, function and emotions (Gawali 2003; Datta et al. 2002; Pal et al. 2002). While this is a universal phenomenon, within the Indian context it becomes traumatic because of cultural conceptions of a 'disabled' child being dependent, immature and incapable of taking decisions about his/her own life (Dalal 2001). Cultural perceptions of 'disability' have not emerged in a vacuum. They are informed by pathologizing discourses of psychology and medicine. Goodley (2007a, 2007b) introduced parents of 'disabled' babies as 'lines of flight'. Parents see their 'disabled' babies as gifts attempting to break free from societal definitions and the restrictions of 'disability'.The effects are not restricted to the immediate family, as children are the shared responsibility of wider social relationships (Saxena and Sharma 2000). Such a context mandates that children's own experiences and interpretations should be understood (Barnes 2003; Bhattacharjee 1999). The present study is an attempt to understand the children's experiences of 'disability'. The construction of the self of a 'disabled' child (specifically mobility 'impaired') vis-à-vis a 'non-disabled' child would comprise of and be influenced by several different factors that vary in relevance. Anything that strays too far from a 'perfect body' is viewed with disdain (La Fontaine 2002, 44). Understanding the 'disabled' child's development of his/her sense of self would necessitate abandonment of the view of 'disabled' children as a homogeneous category.

The literature highlights some of the negative assumptions that underlie the construction of 'disabled' children in contemporary society (Jayawant and Pathak 1995; Bharadwaj 1999; Priestly 2001; Christy and Nuthetie 2002; Khanna and Ghai 2005). The themes evident within the Indian scenario are as follows. 'Disabled' children have typically been categorized as silent, voiceless victims (Corker and Davis 2000) and denied agency because they are incapable of making choices. Within the Indian context research with 'disabled' children largely remains quantitative and atheoretical (Ghai 2008). The focus has been more on the 'psychopathology of disability' rather than a 'psychology of disability' (Ghai 2006; Goodley and Lawthom 2005; Finkelstein 1980). A fixation on 'impairment' points to a preoccupation with bodily perfection and physical and intellectual fitness. Judged against normative yardsticks, the 'imperfect' bodies of 'disabled' children are inferior or 'backward'. Attention has been on the vulnerability experienced by children. Both 'disability' and childhood are presented as dependent states, in terms of 'care' needs. Consequently, the emphasis has been on service delivery, focusing primarily on health and schooling. A reductionist approach which constructs 'disabled' children as 'pupils', 'cases' or 'service users' is evident. Such a concern is seen in the domestic sphere, where the 'disabled' child's concerns have been subsumed into the collective notion of the 'disabled family'. The danger then is that the experiences of the 'disabled' child are overshadowed by the needs of adults and their institutions. Further, Watson et al. (1999) argued that the main problem facing 'disabled' children is that they live in a society that devalues their difference and views their existence as problematic and undesirable. Research should therefore focus on the physical, structural and institutional barriers to social exclusion that 'disabled' children face (Deb et al. 2002; Ghai 2001). Such research has to be cautious that it does not speak and act on behalf of these children whom it inevitably constructs as inexperienced, passive and intellectually immature. Presuming that 'disabled' children have a unitary identity as 'disabled' leads to a denial of other significant aspects of their experience. Davis and Watson (2001) and Khanna and Ghai (2005) indicated how 'disabled' children encounter discourses of 'normality' and 'difference' in school, arising from institutional factors and everyday cultural practices. In Goodley's (2007a, 319) words, 'deficit thinking surrounds disabled people'. Thus, 'disabled' children need to be understood as social actors, as controllers and as negotiating their complex identities within a disabling environment.

Methodology

The research was conducted in the context of very marginal attention paid to inclusive research practices with the 'disabled'. It was carried out in fulfillment of the first author's bachelor degree requirements. All costs were borne by her. We followed a participatory research methodology that has an immediate, positive impact on the lives of 'disabled' children. Emancipatory research, which is distinct from participatory research, is increasingly being used in 'disability' research, the former being constituted as much by political as by empirical activity (Walmsely 2001)

The research used qualitative in-depth interviews with children living with mobility 'impairments'. The aim of the interviews was to explore the theme of identity formation, stories and knowledge relevant and important to them. The aim was to avoid the tendency of fully structured interviews or survey questionnaires to impose biomedical-diagnostic interpretations. With the consent of the participants the interviews were audiotaped for later transcription and to ensure the accuracy of data interpretation and attention to the nuances of the language people used. Keeping the above considerations in mind, the following measures were used: (1) semi-structured interviews; (2) human figure drawings made by the children; (3) focused group discussions (FGD).

The participants in the study comprised 14 children, seven boys and seven girls, with mobility 'impairments', aged 11–16 years (average age 13.21 years) from a lower socio-economic background. As they were in a period of transition from childhood to adolescence, the child's sense of self was being established and was highly sensitive to societal and peer influences. The participants were chosen from a school providing integrated education using a purposive sampling method. After obtaining the necessary permission to carry out the research, each child was interviewed during his/her free time. After the individual interviews two FGDs were conducted. The interviews and FGDs were recorded with the aid of a micro-cassette recorder and any behavioural observations were noted down. The interviews and FGDs were transcribed and, along with the drawings, coded according to recurrent themes. All the data were content analysed. The categories, however, are not exclusive and there might be contradictions within the same narrative. Themes that emerged upon coding the interviews and FGDs are presented below.

Main findings and discussion
Notions of self
Understanding the 'disabled' self

The interviews and drawings, as well as the FGD, indicated that the interpretations of 'disability' showed distinct individual variations. For instance, 7 of the 14 participants said they were no different from 'normal' children. Some of them acknowledged that there were activities in which they experienced limitations, such as an inability to run. Nevertheless, they were confident that they could do whatever they decided to do. A desire to appear the same as everyone else was evident. For instance, sentiments such as 'I can also run, though a little slowly' or 'I can do all my work myself' were expressed. Past researchers have validated this desire (Law et al. 2005).

However, there were some who felt that 'disability' made them different. For instance, Sonam said:

> Yes, I am different, others are normal. Disability is when one is helpless and can't do his/her own work we don't have that life, that power which normal people have.

Terms such as 'normal' and 'handicap' were used frequently. The children had internalized the societal understanding which validates the 'non-disabled' mode as the 'normal' mode'. Children identified feeling 'disabled' at times when they could not perform certain activities. Provision of assistive devices was associated with 'normality'. As Mohi put it, 'I will become normal when I get my calipers'. Their responses clearly reify the understanding of the social model that environmental constraints cause 'disability'. Children seemed to have internalized the labels. For instance, many children used the word *viklang*.[1] The children's responses can be conceptualized in terms of the individual or medical model of 'disability', which emphasizes the meta-narrative of 'deviance, lack and tragedy' (Corker and Shakespeare 2002, 2). The underlying assumption is that 'disability' is 'logically separate from and inferior to normalcy' (Ghai 2006; see also Ghai 2003; Dalal 2001). That a hierarchy of 'disabilities' exists in children's minds is evident when Sonam said 'I consider myself better than those who cannot speak, see or write anything'. In drawing 'myself' children drew 'disability' and assistive devices. However, in drawing 'me and my friends' (7 of 14), as well as 'me and my school' (10 of 14) (Figures 1 and 2), children did not present themselves as 'disabled' and mobility aids were omitted. Evidently, mobility aids became signifiers or symbols of 'disability'. They not only have an impact on the way the individual constructs his/her own self but also influence other's construction of the 'disabled' individual, for instance as a patient dependent on others (Sapey et al. 2005).

Children's evaluations of 'disability' were based on their inability to perform certain tasks. Such an evaluation/understanding is congruent with Priestley's (2001) claim that perceptions about 'disabled' children arise from a preoccupation with pathology and 'impairment'. Some children, such as Sonali, Surjeet and Rani, did not know the meaning of 'disability'! That 'disability' is not understood in any unilateral way is clearly indicated by this study. Although from a different location, similar observations were reported by Watson et al. (1999), who found a similar fluidity in children's identification with 'disability'. The explanation of 'disability' varied in terms of its specific and practical impingements. As Gallagher (2001, 643) observed, 'disabilities exist because we as humans view ourselves and each other from within a particular context'.

Figure 1. Drawing by Sonal.

Figure 2. Drawing by Mohit.

That 'disability' is part of the personal self not open to questioning is clear from the respondents' reluctance to reveal it to strangers who do no know about it. For instance, 7 out of 10 children were unwilling to share this information in telephone conversations, indicating an aversion to be identified solely on the basis of their 'disability'. Responses such as 'he didn't ask, so why should I tell?', 'it is not important to tell' or 'he is not my relative, so why should I tell?' perhaps indicate both their apprehension and anger. The children worried that 'telling will lead that person to poke fun and say silly [*ulti-seedhi*] things' or that they would experience feeling ashamed. In fact, the responses of six children indicated that they experienced shame on account of their 'disability'. A desire to become 'normal' points to the dominant discourses of 'normality' as an oppositional category to 'disability'.

'Disability' is thus like any other identity category, a term with multiple meanings. In a constant battle with the disabling barriers and institutions, 'disability' as a category keeps evolving and transforming the self (Linton 2006). A need to consider 'disability' as multifaceted and fluid rather than as a fixed concept is evident. Often one finds 'disabled' described as 'deficient', as 'victims' or sometimes even as 'super achievers'. Portrayals of the 'disabled' as 'normal' and 'ordinary' persons are rarely found. A deeper, more complex and nuanced understanding of the 'disabled' experience is required to make 'the terrain of disability and disabled people less alien' (Mitchell and Snyder 2000, 173).

Attributions of 'disability'

As is evident from Table 1, children listed several causes for their 'disability', including both existential and material causes, such as polio dan physical injuries. The

Table 1. Frequency analysis of themes under 'Understanding the disabled self'.

Theme	Frequency
Notions about self	
Self perceived as disabled/different	7
Self perceived as same as non-disabled peers	6
Meaning of disability	
Synonymous with 'handicap'	5
Limitation (inability to walk/use hands)	8
Impact of disability	
Fully independent	3
Dependent for critical tasks	9
Limitation	
Standing/walking/running	9
Studying/drawing	4
Desire to change aspects of self	
None	4
Disability	4
Attributions for disability	
Existential (fate/destiny, God, etc.)	9
Material (physical injury, polio)	5
Areas of perceived competency	
Drawing	1
Helping others	1
Understanding others	3
Studying	3
Future aspirations	
Doctor	5
Teacher	4
Other (engineer, painter, social worker)	5
Possibility of change in experienced disability	
Disability as evolving	5
Uncertain	5
Disability as fixed	4

Table 2. Frequency analysis of themes under 'Emotional responses'.

Theme	Frequency
Shame	4
Guilt/self-blame	6
Resignation/acceptance	7
Anger towards others	6
Hope for future	5
Dependence	7
Frustration	4
Wish to be independent	5
Worthlessness	4
Loneliness/isolation	3
Helplessness	7
'Why me?'	3
Anger towards God	1
Gratitude	2
Belief in being independent	5

Table 3. Frequency analysis of themes under 'Societal experiences'.

Theme	Frequency
Societal reactions/attitude	
Experience of being stared at	9
Pity/charity	4
Mocking	5
Curious	5
Response to societal reaction (bullied/teased)	
Complain to authorities	5
Retaliate	2
Ignore	6
Avoid outings	8

Table 4. Frequency analysis of themes under 'Familial experiences'.

Theme	Frequency
Attitude of parents	
Encouraging	3
Worrying	6
Protective	3
Blaming	5
Experience of being treated differently from siblings	9
Experience of causing disruption in family life (mobility, economic, emotional)	8
Attitude of sibling	
Bullying	3
Protective	1
Resentful	1

Table 5. Analysis of drawings of 'Myself'.

Subject	Drawing
A Sonal	Smiling, wheelchair, few plants and sky
B Mohit	Small figure, wheelchair, face unclear, small house, tree, sky, sun, birds
C Sangeeta	Small figure, standing, no disability, smiling, well-clad
D Nausar	Standing, face with eyes but no mouth, no disability
E Sonam	Drawing titled 'this is Sonam Bhawnani', Smiling, wheelchair, in school uniform
F Sanjay	Crutches, smartly dressed, smiling, sky, trees, birds, very colorful
G Hushna	Smiling, crutches not touching ground, name of school written
H Ram	Standing, crutches, lots of brown patches
I Rani	Big face, design of clothes will hide disability, smiling, very elaborate dress
J Preeti	Crutches, smiling, in school uniform and with bag, hair fashionably tied, grass
K Satish	No disability, smartly dressed, smiling, red lips
L Chand	Crutches, smiling, well-dressed
M Amit	Disability identified, smiling
N Surjeet	Crutches, smiling but sense of emptiness in drawing

predominant cause seems to be God's will or retribution for past sins. As Amit put it, 'whatever is written has happened … whatever has to happen to everyone will happen'. Similarly, Sonam believed 'I must have done something in an earlier life. … I feel it'. Others, like Sanjay, said 'This is because of God. He only has done this'. Similarly, Hushna said 'because I am disabled, my parents ask God for his blessings, but he never grants them [*dua poori nahin karte*]'. The observations are in line Berry and Dalal (1996) and Ghai (2003), who indicated that within the Indian context people attribute 'disability' to their past Karma or to God's will or supernatural powers.

There is an indication that a belief in an afterlife is used by parents to generate hope for the future. As Sonam put it, 'my parents say it's good that this has happened to you in this life [*janam*], which will pass. In the next life you will be able to walk.' The idea that penance is being made beforehand precludes retribution in any future

Table 6. Frequency analysis of drawings.

	Frequency
Self with disability	10

Table 7. Frequency analysis of themes under 'Notions of self'.

Theme	Frequency
Refusal to reveal disability to stranger (over phone)	8
Experience of disability as associated with shame	6
Fantasy	
Being able to play (cricket, football, cycle, etc.)	3
Become a bird and be free	1
Become a magician make make aeroplanes	1
Many things –toys, crayons, car, mobile, computer, money, travel	4

life. There were some instances in which parents were blamed for the 'disability'. As Rani explained, 'The doctor told mother that her milk is bad [*kharab*]. Mother made me have her milk, which is why this has happened'. A similar observation was made by Ghai (2000) in her work with mothers of 'disabled' children. These strong convictions are rooted in adult attributions.

Recognition of strengths and limitations

Children's narratives challenged the expectation that 'disabled' children are 'different' or 'deficient'. The belief that these children need to be taught separately, require special assistance/attention, etc. was not upheld. Children's responses indicated that their participation in any activity could be as good/as bad as that of any other child. Children identified strengths in various activities, such as sewing, weaving, using computers and study of aesthetics, along with doing well in academic studies. The results confirm Watson et al.'s (1999) belief that self-identity is about 'what they can do'; it has no relationship with their 'disability'. As Hushna asserted during the FGD, 'Our legs are disabled not the hands'. Amit said 'I take part in everything and come first in school in racing'. Many, such as Hushna, Sonam and Ram, also felt that 'disability' gave them a better understanding of others.

One noticeable feature was a desire to draw pretty pictures. The drawings indicated that the children highlighted diverse aspects of self. Using detail and specificity, most children drew their unique selves painstakingly. Satish would regularly cross-check to ensure that the colour schemes matched. Children identified trees, flowers, birds and the sky with a rich combination of colours. In some drawings children conveyed their insignificance by either drawing very small figures (Mohit, Figure 2; Sangeeta, Figure 3) or missing out the face (Nausar, Figure 4). Notwithstanding the immense value that children attach to their multiple facets, society usually gives them a 'global categorization' only in terms of their 'disability'. Thus there is merit in accepting the heterogeneity inherent in 'disabled' children's conceptualizations of self.

That children were realistic in their appraisals was evident in their recognition of limitations. Many (9 of 14) of them, such as Sanjay, Amit and Rani, realized that they

Figure 3. Drawing by Sangeeta.

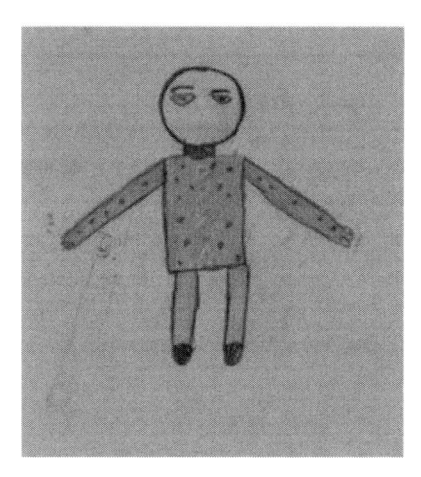

Figure 4. Drawing by Nausar.

could not participate in certain games/sports, such as cricket and football. Instead, they chose to stay indoors. However, there was an indication that the children experienced the pain of exclusion when 'non-disabled' children did not engage with them. As Rani put it, 'nobody plays with me ... they all start running. Sometimes I wish that I were normal'. This concurs with Tregaskis's (2003) assertion that 'disability' is experienced most acutely in the domain of relationships with the 'non-disabled'. 'Disability' was associated with inability, lack or 'deficit' in nine narratives. However, in the FGD many children backtracked and refuted such claims.

Terminology: issues of labelling and categorization

The interviews and FGD indicated that the children replicated labels assigned by the wider society around them. Children often used the terms 'disabled' and 'impaired' (*viklang*) as well as a categorization of 'like us'/'like them'. The hegemony of 'normality' clearly influenced their understanding. As Surjeet explained, 'I am disabled but you are normal'. Labels such as *tunda* (impairment of hands) and *loola* (mobility impairment) were used. These labels operate to establish the essential nature of the person being described and by which we understand the person in the world (Barton 2001). As Ghai (2008) put it:

> The concern with the proliferating effects of the deficit vocabulary and maintenance of the very problems it attempts to describe becomes fairly acute, when one acknowledges the serious impact it has on the lives of disabled people. It thus becomes vital for research to identify and intervene in the process through which both disabled persons and those who interact with them apply derogatory language.

Aspirations for the future

Children spoke of their future desires and possibilities with strong conviction and hope. They, like their 'non-disabled' peers, aspired to be doctors (5 of 14), teachers (4 of 14), computer engineers (2 of 14), etc. The choice of the medical profession may be an unconscious desire to search for cure, as Mohit explained: 'I want to cure people'. Children on the whole did not allow their choices to be guided by limitations imposed by their 'impairment'. Hope, confidence in their own selves and a belief in God/destiny were seen as possible agents in fulfilling their aspirations. Sonam said 'Its all in God's hands ... although I know that my life will become golden [*sunehri*]'. Hope was most clearly expressed through drawings, with smiling faces. Although there were concerns about the future, the results challenge the societal view of 'disability' as being a pitiable condition. As the literature shows, overcoming 'disability' can be a predominant concern (Ghai 2006; Joshi 2001; Oliver 1996).

Almost all the children considered education as playing a key role in determining the future. Children also spoke of their individual wishes, such as fantasizing being a bird (Hushna) or making an aeroplane (Satish). These responses are significant, as both birds and aeroplanes are symbolic of the absence of barriers to movement.

The impact of 'disability'
Emotional responses

Whether children accept stigmatized identities or not, it is clear that 'disability' does leave emotional scars. Half of them, including Rani, Sonam and Sanjay, expressed a feeling of dependence and helplessness. For instance, Sonam said 'we are helpless and can't do anything ourselves'. Other emotions expressed by the children included feelings of being a burden on their family (8 of 14), resignation (7 of 14), frustration (4 of 14) and worthlessness (4 of 14). Self-blame was evident, which produced a sense of shame. For instance, Rani said 'I know, I have myself become like this ... what do I do?' The emotional responses of the children clearly convey a feeling of being stigmatized (Goffman 1997) and exhibit feelings of worthlessness and being a burden, which arise as they continuously managethe negative and discriminatory social reactions and behaviours (Thomas 2006).

Societal reactions

The narratives revealed that pity/charity and mocking attitudes were predominant reactions. As. Ghai (2002a, 2002b) argued:

> charity and philanthropy remain the predominant responses to the predicament of 'disability ... . Charitable gestures are made not out of a sense of commitment to the issue of 'disability' but as a response to a cultural expectation to do one's dharmic [religious] duty towards the needy. (p. 92)

Another noticeable feature was that children were aware of other people's stares and gaze. 'Disability', according to many, invited enquiries as to their well-being on a daily basis. As Sonam put it, 'Am I an unusual [*anokhi cheez*] entity'. Whether other's gaze was directed at assistive devices or whether they were different because they could not walk like others (Chand), this staring touched the children, making them feel 'disabled' or 'strange'. The desire to retaliate by 'giving them two slaps' was, however, repressed. As Ghai (2003) observed, 'staring turns the "disabled" object into a grotesque sight'. Staring results in a 'public stripping', leaving the object in a state of humiliation, highlighting their vulnerability in a very intense way. Power staring leaves the 'disabled' people with experiences of shame and invalidation, resulting in 'impairment' becoming a totalizing identity (Malacrida 2005; Foucault 1994).

Responding to societal reactions

The responses to societal reactions were largely passive in nature. The goal was to control information and avoid negative encounters. Eight children said they 'just didn't go out' or 'kept quiet'. Although angry, Hushna did not venture out. As Rani said, 'I quietly move on and do not say anything'. Sometimes they complained to the authorities if they were bullied/teased. The rationalizations offered by parents were accepted. Rani said 'my mother says let them speak, when they also become "disabled" in their next life then you can say the same to them'. Some were taught strategies of not attending (Sonam and Sonal). Children were sensitive to the negative impact of their experiences on their parents and consequently did not communicate every negative encounter to them. Sonal said 'I feel bad because when people ask about my disability, mother starts to cry'.

Congruent with recent literature, the children's narratives show that interactions within the family create the complex identities that children negotiate in the face of the negativism imposed on them (Breivik 2005; Haualand, Gronningsaeter and Hansen 2003; Low 1996).

Familial reactions

Socialization of the child begins very early in infancy and the family is the first agency to impart this training. Not only are the children affected by their families, the children's 'disability' has a significant impact on the family (Najarian 2006; Tripathi and Agarwal 2000).

Parent's responses – worry and protection. Six children felt that their parents were anxious and worried and overprotective. As Rani said, 'I am not made to do any work ... father scolds mother when she gives me work'. Greater attention on the part of parents in comparison with siblings was indicative of parental love and close affectional ties (Sonal and Chand). However, some children, such as Rani, felt that their parents blamed them for the 'disability'. Such an attitude of blame may preclude opportunities for more positive and productive parent–child interactions. Further, there were instances when the parents limited the child's exposure to and experience of the outside world. As Hushna said, 'my parents say you are not capable/worthy [*layak*] of going anywhere'. Similarly, many children (5 of 14), including Preeti, Sonam and Amit, were encouraged to stay at home, with no interaction with the outside world. Perhaps the parents wanted to protect their children from negative societal reactions such as teasing, bullying, etc.

Differential treatment was experienced in comparison with their siblings. They did not fail to notice discouragement and subtle hostility and blame. Sanjay said 'they don't let me do any work, mother scolds my brother and sister – says how can he do this work? You can do it'. Researchers such as Villa et al. (2003) and Mohapatra (1995) have warned against the dangers of overprotection as it can be instrumental in generating dependence or insecurity and ultimate alienation from the family. That parents are often desperate for a cure is indicated by their willingness to believe in supernatural powers. Sanjay said:

> One uncle has told us about a place where there is a well. If you take a bath in that water you will become fine. We will go there in 5 days. If God wants, I will become fine.

Despite anxiety and overprotection, most parents were positive and hopeful. For instance, Chand said 'Father says I can do everything'. Amit recalled that his parents motivated him to attend his school regularly. Hubert (2006) observed that parents had serious anxieties about the future of their 'disabled' child.

A desire to protect the parents from the disruptive influences of 'disability'. Despite positive interactions, children felt responsible for desynchronizing and deharmonizing the balance in their parents' lives. Whether it was movement restrictions or difficulties with travel, children could not locate larger forces as playing a role, which reinforced their dependency. Satish said 'Mother and father make me wear my knickers and calipers'. Children were sensitive to the emotional trauma of their parents, as well as societal reactions to their 'disabilities'. Sanjay, for instance, said 'my parents feel bad'. Parents too were labelled and marked by society. Hushna said 'I do not go anywhere because father has to pick me up and now I have even started to feel shy/ ashamed'. Joshi (2001) pointed out that parents tended to avoid situations where 'impairment' could be discovered or become a topic of conversation. The 'burden of caring' for the 'disabled' child taxes family members emotionally, socially and economically (Laville 2005; Sapey et al. 2005; Rolph et al. 2005). As Satish put it, 'once father's entire salary was spent on my medication'. Consequently, children suppressed their own desires to make things easier for their parents. Refusing to go on outings organized by the school was one such way. Sonal said 'I don't go because father will have to pick me up from school and it will disturb him'. Children also expressed a desire to be independent, saying 'I wouldn't have been so dependent had I not been disabled'. Similarly, children wanted to reduce perceived difficulties on the economic front by earning. The resilience that close family ties provide cannot be underestimated in India. As Ghai (2008) pointed out, 'despite hardships, the family is the agency that provides emotional strength'.

Response of the siblings. Relationships with siblings were characterized by ambivalence. Some children were bullied/teased by their siblings. As Ram stated, 'My brother calls me *loola* ... so I beat him up'. Children retaliated or complained to their parents. Hushna said 'I get very angry and even say bad things when my sibling teases me'. However, many siblings were caring. Sonal talked about how her elder sister took care of her. That some siblings were indifferent was indicated by Rani, who said 'My younger brother goes out to fly the kite and doesn't do any work'. However, it could be more a consequence of patriarchal structure rather than 'disability' per se. Previous research indicates both protective as well as resentful attitudes on the part of the siblings of 'disabled' children (Ghai 2001; Boer 1990; Dunn and Kendrick 1982).

Concluding remarks

The present study focused on understanding the phenomenological realities of children living with mobility 'impairments'. The key themes identified through content analysis indicated no uniform understanding of 'disability', as each child had his/her own notion of what being 'disabled' means. There were times when they idealized 'non-disabled' people and experienced limitations in many walks of life. Experiences of being labelled, stared at and bullied were a source of pain. 'Disability' was attributed to both existential (God, fate) and material (polio, physical injury) causes.

Families were perceived as ambivalent – sometimes looking on the child as a burden, causing worry and disruption in the family, while also being loving, encouraging and overprotective. Our findings are significant, as they elucidate what young people are going through during the important years of identity formation. Exposure to encouraging environments is crucial during this period, as it lays the foundations of self-confidence and self-worth for the years that follow. Although there are structural inequities in India, most of the 'disabled' children construct themselves as did other 'normal' children with everyday lives. The possibility is that they might be minimizing their differences because disability carries negative connotations. Highlighting the voices of the children indicates that they do not play a passive role. The present research is a pointer to the fact that disabled children have a unique perspective and would like to influence their own lives. 'Disabled' children in the present research appear as independent, having made the decision to control their disabilities. What needs to be understood is that if the agency of disabled children is to claim space, voice and power, there is a critical need to disrupt the hegemonic discourses of normality.

As the present study only explored the children's perception/experiences, the views of parents, siblings, teachers and 'non-disabled' peers could not be incorporated. Future research could attempt to include 'significant others' and obtain a holistic picture of the families of 'disabled' children. The study could have benefited with the inclusion of children living with other 'impairments'. Exploring and comparing life experiences of children living with other 'impairments' could throw light on the common as well as unique significance of the 'type' of 'impairment'. Further, experiences of special, integrated and inclusive schools need to be compared. As the experience of 'disability' is affected by class, future research needs to obtain to a more nuanced understanding of class and its relationship to 'disability'.

Note
1. The term *viklang* is roughly equivalent to disabled. There is a tendency within the Indian context to use pejorative labels such as *langra* (cripple) and *aandha* (blind)

References
Barnes, C. 2003. Reflections on emancipatory research. *Disability & Society* 18, no. 1: 3–17.
Barton, L. 2001. Textual practices of erasure: Representations of disability and the founding of the united way. In (Eds.). *Embodied rhetorics: Disability in language and culture,* ed. J.C. Wilson and C. Lewiecki, 169–99. Carbondale, IL: Southern Illinois University Press.
Berry, J.W., and A. Dalal. 1996. *Disability–attitude–belief–behaviour study: Report on an international project in community based rehabilitation.* Kingston, Canada: Queen's University International Centre for the Advancement of Community Based Rehabilitation.
Bharadwaj, R.L.C. 1999. Assessment of psychogenic needs of 'normal' congenitally blind and cerebral palsied children. *Disabilities and Impairments* 13, nos. 1–2: 86–93.
Bhattacharjee, N. 1999. Through the looking glass: Gender socialization in a primary school. In *Culture, socialisation and human development,* ed. T.S. Saraswathi, 336–55. New Delhi: Sage.
Boer, F. 1990. *Sibling relationship in middle childhood.* Leiden: DSW Press.
Braathen, S.H., and B. Ingstad. 2006. Albinism in Malawi: Knowledge and beliefs from an African setting. *Disability & Scoiety* 21, no. 6: 599–613.
Breivik, J.K. 2005. *Deaf identities in the making: Local lives, transnational connections.* Washington, DC: Gallaudet University Press.

Brown, H. 1994. An ordinary sexual life? A review of the 'normalization principal as it applies to the sexual options of people with learning difficulties. *Disability & Society* 9, no. 2: 123–44.
Burns, J. 1992. Normalisation through the looking glass. *Clinical Psychology Forum* 39: 22–4.
Christy, B.S., and R. Nuthetie. 2002. Self perceptions of visually 'impaired' children aged 3–10 in India. *Journal of Visual 'Impairment' and Blindness* 96, no. 8: 596–8.
Corker, M., and J.M. Davis. 2000. Disabled children – invisible under the law. In *Disability and the law*, ed. J. Cooper and S. Vernon. London: Jessica Kingsley.
Corker, M., and T. Shakespeare, eds. 2002. *Disability and postmodernity: Embodying disability theory*. London: Continuum.
Dalal, A.K. 2001. Health psychology. In *Psychology in India revisited: Developments in the discipline*, ed. J. Pandey. New Delhi: Sage.
Dalal, A.K., and N. Pande. 1999. Cultural beliefs and family are of the children with Disability. *Psychology and Developing Societies* 11: 55–75.
Datta, S., P. Russell, S. Swamidhas, and S.C. Gopalakrishna. 2002. Burden among the caregivers of children with intellectual disability: Associations and risk factors. *Journal of Learning disabilities* 6, no. 4: 337–50.
Davis, J., and N. Watson. 2001. Where are the children's experiences? Analysing social and cultural exclusion in 'special' and 'mainstream' schools. *Disability & Society* 16, no. 5: 671–87.
Deb, S., C. Duggal, and A. Sarkar. 2002. Problems encountered by sightless children. *Disabilities and Impairments* 16, no. 2: 93–104.
Dunn, J., and C. Kendrick. 1982. *Siblings: Love, envy and understanding*. London: Grant McIntyre.
Finkelstein, V. 1980. *Attitudes and 'disabled' people: Issues for discussion*. New York: World Rehabilitation Fund.
Foucault, M. 1994. *The birth of the clinic: An archeology of medical perception*. New York: Vintage Books.
Gallagher, D.J. 2001. Neutrality as a moral standpoint, conceptual confusion and the full inclusion debate. *Disability & Society* 16, no. 5: 637–54.
Gawali, G. 2003. The impact of psychological intervention on parental involvement in the rehabilitation process of mentally 'retarded'. *Disabilities and Impairments* 17, no. 1: 25–30.
Ghai, Anita. 2000. Towards understanding disability. *Psychological Studies* 45, no. 3: 145–49.
Ghai, Anita. 2001. Marginalisation and disability: Experiences from the third world. In *Disability and the life course: Global perspectives*, ed. M. Priestly. Cambridge: Cambridge University Press.
Ghai, Anita. 2002a. Disability in the Indian context: Post-colonial perspectives. In *Disability and postmodernity: Embodying disability theory*, ed. M. Corker and T. Shakespeare. London: Continuum.
Ghai, Anita. 2002b. How Indian mythology portrays disability. *Kaleidoscope* 45: 6–10.
Ghai, Anita. 2003. *(Dis)Embodied form: Issues of 'disabled' women*. New Delhi: Haranand Publications.
Ghai, Anita. 2006. Education in a globalising era: Implications for 'disabled' girls. *Social Change* 36, no. 3: 161–76.
Ghai, Anita. 2008. Gender and inclusive education at all levels. In *Perspectives on education and development: Revising education commission and after*, ed. V. Prakash, and K. Biswal. New Delhi: National University of Educational Planning and Administration.
Goffman, E. 1997. Selections from stigma. In *The disability studies reader*, ed. L.J. Davis. New York: Routledge.
Goodley, D. 2007a. Towards socially just pedagogies: Deleuzoguattarian critical disability studies. *Disability & Society* 11, no. 3: 317–34.
Goodley, D. 2007b. Becoming rhizomatic parents: Deleuze, Guattari and 'disabled' babies. *Disability & Society* 22, no. 2: 145–60.
Goodley, D., and R. Lawthom. 2005. Epistemological journeys in participatory action research: Alliances between community psychology and disability studies. *Disability & Society* 20, no. 2: 135–53.

Haualand, H., A. Gronningsaeter, and I.L.S. Hansen. 2003. *Uniting divided worlds: A study of deaf and hard of hearing youth*. Norway Centraltrykkeriet AS. http://www.fafo.no/pub/rapp/412/412.pdf#search='haualand'.

Hubert, J. 2006. Family carers' views of services for people with learning 'disabilities' from black and minority ethnic groups: A qualitative study of 30 families in a south London borough. *Disability & Society* 21, no. 3: 259–73.

Jayawant, M., and P. Pathak. 1995. An exploratory study of deaf children in integrated units of 'normal' schools. *Disabilities and Impairments* 9, no. 1: 21–9.

Joshi, P. 2001. Understanding the experience of disability through children's expression. Paper presented at the International Special Education Congress, July 24–28, in Manchester, UK.

Khanna, R., and A. Ghai. 2005. Meaning of disability: Through the voices of children. Project report submitted in partial fulfillment of the requirement for the Bachelor of Arts (honours) degree in Psychology, University of Delhi, India.

La Fontaine, M. 2002. *Perfect? Analysis of global human genetics fix. In Women, disability and identity*, ed. A. Nans and A. Patri. New Delhi: Sage.

Laville, S. 2005. Mother who killed son with Down's syndrome gets suspended sentence. *The Guardian*, November 3. www.guardian.co.uk/uk-new/story/0,3604,1607106,00.html.

Law, J., S.B. Bunning, F.S. Arrelly, and B. Heyman. 2005. Making sense in primary care: Levelling the playing field for people with communication difficulties. *Disability & Society* 20, no. 2: 169–85.

Linton, S. 2006. *My body politic: A memoir*. Ann Arbor, MI: University of Michigan Press.

Low, J. 1996. Negotiating identities, negotiating environments: An interpretation of the experiences of students with 'disabilities'. *Disability and Society* 11, no. 2: 235–48.

Malacrida, C. 2005. Discipline and dehumanization in a total institution: Institutional survivors' descriptions of time-out rooms. *Disability & Society* 20, no. 2: 523–39.

Mitchell, D.T., and S.L. Snyder. 2000. *Narrative prosthesis: Disability and the dependencies of discourse*. Ann Arbor, MI: University of Michigan Press.

Mohapatra, S. 1995. Acceptance of the 'disabled' in society. *Social Welfare* 41: 19–20.

Najarian, C.G. 2006. Deaf mothers, maternal thinking and intersections of gender and ability. *Scandinavian Journal of Disability Research* 8, nos. 2–3: 99–120.

Oliver, M. 1996. *Understanding disability: From theory to practice*. London: Macmillan.

Pal, D.K., G. Chaudhury, T. Das, and S. Sengupta. 2002. Predictors of parental adjustment to children's epilepsy in rural India. *Child: Care, Health and Development* 28, no. 4: 295–300.

Priestley, M. 2001. *Disability and the life course: Global perspectives*. Cambridge: Cambridge University Press.

Rolph, S., D. Atkinson, M. Nind, and J. Welshman, eds. 2005. *Witnesses to change: Families, learning difficulties and history*. Kidderminster, UK: Bild.

Sapey, B., J. Stewart, and G. Donaldson. 2005. Increases in wheelchair use and perceptions of disablement. *Disability & Society* 20, no. 5: 489–507.

Saxena, M., and N. Sharma. 2000. Growing up with the mentally 'retarded' child: A study of adolescent siblings. *Journal of Personality and Clinical Studies* 16: 16–23.

Thomas, C. 2006. Disability and gender: Reflections and theory and research. *Scandinavian Journal of Disability Research* 8, nos. 2–3: 177–85.

Tregaskis, C. 2003. *Constructions of disability: Researching the interface between 'disabled' and 'non-disabled' people*. London: Routledge Falmer.

Tripathi, I., and A. Agarwal. 2000. Chronic illness, symptoms and efficacy in children as related to some psychological characteristics of mothers. *Psychology and Developing Societies* 12, no. 1: 31–42.

Villa, R.A., L.V. Tac, P.M. Muc, S. Ryan, N.T.M. Thuy, C. Weill, and J.S. Thousand. 2003. Inclusion in Vietnam: More than a decade of implementation, research and practice for persons with severe 'disabilities'. *Disability & Society* 28, no. 1: 23–32.

Watson, N., T. Shakespeare, S. Cunningham-Burley, C. Barnes, M. Corker, J. Davis, and M. Priestley. 1999. *Life as a 'disabled' child: A qualitative study of young people's experiences and perspectives*, Final Report. Edinburgh and Leeds: Universities of Edinburgh and Leeds.

Walmsley, J. 2001. Normalisation, emancipatory research and inclusive research in learning disability. *Disability & Society* 16, no. 2: 187–205.

Constructing 'normal childhoods': young people talk about young carers

L. O'Dell[a], S. Crafter[b], G. de Abreu[c] and T. Cline[d]

[a]*Faculty of Health and Social Care, The Open University, Milton Keynes, UK;* [b]*Psychology Division, The University of Northampton, Northampton, UK;* [c]*Psychology Department, Oxford Brookes University, Oxford, UK;* [d]*Educational Psychology Group, University College London, UK*

> There has been a great deal of attention paid to young carers in recent research, social policy and service provision. In this paper we report on a survey and interview study of 46 young people aged 15 to 18, nine of whom had experience as young carers, to explore the ways in which young people construct the young carer and their disabled parent. A key theme arising from the interview data analysis is the construction of a series of normative assumptions about 'normal' childhood through which young carers and their disabled parent are viewed as non-normative and deficient. The predominantly negative construction of both parent and child/carer is critically analyzed and alternatives suggested in the discussion of these findings.

Points of interest

- Young carers are children who help care for a disabled person in their family.
- A lot of research on young carers says that caring for someone with a disability in your family can be bad for young people.
- We argue that all families are complicated and if we only see caring for a disabled family member as a problem we are missing out on lots of information.
- We are worried that by seeing young carers in a bad way it also means that we might also see disabled family members badly too and will not see the good side of family life.
- Young carers who took part in our research talked about how they want to help their disabled parent.
- The young carers in our project said that they could arrange things so that they could help to care for their parent, but also do things that other teenagers do, like seeing their friends.

There has been widespread concern about young carers within social policy debates and research activity over the past fifteen years. Within the Carers Act (1995) young carers are defined as 'children and young people [under 18] who provide or intend to provide a substantial amount of care on a regular basis' (cited in Underdown 2002, 57). It is difficult to estimate the number of children and young people who act as young carers and the exact numbers remain unknown (Siddall 1994; Olsen and Clarke 2003). Almost three million children in the UK live in households with a family member who has chronic illness or disability (Butler and Astbury 2005). The 2001 census recorded 175,000 young carers in the UK (supported by Becker 2004) and in the 1990s, the Office of National Statistics estimated 51,000 young carers in the UK (Walker 1996). The variability in prevalence rates is due, in part, to varying definitions of what constitutes a young carer (see Newman 2002 for a critical discussion of defining the young carer).

The overwhelming view within debates about young carers is that caring for a disabled parent or family member causes serious problems for the child (Siddall 1994). However there has been little research into the psychological consequences of being a young carer (Aldridge 2006). Research evidence suggests that young carers may feel different to other children and under pressure to keep their family outside of social services' gaze (Aldridge and Becker 1993). A major concern within policy debates is that young carers may actively hide their family situation from outside agencies, for example in many instances schools are unaware of the caring duties performed by their pupils (Underdown 2002).

A key concern in discussions about young carers is that caring involves a loss of opportunities to socialize with their peers and participate fully in school (Earley, Cushway and Cassidy 2007); 'Thus we have a picture of children committing themselves to caring for their loved ones in a lonely and isolated environment, exacerbated by the disinterest of others' (Aldridge and Becker 1993, 14). Consequently young carers are seen to have lost out on significant aspects of a 'normal' childhood. This is exemplified in one of Becker and Aldridge's first papers outlining their research findings on young carers in the UK, titled 'The Lost Children' (Becker and Aldridge 1993). Loss of opportunities to engage in 'normal' childhood activities may be conflated with a sense of loss of childhood in an abstract way, where young carers are positioned as having symbolically lost out on their childhood.

Whilst we do not intend to minimize or dismiss concern about young carers our view, drawing on theoretical work in critical developmental psychology and sociocultural theory, is that when the experience of young carers is evaluated against an ideal of a supposed 'normal' childhood, there is a risk of over-simplifying complex family systems, ignoring young people's agency and depreciating disabled parents' actions and wishes. In this paper we draw on theoretical insights in the social construction of childhood to argue that dominant representations of child development construct a notion of universal childhood development that is invoked as a benchmark against which to negatively judge the activities of young carers. The taken for granted assumption of developmental psychology is that of an ordered progression from dependency to maturity and independence, where dependency is devalued within the cultural priorities of a Westernized, individualistic notion of development (Fleer 2006). Children are viewed as in a state of becoming and positioned as vulnerable and unable to negotiate the world of adults. Within this mainstream view, social competence is accorded at particular ages (Fleer 2006) and therefore young carers transgress taken for granted assumptions about the competence and abilities of children, where the assumption is that children are to be cared for rather than care for others.

Drawing on the notion of a universal childhood where children are dependent upon their family for care, the assumption from public policy debates and the young carer research is that performing particular kinds of caring duties produces a premature level of responsibility and maturity in a child. In debates about young carers the concern is that by caring for an ill or disabled parent the child becomes responsible for them, so that the roles in the family are reversed (Siddall 1994). Young carers are often characterized in research and policy as their parent's parent (Olsen and Parker 1997) and positioned as 'parentified children' (Mahon and Higgins 1995; Early, Cushway, and Cassidy 2006). Within this view of caring the disabled parent is constructed as dependent upon their child and the child is forced (due to family dynamics and possibly by lack of social work intervention) to care for their parent.

An implication of the current debates on young carers is an implicit construction of the disabled parent. Olsen and Parker (1997, 127) argue that 'the rhetoric of much, though not all, current "young carer" service provision involves some kind of substitution of, rather than support for, the parental role'. Commentators such as Keith and Morris (both disabled mothers) have argued that lack of services and support for disabled parents serves to compound their dependency on their families (Keith and Morris 1995; Prillenltensky 2002). Disabled parents are seen as passive and often part of the 'problem' concerning their children (Olsen and Parker 1997). Newman (2002) argues that the young carers debate represents disability as hazardous to family life and leads to pathologized and distorted images of disabled parents. Thus the disabled parent is positioned as dependent and marginal in discussions about the young carer and the young carer is represented as having lost out on their childhood through their caring activities.

The research presented in this paper aims to explore ways in which young people both with and without experience of young caring construct young carers and the disabled parent. The data are part of a larger project that examined the working activities of young people, including young caring and language brokering (young people who translate for a family member – see Crafter, O'Dell, de Abreu, and Cline 2009). The project aimed to examine the taken for granted assumption that the move to adulthood is accompanied by a gradual increase in engagement in more adult-style responsibilities and thus children's involvement with work increases with age (Hobbs and McKechnie 1997, cited in Leonard 2004). Children who act as young carers and language brokers are positioned in unique circumstances due to their engagement in activities that are typically viewed as adult work. These activities were chosen as a focus for the project because they represent activities that are not generally defined as 'work' in that they are normally unpaid and are undertaken for family members or friends within a nexus of obligations negotiated within a family unit.

Method

The findings reported in this paper form part of a larger study of childhood and what are viewed as 'atypical' roles for young people funded by the ESRC (RES-000-22-0549). A key aspect of the project was to examine diverse constructions of childhood, particularly in relation to social diversity. The project collected data in two phases; an initial survey of (very broadly defined) working activities of 1002 young people in two year groups at school, and a second phase of in depth interviews with 46 young people identified as being either young carers, language brokers or young people who engage in more 'typical' work roles such as having a Saturday job. Participants were recruited from six schools and colleges in the South East and

South Coast of England. These were selected to represent a diverse range of types of institution, location and ethnic composition.

The initial data generated from phase one of the project allowed us to identify for possible inclusion in the second phase those who had experience as a young carer. The survey included an extensive list of work-related activities which a young carer may engage in, such as helping a disabled parent, as well as activities such as helping get younger siblings dressed and making the family dinner, as these could possibly be linked to the activities of a young carer. Participants for the one-to-one interviews were selected on the basis of their answers to these questions. The survey permitted respondents to self-define as a young carer or to describe their activities rather than a defined role. The survey was designed in this way to address issues raised by Keith and Morris (1995), who, as feminist academics and disabled mothers are critical of the young carers debate for framing young people's lives around professional terminology and assumptions about family relationships.

A preliminary short interview was conducted with possible participants for the interview phase of the research to ascertain the level of caring duties undertaken by the young people. Of the 46 young people who were interviewed, nine young people (four young men and five young women) reported performing substantial caring duties for a member of their immediate family.

Procedure

The research team liaised with the schools and colleges to ensure that students and their parents were given information on the project and were able to consent (or not) to take part in the research. In phase two (the interview study) the research team asked for young people to volunteer to talk about their working activities and thus young people were not identifiable as young carers or language brokers by consenting to take part in the research. Interviews were conducted in the students' schools by two of the research team. The students were assured that their contribution would be totally confidential and that no personally identifiable information would appear in any report of the study.

Materials

The interview study used a series of vignettes to structure the discussion and provide prompts for participants. The vignettes, which were piloted in similar areas to those sampled in the main study, were designed to represent aspects of children and young people's work that were identified by the research team to be of significance theoretically. The characters were 14 years old, slightly younger than the participants to allow them to identify with the characters and feel that they were familiar (a point confirmed by the pilot participants). The vignettes implied a variety of cultural backgrounds (indicated by culturally specific or ambiguous names such as Samuel and Mira) and in their gender. The character in each vignette performed a different form of work: Samuel had a Saturday job; Mira was a babysitter and cleaner; Eduardo was a language broker and Mary was a young carer. All the respondents were asked questions that relate to the lives of young people such as 'What advice would you give this person if you were their friend?' and 'What do you think their teacher would think about what the character is doing?' In this paper we focus on the vignette of the young carer 'Mary':

Mary is 14 years old and lives with her dad and her brother who is 15 years old. Mary's dad is disabled and needs help during the day with activities such as getting out of bed, getting dressed and making lunch. Mary loves her dad and is happy to be there for him. However she also misses school some days if her dad has a bad day and needs extra help. Sometimes Mary wishes that she could see her friends after school like her brother does.

The vignette of Mary was designed to embed ideas about gender in the construction of the vignette to provide a context for issues in relation to care to be discussed if they were important to the participants. The project sought to examine social diversity including the intersections of culture, ethnicity and gender. It is interesting to note that from the 1002 respondents to phase one of the project (a survey) 6.4% of the young people who responded reported that they had acted as a carer for an adult at home, of whom 64.5% were female. In phase two, the interview stage of the project nine young carers were interviewed; four young men (all White-British) and five young women (three White-British and two from a cultural or linguistic minority group).

Analytical procedures

The interview data were transcribed and the text was interrogated in relation to the main research questions and emerging themes were identified. The coding strategy was based on identification of key issues and conceptual themes from our earlier theoretical analysis which enabled us to develop themes from an iterative interrogation of the data. In this paper we discuss four broad themes:

- Mapping 'normal' childhood
- Loss of childhood
- Mapping the 'abnormal' parent
- Possibilities: young people talk about caring

Mapping 'normal' childhood

All the interview respondents articulated a sense of 'normal' childhood against which the 14 year-old vignette character Mary was judged. In discussing which vignette character has the hardest job, a young carer discussed the notion of normality:

Mary [has the hardest job], just because, I think it is a mixture between these two [Eduardo, a boy who translates for his Mum, and Mary] because they both, both of them have to deal with the fact that they are different. They are extremely different from what, what we as a society call normal. A normal teenager would be somebody who has a mum and a dad, who have full functioning bodies, who speak English who have decent jobs, maybe and couple of brothers or sisters. But they're not typically normal. (Year-13, White British girl, young carer)

Participants drew on an understanding of development as age graded, in which age defines roles and responsibilities. Thus, Mary is constructed as different because she is seen to be too young for her role as a carer:

… she's got a lot of responsibility for 14 years old to be honest. (Year-11, White British girl, young carer)

Erm. I think she's … it's really nice I think, it's really a difficult, it's really difficult for her 'cause 14 is a time when you do get to see friends, and like go cinemas, that's what

I do, other people have a really good time at 14 and because she has her dad, its difficult she, 'cause she has to stay home ... and like she has got a responsibility like an adult. ... 'Cause if you're 14 I used I didn't have to worry about that kind of stuff only school and that's it, school and homework and it's really good after school to go and see your friends so I would say yeah she really needs that. (Year-13, White Brazilian boy, language broker)

The construction of a 'normal' childhood (and teenage years) as a time of limited responsibility and a time for play and socializing serves to position young carers as different. Caring is constructed as a task for adults rather than children and young people. Therefore young carers' lives are viewed as 'not real', not an authentic or typical way in which young people should be living:

How would you feel do you think if you were in Mary's situation?
Um, trying to say this without ..., I'd be very upset ... Yeah, she doesn't really have a real life, she's got school and then home to help her dad, school and home, school and home, so no social life and well, hardly any. (Year-13, White European Portuguese boy, language broker)

Loss of childhood

Young people with and without experience of caring for a disabled family member discussed caring as a loss in terms of opportunities and experiences of 'normal' teenage life:

I don't think she [Mary] would have that much of a social life 'cause she would have missed out quite a lot basically where, that's the most important place where you get, that's where you have lots of friends basically, at that stage of school. (Year-13, Black Caribbean/Guyana girl, young carer)

The next participant, who identified herself as her mother's carer, discusses how loss of opportunity to engage in the everyday aspects of school life made her feel marginal and different:

(When I was 16,) because I went through year seven, eight, nine, 10 and a lot of year 11, 'cause aside from the fact that I did not have a good time because of my undiagnosed dyslexia and through the fact that, because of things with my mum being disabled, I didn't fit in well with other people because when it came down to it the way I saw it was 'well I will try but they don't understand where I'm coming from so it's very hard to relate to them because I don't go through typical issues that they do'. I mean, they would come on to the school going 'oh my mum's a bitch, she won't let me do this, she won't let me do that' and I'm sitting there thinking 'oh my God, how superficial are you, you don't even know what the hell you're talking about'.

So did people bully you or tease you?

No, you get left out, you get left out because when it gets down to it um, if you're not there all the time in school you miss out on so much because in secondary school life is, it's always about each day so if you're not there one day and miss something major and then you go in the next day 'so what about XXX' and you can't actually get that experience because it's just second hand information to you. (Year-13, White British girl, young carer)

Drawing on a view of Mary as a child in the process of developing, the loss of time and opportunity as a child/carer was seen to have a potentially negative impact on her later life:

What do you think will happen when she grows up?
I don't know probably similar sort of thing to Eduardo, she won't be able to develop fully while she's looking after someone else and she might feel under pressure to get out there and work as well as to bring money back as well as having to be there to look after her dad. (Year-13, White British boy, performs 'typical' work roles)

Caring is seen to force premature entry to adulthood thus producing a loss of opportunities to engage in the 'normal' activities of a 14 year-old. Helena above discussed being left out of 'normal' school life and school-based peer relationships. This construction of young carers as losing out was also evident in a more generalised, more symbolic sense of loss. Here a participant is discussing Mary:

What do you think will happen when she grows up?
I think she will be responsible because at such a young age she is learning to look after someone else but if she goes on without any help she wouldn't be, she would lose most of her childhood so. (Year-11, White European, Albanian girl, language broker)

Thus the dominant construction of a young carer is a profoundly negative view. The construction is based on an assumption of loss. Young caring is constructed as producing a loss of opportunity to be a 'normal' teenager, which may have serious implications for the development of friendships. The loss of opportunities to engage in 'normal' activities is seen to disrupt Mary's development, and a more abstract notion of 'losing out on childhood' is drawn on by participants. Caring is not viewed as a 'real life' but a hindrance from the 'reality' of being a teenager. Here, participants are drawing on an idealized normative view of the family life of a 'normal' teenager which is free from family disability and any form of serious difficulty.

Mapping the 'abnormal' parent

The discussion of the fictitious young carer, Mary elicited comments about the role of her father, a disabled parent, in her life. Young people in our study drew upon dominant understandings of development and the role of the family in which parents are the carers of dependent children. This is illustrated in the extract below:

What do you think about what Mary is doing?
Um, I don't think she should have to do that at her age, I think her dad should get like a carer or something, someone who comes in and helps him do stuff like that. He shouldn't be depending on her, especially at her age. (Year-13, Black Carribean Guyana girl, young carer)

Talk about the disabled parent draws on the mainstream construction of families in which parents care for their (dependent) children. The family system is constructed as a collection of individuals in which the role of the young person is to develop as an individual and to lead their own (separate) life:

It's not up to a 14 year-old girl to help, you've got your life to live. (Year-13, White European Portuguese boy, language broker)

Any transgression from prescribed roles for family members is viewed negatively and acknowledged as psychologically difficult. In the quote below a participant articulates an emotional response to Mary's father who is viewed as unable to perform their assumed parental roles:

Because it takes, it seems like a lot of hard work for her to like take on all this responsibility of looking after her disabled dad. Not just mentally but physically as well, 'cos it's tiring and it might be disturbing for her as well. (Year-13, dual heritage White and Black African Seychelles boy, performs 'typical' work roles)

Implicit within talk about Mary's father is the assumption that he is failing to fulfill his role as 'father' by 'depending on her' (significantly, discussions by participants focused attention on Mary as a provider of care, rather than discuss the absence of her brother in providing support for his father) and, thus, not allowing for the 'normal' path of development for his child:

I think Mary's dad may feel a little guilty because at one point he loves his daughter but at the next point he may feel that he is taking her away from being a normal child. (Year-11, White British boy, performs 'typical' work roles)

What about her dad? How do you think he feels about the situation?
I think he feels a little bit bad because he knows that his daughter and she wants to be playing outside and going to the cinema with friends, talking to boys, doing things that normal fourteen year-old girls do. But she has to stay home and look after her dad so he's feeling a bit bad that he's like, like pulling her back. But I'm also sure that he probably feels loved because his daughter's doing that for him. (Year-13, Black African girl, performs 'typical' work roles)

A further theme in participants' observations on Mary's father was to highlight his lack of agency as 'parent'. The implicit assumption was that Mary's father had no choice in using Mary to help him and was therefore constructed as a passive recipient of his care.

What about her dad, how do you imagine her dad would feel about the situation?
He doesn't really have a choice in it, but um, I think he wouldn't be too pleased to have his 14 year-old daughter having to help him in and out of bed, and just, you know, just helping him do thing. (Year-13, White European Portuguese boy, language broker)

How do you think Mary's dad feels?
Probably the same as my mother, grateful for the help but feels guilty for the, having to take up the time. Because many times she's said that she feels guilty because she's having to get us to do things that she should be doing.

How do you feel ...?
I don't mind doing the things that need doing but it can be a little upsetting at times when mum gets upset because she can't do the things she wants to do and she has to get us to do it. (Year-11, White British boy, young carer)

Within the study, the construction of Mary's disabled father was exclusively a negative view of a passive recipient, dependent upon his child for care. The disabled parent is constructed as to blame for the situation but powerless to act to improve the lives of their family. Some of the young people responded to that dilemma with empathy, imagining how a failure to live up to the normative expectations of a father's responsibility might make a man feel. Their preoccupation in constructions of the father appeared to be the impact of his situation on his daughter's enjoyment of (and benefit from) her childhood.

Possibilities: young people talk about caring
The mainstream construction of young carers positions the young person as a tragic victim of circumstance. An exception to this dominant construction of young caring

as a loss of potential and a loss of childhood was articulated by some of the young carers when reflecting upon their own activities. A far more pragmatic view of caring was evident in the ways in which they saw themselves as negotiating their responsibilities. The young carers in our study discussed ways in which they managed their lives and were not passively implicated within a hazardous family system. For one young carer, this involved making decisions that, to outsiders might appear to be counterproductive, but allowed her a sense of agency:

> So you have the stress of school but you also have the stress of family and everything else and so teachers do understand but at the same time they don't because it's like different people react differently. Like, for me, I used my, I hate to say it but I did use my mum as an excuse to get out of school because I was not having a good time and everyone thought I was dumb. (Year-13, White British girl, young carer)

Whilst young carers in our research drew on a construction of caring as involving loss, they also reported that they *wanted* to care for their disabled family member. There are complicated and often contradictory pressures for the young carer. In the extracts below two young carers discuss their own lives and illustrate the emotional 'pull' of family and, in the second extract, the 'pull' of their (constructed as separate) lives with their peers:

> *Would you change anything?*
> Um, no not really 'cos I like helping out with my sister, 'cos I don't like leaving my mum to do it all 'cos she has to look after my sister a lot. (Year-11, White British girl, young carer)

> *What do you think about what Mary is doing?*
> That's the same as me, that's the same as I did in high school, it's the same thing, you know, you take, if you have a disabled parent it's kind of like you're split ok, you have the side that just wants to be you. You want to be able to go out, have a kick about, you wanna be able to go to the shops and buy Nike, all the retail stuff. You wanna be able to just go over to your friends and watch movies and go 'ha, ha, ha'. But then on the other side you've got your obligations to your family because no matter how much you may want to be a normal person you also, if you tried being a normal person you'd feel guilty and I mean, so yeah, I understand where Mary is coming from because I've been there too. (Year-13, White British girl, young carer)

The dominant Western view of a family as a group of individuals with individual (and sometimes competing) needs is evident in the discussions in which young carers are positioned as having to choose between two competing duties, one to their family and the other to themselves, their friends and their development as a 'normal' teenager. For example, the young carer below discusses how it is through individual action that she must develop:

> I had a conditional offer as long as I got my, as long as I got five Cs I'd be fine and my GCSE grades came in, flopped, Es and Ds. At that point when I got rejected I was like 'do you know what, I've got to sort this out' you know 'I've got to get my GCSEs, I can't go through life thinking oh yes, this is difficult, I've got to run away, I'll hide behind my mum's disability, if I want something in this life I've got to get it for myself'. (Year-13, White British girl, young carer)

There was a limited discussion of positive views of caring and of the skills gained from caring by either the young carers or their peers in our interview sample. The examples of where it was drawn on were, interestingly, not by young carers but by young people who had acted as language brokers for their family. Their activities as language brokers may have made them more aware of the complex family dynamics involved. There was, however, evidence in the transcripts of a small number of participants portraying caring skills in a positive light partly because they viewed them in terms of a perspective on family obligations and family relationships that was culturally embedded within their own families who had arrived from overseas comparatively recently:

> ... in a long run she could benefit from, from what she's doing
>
> *In what way?*
> In what way, that err, it's like as I said before if she's planning to take any courses or ... it's not just about a courses really it's like err having relationship or communication with anyone ... it's not just someone with disability just anyone ....
>
> Because it's, it's quite, a it's quite a skill really to be able to communicate so ....
> (Year-13, East Asian Filipino boy, language broker)

The competing 'pull' of family obligation and (constructed as separate) friends and social life was articulated by the young carers in the study. However, young carers also talked about active ways of managing their lives. It is significant that only a few discussed the skills developed through caring. Positive skills and enriched development as a result of caring for a family member were evident but muted in discussions of most young carers. This may partly be because the tension from the dominant representation makes it difficult to reconcile with their experiences.

Discussion

The young people in our study drew on a predominantly negative construction of young carers in which carers experience a loss of engagement in 'normal' activities of teenagers. Participants drew on a construction of 'normal' age-related development through childhood and teenage years against which young caring was viewed as different and problematic. The assumption was that the lives of young carers are characterized by loss of opportunities to engage in 'normal' activities of young people such as socializing and studying at school. This construction was drawn on by those who had no experience of young caring as well as by young carers themselves. As a group of young people the participants all discussed the importance of friends and the ways in which friends may lose interest in a young carer who had little time to spend outside the house. Caring was viewed as not a 'real life' but an obstacle in the way of achieving the 'reality' of being a teenager, a view that reflects the dominant view of caring in Western, individualized cultures. The participants in our study drew on a normative view of the family life of a 'normal' teenager which is free from disability and any form of serious difficulty.

Using a model of development that benchmarks proficiency by age-related stages provides a comparison against which all children and young people who have lives outside of the idealized norm are judged as different and deficient. A criticism of early research on young carers such as Aldridge and Becker's (1993) work is that it positions young carers in comparison to an idealized 'normal' childhood (Olsen and Parker 1997). Drawing on socio-cultural theory, if we reject a conceptualization of development as a universal process of age-related stages of increasing proficiency but rather theorize development as about increasing participation in a full range of cultural activities (Rogoff 2003) then we open up possibilities of acknowledging that the different institutions and cultural arenas in which children engage will impact on their abilities, proficiencies and competencies. Rather than assume a universal template of appropriate childhood activities, theorists and practitioners could acknowledge the diversity of children's lives which impact upon them to produce different kinds of children with different kinds of skills, rather than holding up one version against which all whom are different fail. A focus on specialized child-focused activities during childhood is more prevalent in societies in which children do not participate in adult work activities (Morelli, Rogoff, and Anglelillo 2003). Within the young carers literature there is increasing acknowledgement that care can be conceptualized as part of the normative developmental process for many families (Cass 2007). The presence of young carers in our society creates a variant on the assumed 'norm' that requires an extension to how child development is understood within a diverse society, an extension that parallels the shift across diverse cultures (Morelli, Rogoff, and Anglelillo 2003). The need is thus to consider the broad cultural context in which the child develops.

We argue for a view of child development, and thus a view of young carers, that acknowledges the complexities of many children's lives. Our work adds to a growing body of knowledge that suggests that there are differing constructions of childhood that may co-exist in society. An example of this was given in our project by a young carer, who had a difficult time at school, was now studying at a diverse, multicultural college in a large city in the UK. She reflected upon the need to encourage diversity:

> Yeah, it's all about the differences between people. I mean, among different religions we've got blacks, whites, Asians, you know, we've got a wide range. It's good because it brings in all the differences and in a college like this where it brings in all the differences it doesn't matter if your mum's disabled or not, it doesn't matter whether you have to be a carer or whether you have to get a part time job to help finances, you know, we all support each other here. (Year-13, White British girl, young carer)

In the wider project we undertook, young people who acted as language brokers for their families were often able to draw on a sense of community (largely due to patterns of immigration and settlement) and a sense of being part of a wider group of young people who undertook this task for their families. For example, a year-11 language broker noted that 'my friends all speak Spanish, it's normal for us because everyone has to do the same thing and for others, no they think it's alright'. However the young carers in our research did not appear to have access to a sense of community that enhanced a feeling of pride in their caring activities. This echoes a broader concern in disability research with the notion of disability being medicalized and individualized. The construction of 'care' as an individualized activity performed within families, usually adult women, towards passive care recipients does not fully address the complexities of the relationship or the ways in which, for many young carers, caring is part of the collective activity that takes place in families.

Whilst a predominantly negative construction of young carers and their disabled family members was evident in the research presented here, there is a developing body of literature which argues that caring may not be a wholly negative experience for children. The young carers in our study talked about complicated feelings of obligation and responsibility towards their family in which they discussed managing their caring duties and attempting to balance this out against their social lives outside the family. It is important that strategies for supporting young carers and their families operate in ways which do not individualize the activity of caring to focus solely on the carer or force young carers into a position where they must choose between family and other aspects of their lives including friends at school. Prilleltensky (2004) argues for a focus on the family as a whole and an examination of factors such as support/isolation, the impact of poverty and inaccessible environments on the ways in which families experience disability. It is also important to acknowledge young carers' participation in their family's lives and the very specific skills learnt from caring. Like our construction of 'childhood' itself, our perspectives on young caring need to expand to take account of the increasing diversity of childhood experience in a more complex society.

Acknowledgements

The authors wish to thank the Economic and Social Research Council for their support in funding this project.

References

Aldridge, J. 2006. The experiences of children living with and caring for parents with mental illness. *Child Abuse Review* 15: 79–88.

Aldridge, J., and S. Becker. 1993. Children who care. *Childright* 97: 13–14.

Becker, S. 2004. Carers. *Research matters* August special Issue: 5–10.

Becker, S., and J. Aldridge. 1993. The lost children. *Community Care* March: 23.

Butler, A.H., and G. Astbury. 2005. The caring child: An evaluative case study of the Cornwall Young Carers project. *Children & Society* 19, no. 4: 292–303.

Cass, B. 2007. Exploring social care: Applying a new construct to young carers and grandparent carers. *Australian Journal of Social Issues* 42, no. 2: 241–54.

Crafter, S., L. O'Dell, G. de Abreu, and T. Cline, T. 2009. Young people's representations of 'atypical' work in English society. *Children & Society* 23: 176–88.

Early, L., D. Cushway, and T. Cassidy. 2006. Perceived stress in young carers: Development of a measure. *Journal of Child and Family Studies* 15, no. 2: 169–80.

Earley, L., D. Cushway, and T. Cassidy. 2007. Children's perceptions and experiences of care giving: A focus group study. *Counselling Psychology Quarterly* 20, no. 1: 69–80.

Fleer, M. 2006. The cultural construction of child development: Creating institutional and cultural intersubjectivity. *International Journal of Early Years Education* 14, no. 2: 127–40.

Keith, L., and J. Morris. 1995. Easy targets: A disability rights perspective on the 'children as carers' debate. *Critical Social Policy* 15, no. 44: 36–57.

Leonard, M. 2004. Children's views on children's right to work: Reflections from Belfast. *Childhood* 11, no. 1: 45–61.

Mahon, A. and J. Higgins. 1995. '... A life of our own'. Young carers: An evaluation of three RHA funded projects in Merseyside. Manchester: University of Manchester, Health Services Management Unit.

Morelli, G.A., B. Rogoff, and C. Angelillo. 2003. Cultural variation in young children's access to work or involvement in specialized child-focussed activities. *International Journal of Behavioural Development* 27, no. 3: 264–74.

Newman, T. 2002. Young carers and disabled parents: Time for a change of direction. *Disability & Society* 17, no. 6: 613–25.

Olsen, R., and H. Clarke. 2003. *Parenting and disability: Disabled parents' experience of raising children.* Bristol: Polity Press.

Olsen, R., and G. Parker. 1997. A response to Aldridge and Becker – 'Disability rights and the denial of young carers: The dangers of zero-sum arguments'. *Critical Social Policy* 17: 125–33.

Prilleltensky, O. 2004. My child is not my carer: Mothers with physical disabilities and the well-being of children. *Disability and Society* 19, no. 3: 209–23.
Rogoff, B. 2003. *The cultural nature of human development.* Oxford: Oxford University Press.
Sidall, R. 1994. Lost childhood. *Community Care* 9–15 June: 14–15.
Underdown, A. 2002. 'I'm growing up too fast': Messages from young carers. *Children and Society* 16: 57–60.
Walker, A. 1996. *Young carers and their families: A survey carried out by the social survey division of ONS on behalf of the Department of Health.* London: Stationery Office.

Not your average childhood: lived experience of children with physical disabilities raised in Bloorview Hospital, Home and School from 1960 to 1989

Tracy Odell

York University, Toronto, Canada

> Sixteen adults with physical disabilities participated in this emancipatory research study to document their recollection of institutionalization in Toronto's Bloorview Hospital, Home and School between 1960 and 1989. This study suggests that: there were two distinct cohorts of residents, with the latter group having a relatively more positive experience; residents operationalized a hierarchy among themselves; residents experienced emotional, physical and sexual abuse while in residence; peer relationships were valued, both within and outside the institution; residents found creative ways to be rebellious; reprisals took the form of physical abuse related to disability; most residents had difficulty expressing their sexuality; family relationships were highly valued by residents; therapeutic interventions were not valued; recreational programs were highly valued by residents and contributed to self-esteem; and educational experiences were highly valued, but deemed inadequate. Respondents, in retrospect, support an ongoing role for institutions as a resource for technology and for fostering independence.

Points of interest

- Sixteen people tell their stories of living in an institution from 1960 to 1989. The researcher grew up in the same institution.
- There was a pecking order, with those best able to speak and move themselves about at the top.
- People were abused in many ways both by staff and other residents. Punishment was often done in ways that took unfair advantage of their disability, such as taking away one's wheelchair, or giving higher doses of medication to quiet them down. People found creative ways to fight back.
- People did not think the schooling or therapy they got was useful, but felt that friends, family and recreation programs gave them self-esteem and a positive future.
- People said that institutions today should show new technologies and teach people ways to be independent.

Dedication

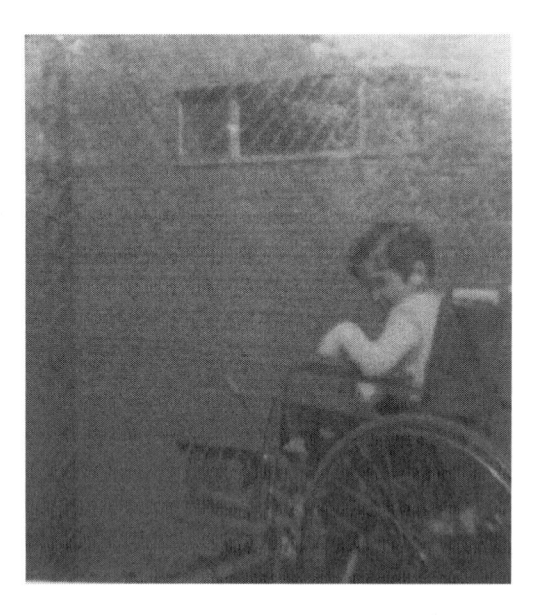

Marie (1956–1975). On the Veranda, c. Summer 1966. Researcher's personal collection

This research is dedicated to the memory of Marie, who, like many of my friends who lived at Bloorview, spent her entire life in an institution.

Introduction

This research documents the perspective of adults with physical disabilities of their experiences as children who were placed in Bloorview Hospital, Home and School between the years 1960 and 1989. During this period, Bloorview admitted children with physical disabilities from across Ontario, Canada in order to provide care, treatment and education that were not offered to children who remained at home.

My interest in this topic arises from my own experience of living at Bloorview from 1965 at age seven, until 1976. Many of the individuals interviewed for this paper are people known to me, although, in most instances, there had been no direct contact between us for over 30 years. The findings outlined in this paper are based on the explanations, reflections and conclusions of the survivors I located and interviewed during the summer of 2005.

The lived experience of people with disabilities is a relatively new area of study. Historically, academic explorations have focused on mental illness (Reaume 2000), developmental disability (Hubert 2000; Jones 1992), orphans (Rooke and Schnell 1983), and chronic pain and suffering (Kleinman 1988).

The primary focus of this research was on the respondents' remembrances of life at Bloorview, rather than on the history of Bloorview itself or on the health care policies of the day. The comments made by respondents, therefore, stand alone. This research explored whether people with disabilities that were raised in institutions as children feel that the gains they received outweighed the cost of living away from home during their formative years.

A brief history of Bloorview

Bloorview's public history[1] describes its beginnings in 1899. Its founders, about 24 white, upper middle-class women, had previously helped to establish the now world-famous Hospital for Sick Children in 1875. These ladies used their connections and influence to establish a small residential institution, initially known as the 'Home for Incurable Children' [sic] as a place for children who needed ongoing care and support after their hospital treatment.

The 1899 building housed 15 children with services donated by physicians. In 1954, it expanded to house 48 children, and in 1966, changed its name to Bloorview Hospital, Home and School. In 1975, the residents were transferred to Bloorview Children's Hospital,[2] a larger, purpose-built facility in the suburbs of Toronto with capacity for 102 children. Following a merger between Bloorview and the Hugh MacMillan Rehabilitation Center in the mid-1990s, it had become the largest children's rehabilitation facility in Ontario, providing medical services and community outreach to about 6500 children and youth with disabilities and their families each year.[3] In 2006, the re-named Bloorview Kids Rehab re-opened in a $100 million state-of-the-art, accessible, five-storey clinic and residence.

Methodology

An emancipatory approach was selected consistent with Oliver's (1997) conceptualization of research controlled by the researched, not the researcher. The study sample was controlled by type of disability (physical), location (Bloorview), and time (1960–1989). This study did not address comparisons across different disability groups, different regions, or historical eras.

The 1960s was chosen as the starting time frame since it was the beginning of an era known for its emergence of modern civil rights awareness. This time frame also served to ensure that survivors could be found to participate in the study. 1989 was selected as the ending time frame on the theory that the lived experience of Bloorview up to that point would have been fairly constant. During this time frame, children with physical disabilities were admitted no younger than two years of age, and discharged no later than age 21 (typically by age 18). Also during this time frame, pre-admission tests screened out children with an Intelligence Quotient (IQ) below 80,[4] to retain the integrity of the facility as a place for children with physical disabilities. By 1991 this criterion was adjusted[5] at which time children having a broader range of physical, medical, and developmental disabilities were accepted for admission.

The study was publicized through personal and electronic networks of people with disabilities. Using 31 interview questions as a guide, face-to-face interviews were conducted with 14 participants using Kvale's (1996) 'InterViews' approach, and telephone interviews were held with two others. Interviews were conducted during the summer of 2005.

All responses were taped, transcribed, and analyzed using a variation on the constant comparative method and supplemental demographic data were collected by questionnaire. Three participants responded using augmentative communication methods and the assistance of a person familiar with their communication style.

The respondents

Eight women and eight men were interviewed who formerly lived at Bloorview between 1960–1989. The diagnoses of individuals interviewed included cerebral palsy ($n = 8$), spina bifida ($n = 3$), muscular dystrophy ($n = 3$), and spinal cord injury/paraplegia ($n = 2$). Three of the respondents with cerebral palsy used word boards or augmentative communication devices to support speech. Respondents ranged in age from 30–50 years. The profiles of the respondents are outlined in Table 1.

The length of stay for respondents varied from two to 17 years, with an average stay of seven years. Figure 1 shows that the majority of respondents resided at Bloorview from age 10 to 18, with some variations on either side of that age range. Figure 2 illustrates that all respondents overlapped their stay at Bloorview with some other respondents.

At the time of the interviews, all respondents resided in the province of Ontario, Canada. Thirteen participants required attendant support services to perform routine tasks of daily living, such as bathing, dressing, toiletry/toileting, grocery shopping and so on. This support was currently being provided in a variety of independent living or group home settings where the respondents lived. All used a wheelchair for mobility, either manual ($n = 8$) or electric/battery powered ($n = 8$).

Some individuals had vivid memories of aspects of their stay but for others, the memories were hazy. The findings which follow are derived from common experiences shared by respondents, as well as responses which were outside of the norms expressed.

Results and emerging themes

Two distinct cohorts of residents existed between 1960 and 1989

Respondents who resided at Bloorview prior to 1975 were more likely to report negative experiences, and residents who resided at Bloorview after 1975 were more likely to report positive experiences as set out in Table 2. While experiences are not always wholly positive or negative in character, the differences in perception of the experience suggests that generally, there were two distinct cohorts or generations of residents within the timeframe of interest to this study.

One reason for this difference in perception of their experience was each respondent's understanding of the differing reasons for his or her admission to Bloorview. In retrospect, some respondents in the first cohort (pre-1975) acknowledged that their placement at Bloorview was because their family members couldn't cope with their needs at home. This group felt they were 'dumped' at Bloorview, confirming Hubert's (2000, 197) postulation that institutionalized people experience abandonment and rejection. Three respondents stated that they were institutionalized because the school principal in their home community refused to request the physical modifications that would have made attendance in the neighbourhood school possible.

The first cohort: 1960–1975

This group was admitted to the older and smaller building located at 278 Bloor Street East in Toronto, Canada. In the 1960s, Bloorview held 48 to 52 children. It had been fairly common to see children admitted at age five or six and stay until they died or until age 18, or even to age 21. When asked about their first impression of Bloorview, the single most common word used by all respondents of both cohorts was 'scary'.

CHILDHOOD AND DISABILITY

Table 1. Respondents' profiles related to stay at Bloorview.

RESPONDENT	Age at Admission	Year	Age at Discharge	Year
R1 – PRE-1975 Female, 50–60 years old Spinal Cord Injury – Paraplegic	2	1956	19	1975
R2 – PRE-1975 Female, 50–60 years old Muscular Dystrophy	11	1962	22	1973
R3 – PRE-1975 Male, 40–50 years old Cerebral Palsy	7	1965	19	1977
R4 – PRE-1975 Male, 40–50 years old Cerebral Palsy	9	1965	19	1975
R5 – PRE-1975 Male, 40–50 years old Cerebral Palsy - Non Verbal	6	1969	16	1979
R6 – PRE-1975 Female, 40–50 years old Spina Bifida	10	1971	18	1979
R7 – POST-1975 Female, 30–40 years old Muscular Dystrophy	10	1979	18	1987
R8 – PRE-1975 Male, 50–60 years old Spina Bifida	10	1964	17	1972
R9 – POST-1975 Male, 30–40 years old Cerebral Palsy – Non Verbal	13	1986	20	1993
R10 – POST-1975 Male, 30–40 years old Spina Bifida	13	1979	19	1984
R11 – POST-1975 Male, 40–50 years old Cerebral Palsy	17	1975	21	1980
R12 – POST-1975 Female, 40–50 years old Muscular Dystrophy	15	1982	19	1986
R13 – POST-1975 Female, 40–50 years old Cerebral Palsy	14	1977	18	1981
R14 – PRE-1975 Female, 40–50 years old Spinal Cord Injury - Paraplegic	10	1969	14	1972
R15 – POST-1975 Female, 30–40 years old Cerebral Palsy – Non Verbal	8	1975	11	1978
R16 – PRE-1975 Male, 40–50 years old Cerebral Palsy	10	1966	12	1968

Notes: R1–R16, Respondent numbers assigned by researcher; PRE 1975, Admitted to Bloorview prior to 1975 (1st cohort); POST 1975, Admitted to Bloorview after 1975 (2nd cohort).

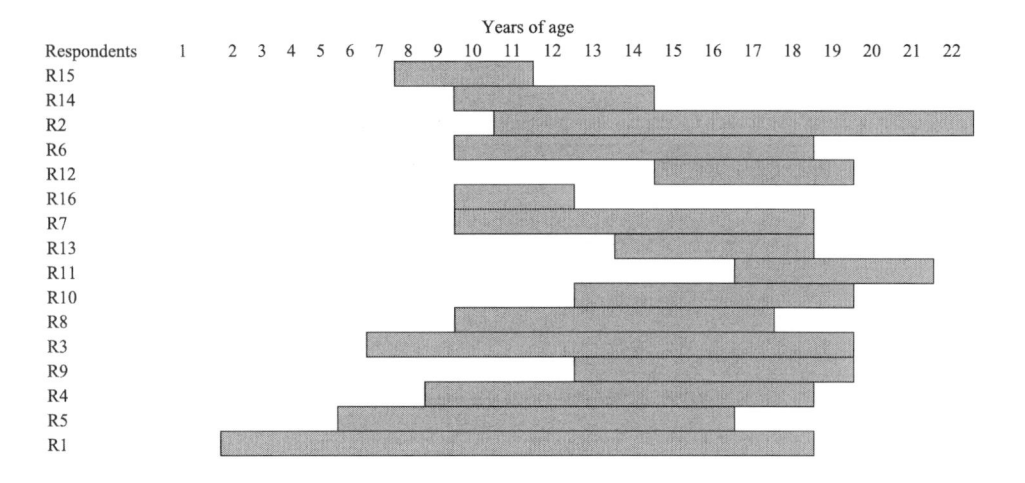

Figure 1. Respondents' relative ages at Bloorview.

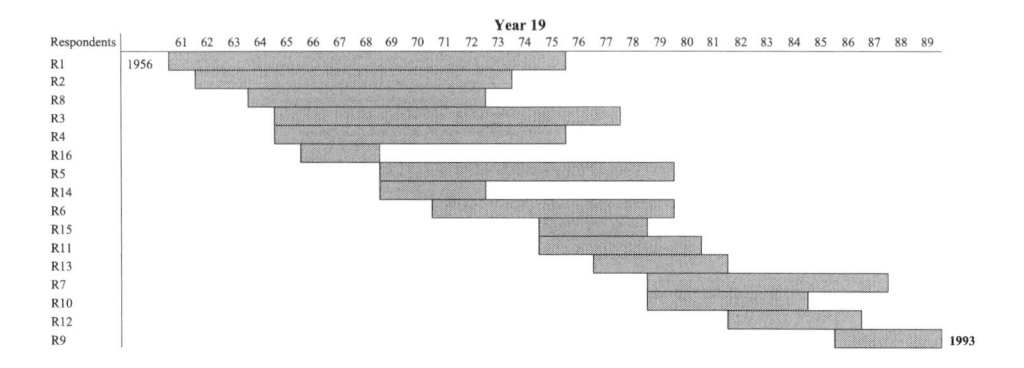

Figure 2. Length of respondents' stay at Bloorview (showing chronological overlap of years 1960–1989).

Table 2. Overall experience of Bloorview by cohort (researcher's summary).

Respondent	PRE-/POST-1975	Overall Experience	Respondent	PRE-/POST-1975	Overall Experience
R6	PRE-1975	Mixed	R13	POST-1975	Mixed
R3	PRE-1975	Mixed	R11	POST-1975	Mixed
R14	PRE-1975	Mixed	R15	POST-1975	Negative
R2	PRE-1975	Mixed	R10	POST-1975	Positive
R4	PRE-1975	Negative	R5	PRE-1975	Positive
R1	PRE-1975	Negative	R12	POST-1975	Positive
R16	PRE-1975	Negative	R9	POST-1975	Positive
R8	PRE-1975	Positive	R7	POST-1975	Positive

Notes: Pre-1975: Positive = 2, Negative = 3, Mixed = 4; Post-1975: Positive = 4, Negative = 1, Mixed = 2.

Many of the individuals in the first cohort had a strong recollection of the plaque at the front entrance inscribed with Bloorview's former name:

> I will never forget that [day] as long as I live. I remember going in to the front door and over the doorway was 'The Home for Incurable Children' [sic] and my first response to my mother was, 'I'm not sick.' (Steven, pre-1975)

Bloorview residents wanted the same experiences that their non-disabled peers had, including experiences of sex, drugs and rock-and-roll. At Bloorview, the desire for rights and freedoms was expressed as a desire to do 'normal' things, and this pursuit forged a new generation of fighters and advocates:

> It was basically a fight a lot of the time just to be as normal as you could. So, it was quite a fight … we got to go to concerts, meet people that were out there and who lived outside of Bloorview so you could have a kind of glimpse of what it was like to not live in Bloorview, basically. So, you know it was not all bad, but it was a fight to get through some of the things that went on there. ('Sally', pre-1975)

The second cohort: 1975–1989

This cohort was admitted to the new building located at 25 Buchan Court in Toronto. With the move to the new building on 31 May 1975 the emphasis at Bloorview shifted overnight to that of a professional hospital (accredited in 1976[6]) and the residents' population grew from 52 to 88 children. The modern building had distinct residential, therapy, school, and recreation areas and the move precipitated some turnover and expansion of staff. This cohort was the first group to benefit from a (then) new accessible municipal transportation system, which had begun operating in 1975.

Generally, older children who went to Bloorview had a say about the decision to move away from home:

> Well, it was my own doing, at that time, because I grew up living with my parents which I felt were getting older, and they couldn't look after me. I also felt that they were over-protective and I was about 17, and I wanted to get away from that life. (Sam, pre-1975)

Other factors that contributed to the overall positive, negative, and mixed perceptions of experiences are set out below.

Residents operationalized a hierarchy among themselves

At Bloorview, where almost everyone used a wheelchair, there was an unspoken but distinct hierarchy among the residents with an individual's position in the hierarchy based on each resident's functional abilities. Children with quick speech who were physically independent were at the top of the hierarchy regardless of diagnosis, as well as outspoken children who were less mobile.

Those with head injuries, those who spoke more slowly or who had difficulty in moving about were much lower on the hierarchy. At the very bottom of the hierarchy were the children who were unable to propel their own wheelchairs and were also unable to speak clearly. Those on the top were often verbally abusive to those lower down the strata, and, in extreme cases, victimized those children perceived to be more helpless.

Residents experienced emotional, physical, and sexual abuse

It has long been understood that people who are institutionalized are vulnerable, and as such, are subject to physical, verbal, medical and even sexual abuse (Sobsey 1994). The Law Commission of Canada (2000, 6) noted that abuse of children in institutions is perpetuated by a lack of proper supervision and oversight of the children's daily activities, level of discipline and quality of care provided.

While some respondents acknowledged that Bloorview rescued them from neglect and over-protective parents, residents at Bloorview were not exempt from abuse. A significant number of respondents spoke of their experience of and/or being witness to physical, emotional and sexual abuses of children both by staff and their more able-bodied peers.

> Well, you know. It is an institution. It is regimented, too many people looking after you, too many authority figures and it confuses people ... too much negativity in a sense, you know. The children around you are being abused psychologically, physically, and it is hard. And, I am sure you have heard the term... we were "warehoused' into this situation. I mean, it was not good. It was rough. It was not good. ('Sally', pre-1975)

Two of the 16 respondents described sexual abuses perpetrated by staff members who preyed on the children in there:

> I saw a lot of sexual abuse happening to both female and male, by both sexes ... And I had experiences with a male attendant that made it look like he was washing me in the shower. For all intents and purposes it would look like he would be washing me properly, but I felt, and a number of other clients felt like, we got fondled by that ... staff ... I got told if I told anybody, the situations would get twice as bad than what they were. ('Joseph', pre-1975)

The following disclosure was elicited from a respondent who uses a word board to communicate. The discussion of this individual's victimization was emotional and heart-wrenching even as it was recalled many years after the incidents occurred:

> Some [staff] were good. Some were awful. [I was] rape[d]. When I was ... only nine. I tried to tell the other staff, but they didn't believe me. It happened over and over again. I am still afraid. I'm still living in fear now, of people around me, in attendant support. It has scarred me for life. Today as I am thinking about it, it is hard. I try not to think about it. The rape. (Lorraine, post-1975)

Abuses were not contained solely within staff–resident relationships. Some of the residents victimized other, weaker or more vulnerable children. Several other respondents commented on the general meanness of the other residents at the time they lived at Bloorview:

> I realized how cruel kids could be to each other. Because I did not speak the language ... I got picked on at first by other kids and I was actually urinated on by one of the kids. (François, pre-1975)

> Some of them were mean. I was really, really hassled by one quick resident, like REALLY hassled when I went there. I was literally terrorized. Like they were the ones that smoked and hung out and were tough. And one of them told me that if I didn't start giving him money, he would come into my room and stab me in the back. (Fiona, post-1975)

In other instances, residents preyed sexually upon other residents who were less mobile, unable to speak, and perhaps less intelligent. Residents used force at times and made threats that they were physically quite capable of carrying out. Siblings living in residence at the same time reported being bullied into performing sexual acts with other residents to protect a brother or sister:

> I remember some of the, some of the girls were threatened at times, if you don't do this, you know, I'll beat up your brother ... I remember that with [J] because her two brothers lived there. Even myself, I even threatened her that I was going to beat up her brother if she didn't do what I asked her to do. ('Andy', pre-1975)

Peer relationships were valued, both within and outside the institution

At least 12 of the respondents were still friends with individuals they had met at Bloorview and these friendships were noted as an important benefit. Peer friendships were often vital to learning about community-based supports.

While 10 respondents were not gainfully employed at the time of their interview, all were living successfully in the community. Of those interviewed, most were content with their current lifestyle, but all expressed plans, hopes or dreams for making continued progress on reaching goals related to employment, education and personal relationships.

Residents found ways to be rebellious

Residents were creative in finding ways to rebel against authority during their teenage years. For example, respondents reported they would smuggle in alcohol, or refuse to sign out when leaving the premises.

> I'd refuse to do treatments, I'd refuse to take meds, I'd, um, not come back when I'd signed out that I'd be back at. Or ... because it was very lax in security and it was so beautifully ravined and everything, it was easy to run away there. And I remember doing things like, if we were assigned to set up toothbrushes, I'd stick Phisohex [medical soap] in them or something. (Mickii, pre-1975)

> The administration had given us permission to have locks on our desks, or night tables, and [one nurse] unilaterally made the decision to inspect everybody's drawers and I remember a group of us locking them back up and singing 'We shall overcome' and stuff like that, and raising shit that way but that was about as far as it went for me. (Steven, pre-1975)

To some extent, residents' rebelliousness was aided by advances in technology:

> When I got my first [electric] wheelchair, I used to stay out past curfew and Bloorview often got mad at me for that. ('Joseph', pre-1975)

Rebelliousness even took the form of consensual sexual relations among residents:

> The Rumpus Room ... Well, you know you go down there for little rounds, like ... at times there was sex and things like that. We enjoyed doing that because this brought us against their authoritarian figures, that was our way of rebelling in a way. It was maybe a type of a way to tackle ... in some ways to be able to participate in a normal way of life. ('Sally', pre-1975)

Reprisals took the form of physical abuse related to disability

Punishments in response to breaking rules and defying authority included the loss of privileges, increased medication, being grounded and even having one's mobility removed:

> Well, I was grounded a few times. Once, I was grounded to the point that I had to stay in bed. They would not let me get up in my chair. I found that to be extremely harsh. (Pina, post-1975)

> If I was getting really emotional and verbal, they'd up my valium on me. They'd get me totally zoned out so that I couldn't overreact, in their opinions, at anything. (Mickii, pre-1975)

The removal of wheelchairs is a form of disability-related physical abuse, since it hampers mobility to an extraordinary degree. As 'Joseph' put it, 'Our wheelchairs are like our legs.' The practise of adjusting medication, as Mickii described above, not only pathologizes healthy acts of adolescent rebellion, but also could be considered as chemical abuse.

Most residents had difficulty expressing their sexuality

Even for residents as old as 21 years of age, there were no condoned opportunities for the healthy expression of sexuality. Participants reported a need to sneak around or collude with other residents to create intimacy:

> I had a couple of girlfriends while I was there. But it wasn't anything, um, 'cause they had certain rules, that you couldn't, like, if you were in your room with a girl, you couldn't have the curtain drawn around your bed, and you definitely could not have the door closed. That was a definite no-no. But I knew people that did, and I would help them. I'd run interference, like, I'd shut the doors. And if I knew the staff were coming, I'd boot back halls and pound on the door, and then they'd stop doing whatever it was they were doing and the staff would come in. (Christopher, post-1975)

In the late 1960s, girls were routinely counselled to take birth control as a matter of convenience for both themselves and the staff. In a few instances, the girls challenged this assumption, as Rosina did when she was sent to see a gynaecologist:

> So I went, and I said, 'Mr. So-and-So told me I have to come here, but I'm not doing nothing!' [i.e. having sex]. And [the doctor] said, 'Well, you know, most of the kids are on the pill or the shot.' And I said, 'Me? (Laughing) No way, I'm on enough already!' (Rosina, post-1975)

By the 1980s, Bloorview staff were less inclined to interfere when they discovered that some residents were sexually active. Residents who obtained their information from friends and from their community high school nurse still found the information to be incomplete, and based on a false assumption that people with disabilities might not form relationships with non-disabled people. For others, the barrier to forming a relationship was others' response to them: being overlooked, dismissed or blatantly rejected as a potential girl- or boyfriend.

At the time of interview, 12 out of 16 respondents (75%) identified themselves as single. This is a significantly higher percentage than for the general Canadian population where 42% of the population are single[7].

Family relationships were highly valued

Frequent and regular family contact contributed to a relatively more positive experience regardless of the timing of institutionalization and, generally, those who were admitted at a later age had a more positive experience than those who were admitted very young (i.e. age two to seven years). Without exception, every respondent commented on the importance of family ties. Whether the family was strong or had internal problems, each respondent felt keenly the benefit of a family connection, perhaps most keenly of all when it was absent.

David (pre-1975) stated his family relationship was 'good' prior to living at Bloorview, and Sam (post-1975) acknowledged that, even though his family may have had low expectations for him, they loved him and cared for him. For Steven, (pre-1975), his family was his 'life-line'. Similarly, Lorraine paints a very warm portrait of her family dynamic:

> It was a typical French-Canadian family where we loved and looked after each other. When we fought over something we had to think about our conduct and somehow, depending on the situation, kiss and make up. Mom was the main caregiver, Dad was the provider. Both sets of grandparents lived close by and helped a great deal. My grandpapa made me my first reclining chair and commode chair. He used his first Canada Pension cheque to pay for my first wheelchair. (Lorraine, post-1975)

During a person's residence at Bloorview in the 1960s, the day-to-day family interaction was severed overnight, since it was believed that the children would make a better adjustment to living at Bloorview if they were not reminded of home. The first cohort experienced what was known as a 'six months policy', whereby family contact was forbidden for the first six months of a resident's stay. This restriction was later reduced to three months, and by the time the second cohort was admitted, had been abolished as a practice. Many respondents commented on how difficult this separation was. Feelings of distance, loneliness, and anger were expressed by some respondents.

> After I went to Bloorview, [my Mom] was still there for me but not as much. As I said, I felt abandoned ... My dad left her and she was all alone so I guess there was no other way ... She thought it was like a boarding school. She did not realize the implications of what it means to be institutionalized. So, I was still close to her but maybe I was having a slight resentment towards her for a while. You know, quite a while. Then, you kind of realize, maybe she did not have any choice at the time. ('Sally', pre-1975)

> As I became an older teenager and more rebellious, I hated my parents for a while to the point that I avoided all contact with them. And I wouldn't even visit them, and I didn't want them visiting me. And I just really hated them, and I blamed them for the misery in my life. I was miserable living at Bloorview sometimes. I mean, I enjoyed parts of it, but other parts, the resentment part, I actually hated it. It was very strong in me, the feeling. So, I translated it to my Mom and Dad, being their fault, and I often lashed out at them. (Pina, post-1975).

Family contact could provide additional support or shielding from institutional problems and policies. Rosina's visit to the gynaecologist might have ended differently had she not called upon her mother to intervene:

> And so, [the gynaecologist] said, 'Well, I'm going to have to put you on something ...' I said, 'Really? REALLY? Wait here for a minute. I'll be right back.' I went up to the pay phone, called my mother, I said, 'Ma! How Catholic are you today?' I said, 'Come

down here! They're trying to give me this little pill.' She did, she flew from the west end ... So, I did, forego that ... It was kind of like, they were trying to stop me from being human. (Rosina, post-1975)

While David (post-1975) reported that his relationship with his parents strengthened after leaving Bloorview, several other respondents spoke about distances that had been created. Most, but not all of this group, were able to build up the relationship with their family once again following their discharges from Bloorview.

Therapeutic interventions were not valued by most residents

One-third of the respondents indicated their need for care and/or therapy, which was beyond the ability of their parents to provide, to be the main reason for placement in the institution, yet most respondents required prompting to recall the therapy or special care they received at Bloorview. When they did mention therapy, they had difficulty remembering the value or relevance of it.

Physiotherapy was the most commonly mentioned therapeutic intervention, followed by weights or weightlifting. Some children received occupational therapy and a few underwent speech therapy. As adults, one person commented that his physical deterioration related to the cessation of physio therapy, stating that the loss of movement in one arm was directly attributed to the unavailability of funding for continuing physio therapy in the community. Few commented on the impact that therapy had, other than in noting that it was a regular interruption of the school day.

Recreational programs were highly valued and contributed to self-esteem

Half of the respondents spoke of Bloorview's recreation department, recreational programs and recreational staff as having a profound impact on residents in their impressionable years, and thus making a positive difference in their self-esteem.

> The younger Rec' people who came in, and just lit the place up with encouragement. ... The recreational programs, to me, were really important, because there was so much in the recreational program that developed who I was. Through theatre, through going to all the arts programs at the museum and live theatre and things like that. And just being able to go out shopping regularly, to go to movies regularly, things like that. To me the Rec' program was ideal. They really did develop a good program ... But, when I was at that location it was great. I really appreciated those programs. They did the best stuff that was there. (Mickii, pre-1975)

Younger staff in the recreation department organized some innovative programs which respondents remembered as a very positive experience. For example, residents were invited to sing and play electric guitar, drums, maracas or tambourines in a Bloorview rock band. Most of the residents were interested in rehearsals and the few who were invited into the band remembered it as a childhood experience which built up their self-esteem.

> Everybody wanted to be like [P]. He was quiet, but I mean, he could draw, could draw very well ... he seemed to be very independent and you could learn from him, his music, you know, and being in a band with him at times. ('Andy', pre-1975)

> One thing Bloorview did for me is ... I remember [V] [in the recreation department] ... and they used to try to teach me ... and I know a little bit of guitar and piano lessons ...

> Yes, it was wild when I was in the band, and it got me away from some school and stuff like that. (Robin, pre-1975)

The recreation department also supported residents who chose to participate in sports. For 'Eileen', the boost to her self-confidence and the exposure to other people with disabilities leading normal lives in the community was a life-changing experience:

> There were staff that were caring. When I got involved with sports, that was a really important change and that was because of one staff person. It was on my initiation because I had seen a film on the 1972 Paralympics and I went to the person [in recreation] and said, 'I want to do that.' And I was 13 or 14 at the time and this person just said, 'OK, let's do it!' And it really happened that way. And that was really an important evolution for me because it allowed me the opportunity to see people with disabilities, other kids and young adults who were fit and active and independent and had girlfriends and boyfriends and some even had kids, and I was exposed to just the potential of what I had not thought of before. So, that was really important and that added a quality to my life as compared to before. ('Eileen', pre-1975)

Educational experiences were highly valued, but inadequate within the institution

Respondents differed in their perceptions of their experiences with both the regular school setting and a special class (i.e. segregated) setting. At Bloorview, students worked on reading, writing and mathematics at their own paces. This posed challenges when they were to go to a school in the community at a set grade level, since they might have been in different grades for different subjects.

Respondents frequently commented on the value of education for eventual success as an adult, as compared to the value of other interventions, such as therapy and surgery. Some respondents questioned the purpose of therapeutic interventions, believing the time it cost would have been better spent on education.

Respondents who relied on augmentative communication reported the most positive experiences with Bloorview's school. They liked the segregated school environment, the teachers, and especially valued the opportunity to learn alternative communication methods, such as Blissymbols®, word boards and/or augmentative communication devices.

> It was good, I went to a special school, and I didn't want to be integrated with kids who didn't have disabilities ... So I could learn at my own pace. (David, post-1975)

Thirteen respondents expressed dissatisfaction with the quality of Bloorview's school experience, especially when accessible schooling had been given as a key reason for their admission. The respondents who went to school in the community, either before arriving at Bloorview or during their stay there, had generally positive comments to make about their integrated experience.

Respondents support a role for institutions as a resource for technology and for fostering independence

Respondents varied in their suggestions concerning an ongoing role for residential institutions like Bloorview. Some of those who had a totally positive experience believed that institutions could play a role in providing a similar level of assistance, friendship and support to that which had been provided to them. Others had a sentiment similar to the following:

> Well, the funny thing is, that it would probably be cheaper for the government to accommodate people at home than to have them in institutions. If I had to get off the fence, I would say that I am anti-institution. I'm sure they play a role for severely disabled kids by providing assessments and equipment and aids, like helping them learn ways to do everything, but I would hate to see anyone spend their whole life in one – especially someone with an active mind – so as I say they play a role in perhaps determining what you can and can't do and in providing equipment. But, in many ways, they hold you back, you know. (Fiona, post-1975)

Those expressing a mixture of positive and negative experiences saw the benefits of an institutional 'hub' that could provide current information and access to technology, especially to those in rural areas where opportunities are more limited. This group of respondents felt that the demands of the therapeutic structure best promoted self-sufficiency and independence, even if for a few weeks of the year:

> All the support is there, the trained people are there, the latest equipment, the latest information, and what kids can and are doing with disabilities in the communities is there for them to see ... Especially the rural kids do not find out generally what is really out there ... And if they have a disability, some parents just won't push them. (Mickii, pre-1975)

Respondents most frequently cited instruction in independent living skills as a role for residential institutions to play today.

Conclusion

This study has begun to document the lived experience of children with physical disabilities who were raised at Bloorview from 1960–1989. Generally, children who lived at Bloorview prior to 1975 had a more negative experience and those who went to live there after 1975 had a more positive experience. It is likely that the sociocultural factors characterizing each era contributed to each person's self-perception and experience of the institution at the time. Increasing expectations of staff as the institution sought and attained a professional standing as a 'hospital' rather than a 'home' no doubt was also a significant contributor to the quality of experience described by respondents.

While this study adds to a body of research on childhood, institutionalization and critical disability studies, it still raises more questions than it answers. Further research is needed to determine the factors that have a strong correlation to adult success, such as gainful employment, community involvement and meaningful personal relationships. Some success factors may be: (1) the ability to speak and advocate for oneself; (2) the maintenance of strong family connections; (3) a role model or ally to provide a glimpse of what adult life could be like; and (4) technological advances. Further research into the history of Bloorview's operations and practices would also be of interest, particularly with respect to the relative impacts of various investments and initiatives from the perspective of the residents (consumers) of those services. Finally, a more comprehensive, follow-up study could further illuminate the experiences of children who grew up in institutions. Exploration into the childhood games played, self-concept related to disability, to the institution, and to society as a whole; what living in an institution meant to them and their perceptions of others' response to them on that basis are just some of the questions that remain unexplored from the residents' perspectives.

As Bloorview's focus shifts from the design and construction of a state-of-the-art building to delivery of service, decision-makers may also be wise to consider the advice of former residents who lived within their walls. Only by understanding the strengths and pitfalls of such institutions can we work to ensure that future service systems benefit people in the ways intended, while safeguarding against doing harm.

Notes

1. See website http://www.bloorviewmacmillan.on.ca/aboutus/history.htm
2. Bloorview-MacMillan archival material (no number).
3. See website www.bloorviewmacmillan.on.ca/aboutus/capitproj.htm.
4. Bloorview-MacMillan archival material (no number).
5. Bloorview-MacMillan archives, cf. document 24/9 1991.
6. Bloorview-MacMillan archival material (no number).
7. Statistics Canada http://www40.statcan.ca/l01/cst01/famil01.htm as modified 21 January 2005 (accessed 12 August 2009).

References

Hubert, Jane. 2000. The social, individual and moral consequences of physical exclusion in long-stay institutions. In *Madness, disability and social exclusion: The archaeology and anthropology of difference,* ed. Jane Hubert, 196–207. London: Routledge.

Jones, Kathy. 1992. Listening to hidden voices: Power, domination, resistance and pleasure within Huronia Regional Centre. *Disability, Handicap & Society* 7, no. 4: 339–48.

Kleinman, Arthur. 1988. *The illness narratives: Suffering, healing and the human condition.* New York: Basic Books.

Kvale, Steinar. 1996. *InterViews: An introduction to qualitative research interviewing.* London: Sage.

Law Commission of Canada. 2000. *Restoring dignity: Responding to child abuse in Canadian institutions.* Gatineau, Quebec: Canada Minister of Public Works and Government Services.

Oliver, Mike. 1997. Emancipatory research: Realistic goal or impossible dream? In *Doing disability research,* ed. C. Barnes and G. Mercer. Leeds: Disability Press.

Reaume, Geoffrey. 2000. *Remembrance of patients past: Patient life at the Toronto Hospital for the Insane, 1870–1940.* Don Mills, Ontario: Oxford University Press.

Rooke, Patricia T., and R.L. Schnell. 1983. *Discarding the asylum: From child rescue to the welfare state in English Canada (1800–1850).* Boston, MA: University Press of America.

Sobsey, Dick. 1994. *Violence and abuse in the lives of people with disabilities: The end of silent acceptance.* Baltimore, MD: Paul H. Brookes Publishing Co.

Facilitating and hindering factors in the realization of disabled children's agency in institutional contexts: literature review

Johanna Olli[a], Tanja Vehkakoski[b] and Sanna Salanterä[a]

[a]Department of Nursing Science, University of Turku, Turku, Finland; [b]Department of Education, University of Jyväskylä, Jyväskylä, Finland

> Disabled children's opportunity to act as agents may be compromised because adults have the power to choose who are entitled to express agency. Disabled children spend much time in institutions and with professionals of different fields. The aim of this literature review was to find out which factors facilitate or hinder the realization of disabled children's agency in institutional contexts. As data we used 19 research articles and analysed them with inductive content analysis. Key factors relate to professionals' attitudes towards diversity, children and themselves as well as professionals' communication skills and institutional factors that enable the child to have an influence or prevent it and which give or do not give room for children's peer relationships. Rethinking the child and adult view and learning dialogical communication are recommended in the education of all fields that work with disabled children.

Points of interest

- Disabled children are not always given the opportunity to influence their own affairs.
- This article combines knowledge from 19 earlier research articles about professionals working with disabled children in school, health or social care.
- Professionals can help the child to have an influence on her/his own affairs by respecting diversity and children as individuals, by noticing their (professionals') own influence on children and by developing their (professionals') own communication skills.
- The structures of institutions and society also need developing in order to enable the child to have an influence and to allow space for children's peer relationships.
- Essential for the future education of all professionals working with disabled children: emphasizing child-centred attitudes and better communication skills

Introduction

Due to the contributions of childhood studies, children have been increasingly considered as active 'beings' and social actors with their own values and rights instead of only 'becomings' and objects of adult goals (for example, James and James 2004; Mayall 2002). From this perspective, researchers have become interested in examining children's agency and its realization in various institutional settings, such as schools (Rainio 2010), daycare centres (Vandenbroeck and Bouverne-De Bie 2006) and hospitals (Alderson, Hawthorne, and Killen 2005).

The concept of agency may be defined in various ways. Some researchers connect the concept to power and consider it as something that only some people have (Ahearn 2001). For example, according to Bandura (2001), the preconditions for the agency of an individual are the individual's capacities for intentionality, forethought, self-reactiveness and self-reflectiveness. In these kinds of definitions, agency has been considered a problematic concept when speaking of small or disabled children, because it has been questioned whether cognitive competence and autonomy as prerequisites of agency are actualized with them. The same interpretation appears in the Convention on the Rights of the Child (United Nations 1989), where the right to express her/his own views is assured only to the child who is capable of forming those views. Likewise, the Convention on the Rights of Persons with Disabilities (United Nations 2006) advises giving due weight to children's views in accordance with their age and maturity. Human right conventions thus promise many rights to children, but at the same time the conventions give adults the power to decide who can use those rights. That places small children with cognitive impairments, in particular, in danger of the disablist presuppositions of adults (Priestley 2003) without giving them the possibility to be heard (Davis and Watson 2000).

In this review the need for agency, or the need to have an influence on other human beings through communication, is understood as part of every human being's essence. According to Mayall (2002), an 'agent' is a person whose interaction makes a difference. The concept of agency is therefore differentiated from the concept of 'actorness', which is confined only to the description of acting, not the consequences (Mayall 2002). In this review, agency is seen as a feature in all human beings and the realization of agency as dependent on interactions with other people. Thus, in interaction a child's agency is realized when her/his need to have an influence is taken into account and responded to. Other peoples' inability to understand a child's self-expression or unwillingness to let the child have an influence may restrict the child's agency from being realized, but it does not eliminate the existence of agency.

Agency may be seen both as an intrinsic value like other human rights and as an instrumental value whose consequences are significant both for the disabled child and society. Important consequences for the child are the actualization of meaningful decisions in her/his life (Davis and Watson 2000; Loijas 1994; Mandich, Polatajko, and Rodger 2003), an increase of self-confidence (Franklin and Sloper 2008; Lightfoot and Sloper 2003; Mandich, Polatajko, and Rodger 2003), control of her/his own life (Loijas 1994) and the experience of being valued (Franklin and Sloper 2008; Kelly 2005). In addition, the realization of agency might increase the child's sense of belonging to a community (Mandich, Polatajko, and Rodger 2003; Milner and Kelly 2009), diversify the child's social relationships and strengthen her/his integration into society (Loijas 1994). From society's point of view, the realization of children's agency is related to the prevention of social exclusion because a lack of influence is related to exclusion from society (Lämsä 2009).

This review discusses studies that have examined disabled children's agency in relation to professionals working with children in different kinds of institutional contexts. As we illustrated earlier, living both as a child and a disabled person at the same time increases the risk of that child's agency not being realized. In addition, disabled children spend more time than other children in special institutional contexts (e.g. healthcare and habilitation/rehabilitation) and in institutions common to all children (e.g. daycare and school); they spend more time with professionals and under their surveillance (Rehm and Bradley 2006; Watson et al. 2000). This puts a great responsibility on professionals to facilitate these children's agency. This review seeks answers from the literature to the question of what factors facilitate or hinder the realization of disabled children's agency in institutional contexts.

Methods

In order to find studies about disabled children's agency, we carried out several searches in the following databases: Cinahl, Medline, Eric, PsycINFO, Sociological abstracts, SocIndex and Ebsco Academic Search Premier. Our search words were different combinations of the following: child*, disabilit*, developmental delay*, impair*, participation, involvement, agent, agency, inclusion and child's/children's perspective*/view*/experience*/attitude*. The searches demonstrated that it is extremely hard to find articles about agency because the word 'agency' has several meanings and because many articles concerning children's agency do not use the concept of agency. The search was made more challenging by the fact that we wanted to find studies conducted from the children's point of view. We approved as data for this review only two articles (Garth and Aroni 2003; Spitzer 2003) from those searches. Other articles included in the data were found by hand search from lists of references, conference presentations, recommendations from others or from searches carried out for other purposes. All the data were from the twenty-first century, although no time limitations were set.

For the final dataset we selected out of all the articles found by different channels those 19 articles that passed the following inclusion criteria: the article is about an empirical research study; the study has primarily sought children's point of view through interviews and/or observation of children's and professionals' interactions; and the study examined disabled children's life at least partly in an institutional context. In seven articles parents and in 10 articles professionals were also interviewed. However, children were the primary informants in all the studies. The majority of the studies were located in the school context, but there were also studies from different health and social care contexts. Detailed descriptions of the contexts, participants and data collection methods are presented in Table 1. We approved as data only studies whose trustworthiness could be evaluated on the basis of a thorough description of their data collection and analysis methods (see also Patton 2002).

The data were analysed by inductive content analysis. All of the expressions in the results sections of articles that described the actions of professionals which affected children's agency (in compliance with the above definition of agency) were underlined. The expressions were condensed into concise phrases that were grouped

Table 1. Description of the data.

Authors and year	Country	Participants	Data collection[a]	Methodological approach	Context
Alton-Lee et al. (2000)	New Zealand	15 children (0–1 class pupils), one professional	Observation (C, Pr) with audio/video records, interview (C, Pr)	Case studies	School
Beresford et al. (2007)	United Kingdom	100 children (2–19 years), parents	Interview (C), observation (C)	Qualitative research	Health/social care
Cameron and Murphy (2002)	United Kingdom	12 young people	Interview (C)	Pilot study	Speech and language therapy service
Cocks (2005)	United Kingdom	Children (age not known), professionals (48 situations during 12 months)	Observation (C, Pr)	Ethnography	Respite care + play and leisure setting
Connors and Stalker (2003)	United Kingdom	26 children (7–15 years), 38 parents	Interview (C, Pa)	Qualitative approach	Health, education and social services
Davis and Watson (2000)	United Kingdom	>300 children (11–16 years), professionals (14 schools)	Observation (C, Pr), interview (C, Pr)	Ethnography	School
Davis and Watson (2001)	United Kingdom	>300 children (11–16 years), professionals (14 schools)	Observation (C, Pr), interview (C, Pr)	Ethnography	School
Davis and Watson (2002)	United Kingdom	>300 children (11–16 years), professionals (14 schools)	Observation (C, Pr), interview (C, Pr)	Ethnography	School
Davis et al. (2000)	United Kingdom	Children (11–16 years), professionals (one school)	Observation (C, Pr), interview (C, Pr)	Ethnography	School
Franklin and Sloper (2008)	United Kingdom	21 children (5–18 years), 24 parents, 76 professionals	Interview (C, Pa, Pr)	Case studies	Social services
Garth and Aroni (2003)	Australia	4 children (6–12 years), six parents	Interview (C, Pa)	Qualitative pilot study	Healthcare
Higgins et al. (2009)	New Zealand	9 + 13 children (primary and secondary school pupils, parents, professionals (two research projects)	Observation (C, Pa, Pr), interview (C, Pa, Pr)	Ethnography + action research	School

(*Continued*)

Table 1. (Continued).

Authors and year	Country	Participants	Data collection[a]	Methodological approach	Context
Kelly (2005)	United Kingdom	32 children (2–16 years), 32 parents, 16 professionals	Interview (C, Pa, Pr)		Social service
Komulainen (2005)	United Kingdom	Children (2–8 years), professionals (two settings, several situations during nine months)	Observation (C, Pr)	Ethnography	Day nursery + assessment centre
Lightfoot and Sloper (2003)	United Kingdom	23 children (13–20 years), 13 professionals	Interview (C, Pr)		Health service
MacArthur et al. (2007)	New Zealand	Seven children (11–14 years), parents, professionals (3 days/month during 3 years)	Observation (C, Pa, Pr), interview (C, Pa, Pr)	Ethnography	School
Nind et al. (2010)	United Kingdom	Three children (4 years), parents, professionals	Observation (C, Pa, Pr), interview (Pa, Pr), documents	Qualitative case studies	Early childhood settings, home
Spitzer (2003)	United States	Five children (3–4 years), parents, professionals (several months)	Observation (C, Pa, Pr), interview (Pa, Pr)	Ethnography	School, therapy, home
Watson et al. (2000)	United Kingdom	>300 children (11–16 years), professionals (14 schools)	Observation (C, Pr), interview (C, Pr)	Ethnography	School

Note: [a]C, children/young people; Pa, parents; Pr, professionals.

by similarity. These groups were given descriptive names and called subcategories. Connectable subcategories were merged into main categories (attitudinal factors, communicational factors and institutional factors), and two themes were constituted: facilitating and hindering factors.

Facilitating and hindering factors of disabled children's agency

The realization of disabled children's agency in institutional contexts is facilitated and hindered by factors related to professionals' attitudes, professionals' communication skills and institutional factors (Table 2). Next, we will analyse these factors on the grounds of the studies selected as the data of this review.

Attitudinal factors

Professional's attitudes towards diversity

Professionals may look at diversity with respect or regard it as a negative deviation from 'normality'. Looking at the different needs and habits of children as a learning challenge in one's own professional practices (Higgins, MacArthur, and Kelly 2009) is an example of an attitude that facilitates the child's agency. In contrast are professionals' expressions that build the otherness of disabled children; for example, 'They are not like us' (Davis, Watson, and Cunningham-Burley 2000).

According to Davis and Watson (2000), building otherness is due to the use of normative and supposedly objective criteria. This places the burden of continuously proving their competency on the children (Davis and Watson 2000; Higgins, MacArthur, and Kelly 2009). In addition, normative-oriented and professional-centred ways of thinking might be barriers to understanding a child's personal way of thinking (Spitzer 2003) when the child's own interpretations of situations, instructions or equipment such as the toys used in tests are not accepted as valid (Komulainen 2005).

A normative idea of diversity may also lead to an emphasis on similarity, so that similar behaviour is demanded of every child, instead of seeing the complexity and skill of the child's actions in relation to the individual child (Spitzer 2003). Considering similarity as a prerequisite for belonging in a group may hinder the realization of the child's agency (MacArthur et al. 2007). Emphasizing similarity may also lead to illogical reasoning in which disability is seen as the only difference and characteristics such as gender are ignored (Watson et al. 2000).

Professionals' attitudes towards subjectivity

Seeing children through personal and cultural ideas of normality and diversity (Davis and Watson 2001) may cause children to be treated as objects instead of subjects (Davis and Watson 2001; Komulainen 2005) with their own views on issues of their lives and with the will to affect those issues. According to Davis and Watson (2000) a child's agency is facilitated by professionals' willingness and ability to believe the child and act on what the child says. Franklin and Sloper (2008) show that it is significant for children to see their opinions as making a difference in professionals' actions or even an institution's structures. When sharing their opinions does not affect their issues, the realization of children's agency is hindered (Franklin and Sloper 2008; Kelly 2005).

The realization of children's agency is facilitated by the possibility to choose their actions and company based on their own interests, not by adults' assumptions (Cocks 2005; Franklin and Sloper 2008). Franklin and Sloper (2008) emphasize that it is not only ideal for children to participate when deciding big issues, but also when deciding small issues such as the menu at a child's institution. However, quite often children are not heard when practices concerning them are planned (Davis and Watson 2001), even though professionals' and children's objectives do not always coincide (Komulainen 2005). A child's personal matters may also be discussed in the presence of the child as if she/he were not there (Watson et al. 2000), or her/his privacy may be violated; for example, by speaking about the child's personal matters in front of her/his schoolmates (Kelly 2005; Watson et al. 2000).

Regarding children primarily as individuals, instead of looking at a child through her/his impairment or a label attributed to her/him facilitates children's agency (Davis and Watson 2000). Also, concentrating on the child's strengths and expecting her/his best effort facilitates agency (Higgins, MacArthur, and Kelly 2009). Adults' belief in a child's competency empowers her/him to make decisions concerning her/his life (Davis and Watson 2000; Nind, Flewitt, and Payler 2010). To this end, Kelly (2005) states that professionals should not only see the services they offer as important, but other aspects of the child's life as well. However, professionals may have prejudices about the impacts of an impairment on the child's life and always see her/him through her/his impairment (Davis and Watson 2002). This may lead to interpreting the child's behaviour that expresses agency (such as disagreeing with adults) as caused by her/his impairment and as punishable, even though the same kind of behaviour from non-disabled children is ignored or is interpreted as a positive expression of agency (MacArthur et al. 2007).

Children feel that professionals' overprotecting practices are an underestimation of their abilities (Davis and Watson 2001) as well as that too low expectations hinder the realization of their agency (MacArthur et al. 2007). Underestimation may be caused by a professional's views on what a child can or cannot achieve in the future (Davis and Watson 2000) or their views that the child's repetitive activity (such as flicking materials) is not a meaningful action, but a symptom of her/his impairment (Cocks 2005; Spitzer 2003). Choice-making that is essentially related to agency may be prevented by a professional ignoring the choice-making ability of a child (Davis and Watson 2000).

Professionals' attitudes towards the influence of their own actions and the environment

Davis and Watson (2000) demonstrate how the realization of children's agency is facilitated when their competency is seen as situated and fluid. In that kind of case, professionals pay attention to the influence of the situation and the context, and do not see all of the children's problems as innate (cf. Komulainen 2005) and caused by their impairment (Davis and Watson 2000). For example, in Davis' and Watson's (2000) study, one child's intended exclusion from 'mainstream' school, ordered because of the child's problematic behaviour, was cancelled when professionals observed the situation with an open mind and discovered that the child's behaviour was not due to his impairment but to other children teasing him.

Professionals may also be incapable or unwilling to evaluate their own actions and their influence on the child or to question their own interpretations of the

Table 2. Facilitating and hindering factors in the realization of disabled children's agency in institutional contexts.

Facilitating	Hindering
Attitudinal factors	
Valuing diversity	Seeing diversity as a negative deviation from normality
Valuing the child • seeing the child as the subject of her/his own life • seeing the child as an individual • concentrating on the child's strengths	Undervaluing the child • seeing the child as an object of professionals' actions • seeing the child through her/his impairment • concentrating on the child's limitations
Taking into account the influence of professionals' own actions, the situation and the environment	Interpreting problems as always caused by the child's impairment
Communicational factors	
Using dialogical communication • having a willingness to create a relationship with the child • changing the power relationship • engaging in a communication process where the meanings and discussion subjects are negotiated	Communicating on professionals' terms • keeping a distance with the child • maintaining the power relationship • holding on to presuppositions or professionals' chosen discussion subjects and presupposed meanings
Solving communication problems by developing professional skills • seeing problems as dependent on the situation and the professionals' skills • reacting to the content of the child's message • using communication methods which enable the child to express her/his own views	Not solving the professional's communication problems at all • seeing problems only as caused by the child's impairment • reacting only to the way that the child's message is expressed • using communication methods which makes the expression of the child's own views impossible
Institutional factors	
Institutional structures enabling the child to have an influence • seeing the child as a client • having enough time to listen to the child • depending on societal values and decisions grounded on respecting diversity and the child's views	Institutional structures preventing the child from having an influence • seeing only parents as clients • not having enough time to listen to the child • depending on societal values and decisions emphasizing quick changes, measurable results and cognitive competence
Establishing a social order which gives room for children's peer relationships	Establishing a strict social order directed by professionals

child's behaviour (Davis and Watson 2000). For example, if only adults' chosen alternatives are given when a choice is to be made, the child may not want to choose any of the alternatives. Professionals may interpret this as the child not being able to choose, even though the alternatives were too limited to choose among (Komulainen 2005). Their view of 'communication difficulties' as a quantifiable, measurable and pathological phenomenon (Komulainen 2005) only focus on the child's communication skills, even though situations interpreted as a child's problem in understanding may be due to the professional's insufficient skill of expressing herself/himself in a way that is understandable to the child (Connors and Stalker 2003; Davis and Watson 2002).

Communicational factors
The dialogicality of communication
There is evidence that communication which facilitates the realization of the child's agency is grounded on the professional's willingness to create a relationship with the child, to change traditional power relationships and to be flexible (Davis and Watson 2001). In contrast, keeping a distance from or ignoring the child hinders the child's agency (Davis and Watson 2002) because the child may feel that the professional does not like her/him and the child may be scared of her/him (Kelly 2005).

Dialogical communication is grounded on supposing that a child's action has a meaning and on avoiding presuppositions of what that meaning is for the child (Davis and Watson 2002). According to Spitzer (2003), understanding the meaning may require seeing the action as meaningful to the child even though it may seem meaningless to an adult. This requires engaging in a communication process in which meanings are negotiated (Davis and Watson 2002) by communicating directly with the child, asking questions and allowing her/him to ask questions (Garth and Aroni 2003). If the child is not allowed to have an influence on the subjects discussed, she/he cannot raise issues that are important to her/him (Lightfoot and Sloper 2003). Professionals' eager prompting may also restrict the child's communicative space (Nind, Flewitt, and Payler 2010).

Solutions to communication problems
As mentioned above, seeing communication problems as a shared problem facilitates the realization of children's agency. Davis and Watson (2002) state that if the professional refuses to change her/him first impression about a failure in communication as the child's fault, the communication will not evolve into dialogue. Sometimes a new opportunity for dialogue is needed and apologizing to the child is necessary if the professional's behaviour has been patronizing (Davis and Watson 2002). According to MacArthur et al. (2007), communication may also fail if professionals respond only to how the child expresses the message (such as with a loud volume), not to the content of the message.

To be able to facilitate the children's agency, professionals need knowledge about and the ability to use alternative and augmentative communication such as signing, picture communication and communication devices. Insufficient alternative and augmentative communication skills hinder the child's agency if the child does not talk or uses talking only as a part of hers/his communication (Beresford, Rabiee, and Sloper 2007; Kelly 2005). Instead, a child's agency is facilitated when she/he has the opportunity to choose among several methods of communication; for example, play, projective techniques, drawing or emotion cards (Kelly 2005) or gaze, action and speech (Nind, Flewitt, and Payler 2010). According to Cameron and Murphy (2002), good features for a communication technique that makes it easy to ask the child's opinion are the following: the child enjoys using it, using it is not grounded on right or wrong answers, answers can be altered and the child is allowed to use as much time with it as she/he wants. In addition, it is useful to take photographs of the result of the conversation so that it is easy to later return to it (Cameron and Murphy 2002). If no concrete instruments for communication can be found, the professional can facilitate the child's agency by learning to infer the meanings of the child's actions from observed cues and from knowledge of hers/his history, or what she/he senses from the child's participation in the activity (Spitzer 2003).

Institutional factors
The child's clientship
There is evidence that many institutions are structured so that the children are approached through her/his parents or a professional responsible for the child. These 'gatekeepers' may facilitate the realization of a child's agency if they think that the child has relevant opinions and feelings that should be taken into account in the professionals' meetings such as the care plan reviews (Kelly 2005). However, they might also prevent professionals from approaching the child in order to ask her/his opinion (Franklin and Sloper 2004). According to Garth and Aroni (2003), children do value being present when issues relating to them are being discussed even if they may not understand the entire discussion.

In some institutions it is unclear whether the client is the child, the parents or both. This structural unclarity sometimes places professionals in a difficult situation if they want to facilitate the child's agency. When a decision regarding professional practices needs to be made, parents are often the only ones asked about matters concerning the needs of the child even though they do not always allow the child's opinions to influence their decisions (Kelly 2005). Sometimes professionals feel forced into the role of a conciliator between the child and her/his parents (Franklin and Sloper 2004), and at times they comply with the parents' wishes; for example, pressuring the child to go to an unpleasant respite care (Kelly 2005).

Institutional factors and the child's possibilities to have an influence
Institutional factors may hinder the realization of children's agency if children's participation in decision-making is not embedded in the culture of an organization (Franklin and Sloper 2008). Moreover, the cultural atmosphere of the institution affects how easy it is for professionals to listen to the child (Davis and Watson 2000).

Essential to the children's agency are circumstances where children can empower themselves (Davis, Watson, and Cunningham-Burley 2000) instead of structural solutions in which the child feels different and incompetent and which the child cannot influence (Higgins, MacArthur, and Kelly 2009). For example, MacArthur et al. (2007) describe a structural solution that ignores the child's opinion placing a girl who has a physical impairment in a class where all the others are boys with 'challenging behaviours'. In that class the girl was bullied and found learning difficult. Another example of hindering the child's agency is giving her/him equipment that she/he does not want to use because it separates her/him from other children in an unpleasant way (MacArthur et al. 2007).

One institutional factor that hinders children's agency is professionals' lack of time (Beresford, Rabiee, and Sloper 2007). As Franklin and Sloper (2008) have noticed, many professionals need more time than usual to observe a child, prepare material in an alternative communication form or to cooperate with adults familiar with that child's style of communication.

Furthermore, wider societal decisions have effects on children's agency. This includes, for example, institutional funding (Davis and Watson 2001; Franklin and Sloper 2008) and national targets in school – if a teacher wants to meet those targets, she/he can only have a few children with learning difficulties in her/his class (Davis and Watson 2001). According to Franklin and Sloper (2008), other factors related to society's structures are rapidly changing environments and the requirement for quick results. These requirements do not take into account that listening to the child's view may produce significant results even if the results are not visible in the short term (Franklin and Sloper 2008).

The management of children's peer relations

Children's agency can be realized in a flexible and changeable social order in which professionals give children room to create their own relationships, as Cocks (2005) describes in her study. Professionals may think that children need constant direction when creating and maintaining friendships, but studies have shown that this is an incorrect assumption (Cocks 2005; Watson et al. 2000). Instead, being under the constant surveillance of adults might keep disabled children from joining their peer group (Connors and Stalker 2003; Kelly 2005; Watson et al. 2000), as might restrictions set by adults such as forbidding the child from visiting their friends (Kelly 2005). When the professional who assists the child steps back, it gives the child space to be part of the peer group (MacArthur et al. 2007). Children's agency can be facilitated by giving them the freedom to choose their own roles in their peer group and to choose companions who share their own interests, not those with similar assumed skills or a similar lack of skills (Cocks 2005).

Sometimes facilitating a child's agency requires professionals to create opportunities where the child can be accepted by other children. For example, situations may be organized for children to make their own decisions in a peer group that is facilitated but not led by a professional (Davis and Watson 2000). Cocks (2005) demonstrates that often opportunities for children to share experiences with others who have a shared history are dependent on adults' organizational decisions. Higgins, MacArthur, and Kelly (2009) describe how children's agency may also be facilitated on occasions where children's 'becoming visible' to each other is made possible; for example, a drama project arranged for both disabled and non-disabled children. Likewise, resisting segregating practices may facilitate a child's agency because the child does not miss the activities of her/his own group (Higgins, MacArthur, and Kelly 2009).

In a group of children a child's agency may be facilitated by offering the child a role that allows other children to notice her/his strengths first, not her/his impairment. A professional can give a child the responsibility of teaching something she/he already knows or of otherwise helping other children (Alton-Lee et al. 2000; Connors and Stalker 2003; Higgins, MacArthur, and Kelly 2009). If a child is being bullied, the professional can make educational (i.e. indirect) interventions in which the child is not a passive object, unlike in disciplinary (i.e. direct) interventions

(Alton-Lee et al. 2000). As MacArthur et al. (2007) demonstrate, professionals may also support the child in defending herself/himself against bullying.

Discussion

In this review we sought facilitating and hindering factors in the realization of disabled children's agency in institutional contexts. Significant factors seem to relate either to professionals' attitudes and communication or to the structural and cultural factors of institutions and society. Underlying all of these factors appears to be professionals' attitudes towards children's diversity and individuality and towards their own contribution in working with the child. Conceptions of disability, childhood and professionality are strongly intertwined.

Health, social and educational sciences have made an attempt to substitute professional-centred, behaviouristic and paternalistic ways of thinking with more child-centred or child-originated and more constructivist theories that aim to empower the client. Yet it seems that the old models live on in the practices of the care and education of disabled children. In this review the data on professional practices concerning agency did not differ according to field (health, social or educational), but differences were found between institutions and individual professionals in all fields. Common to those professionals who facilitated children's agency seemed to be seeing disability in line with the social model of disability and seeing childhood in line with the new sociology of childhood. Also common to them seemed to be that their professional self-efficacy was so strong they could confess their ignorance and could engage in unpredictable dialogue with a child. Listening to and understanding a child seems to require giving up a power relationship in which one person places oneself above another and knows better or acts on her/his behalf. As Sieppert and Unrau (2003) state, children's possibility to influence issues in their own lives may stop where adults think they know what is best for the child and professionals think they know what is best for the client.

In this review the concept of agency is defined somewhat differently from previous research (for example, Ahearn 2001; Bandura 2001), as agency is seen here as a feature of all human beings, the realization of which is dependent on interactions with other people. This led to seeing agency where it would not have been seen with other definitions (e.g. in children with severe cognitive impairments). As data for this review we chose only studies in which children had been heard and their own perspectives valued. Probably due to this, all of the articles aimed at promoting children's agency and identifying best practices for communicating with children. Some of the articles used the same data as other articles (e.g. all of Davis and Watson's articles used the same data, and Higgins et al. and MacArthur et al. partly used the same data), but we included them because every article had some new insights.

Results of this review have been systematically drawn from results of the original studies, and only this discussion section goes beyond the references. However, as always in qualitative studies, we as researchers were the instrument that processed the data and therefore it is useful for the reader to know also something about us (Patton 2002). Our professional and academic experience of the institutional situation of disabled children served as the background for our interpretations: one of us has worked as a nurse with disabled children in a hospital, another has researched professionals' attitudes towards disabled children, and the third is an experienced researcher of sick and healthy children's nursing care. Our academic backgrounds consist mainly of nursing science and special education (both of these with a history of emphasizing the medical model of disability), but two of us also have knowledge of disability studies and childhood studies.

Finding data for this review was challenging, which speaks of how rarely disabled children have been researched from the point of view of agency. All of the data found were from the twenty-first century, so this perspective is quite new and has been the focus of only a few research groups. Especially rare has been research on small children with cognitive impairments in the healthcare context, even though healthcare in many countries is the first stop for interventions for these children. Specifically, small children's views are often ignored even in contexts where there are specific systems for listening to children (such as the family group conference; Heino 2009). It would be important to regard disabled children's human worth and human rights as similar to others from the very beginning. As Cocks (2000) states, segregating disabled children in their own institutions and treating them as passive objects of adults' interventions reflects the fact that people see passive adulthood as suitable for them.

In future it would be significant to emphasize child-centred attitudes and dialogical communication in the basic and further education of all professionals working with disabled children. These are enabled only if professionals can see children as both competent and incomplete, as Cocks (2006), Komulainen (2007) and Lee (1998) suggest. It would be essential for professionals to see incompleteness and fallibility also in themselves – and yet, at the same time, to be able to value themselves and their professionality. This is related to seeing aspects shared with all human beings (such as the need for agency) in both children and in professionals and seeing diversity as a richness in all of us. It might be useful to see that changing professional practices towards facilitating children's agency would also have positive outcomes for professionals: their professional behaviour changes when they realize that they do not always know what is important to children – and that children have much to say that is worth listening to (Karlsson 2009; Lightfoot and Sloper 2003). Most essential would be, however, to concentrate on agency as an intrinsic value (i.e. a universal human right), because seeing agency as an instrumental value gives adults too many opportunities to speculate about who will benefit from it and who will not.

References

Ahearn, L. 2001. Language and agency. *Annual Review of Anthropology* 30: 109–37.
Alderson, P., J. Hawthorne, and M. Killen. 2005. The participation rights of premature babies. *The International Journal of Children's Rights* 13, nos. 1–2: 31–50.
Alton-Lee, A., C. Rietveld, L. Klenner, N. Dalton, C. Duggins, and S. Town. 2000. Inclusive practice within the lived cultures of school communities: Research case studies in teaching, learning and inclusion. *International Journal of Inclusive Education* 4, no. 3: 179–210.
Bandura, A. 2001. Social cognitive theory: An agentic perspective. *Annual Reviews* 52: 1–26.
Beresford, B., P. Rabiee, and P. Sloper. 2007. *Priorities and perceptions of disabled children and young people and their parents regarding outcomes from support services.* York: The University of York, Social Policy Research Unit.
Cameron, L., and J. Murphy. 2002. Enabling young people with a learning disability to make choices at a time of transition. *British Journal of Learning Disabilities* 30: 105–12.

Cocks, A. 2000. Respite care for disabled children: Micro and macro reflections. *Disability & Society* 15, no. 3: 507–19.

Cocks, A.J. 2005. The peer groups of children with learning impairments. In *Another disability studies reader? Including people with learning difficulties*, ed. D. Goodley and G. van Hove, 75–91. Antwerpen: Garant Publishers.

Cocks, A.J. 2006. The ethical maze: Finding an inclusive path towards gaining children's agreement to research participation. *Childhood* 13, no. 2: 247–66.

Connors, C., and K. Stalker. 2003. *The views and experiences of disabled children and their siblings*. London: Jessica Kingsley Publishers.

Davis, J., and N. Watson. 2000. Disabled children's rights in every day life: Problematising notions of competency and promoting self-empowerment. *The International Journal of Children's Rights* 8, no. 3: 211–28.

Davis, J.M., and N. Watson. 2001. Where are the children's experiences? Analysing social and cultural exclusion in 'special' and 'mainstream' schools. *Disability & Society* 16, no. 5: 671–87.

Davis, J., and N. Watson. 2002. Countering stereotypes of disability: Disabled children and resistance. In *Disability/postmodernity: Embodying disability theory*, ed. M. Corker and T. Shakespeare, 159–74. London: Continuum.

Davis, J., N. Watson, and S. Cunningham-Burley. 2000. Learning the lives of disabled children. Developing a reflexive approach. In *Research with children. Perspectives and practices*, ed. P. Christensen and A. James, 201–24. London: Routledge Falmer.

Franklin, A., and P. Sloper. 2004. *Participation of disabled children and young people in decision-making within social services departments.* Interim report. York: The University of York.

Franklin, A., and P. Sloper. 2008. Supporting the participation of disabled children and young people in decision-making. *Children & Society* 23, no. 1: 3–15.

Garth, B., and R. Aroni. 2003. 'I value what you have to say'. Seeking the perspective of children with a disability, not just their parents. *Disability & Society* 18, no. 5: 561–76.

Heino, T. 2009. *Family group conference from a child perspective*. Nordic Research Report 13/2009. Helsinki: National Institute for Health and Welfare. http://www.thl.fi/thl-client/pdfs/da905b95-70f6-4db8-9d82-91b74fe55ed0.

Higgins, N., J. MacArthur, and B. Kelly. 2009. Including disabled children at school: Is it really as simple as 'a, c, d'? *International Journal of Inclusive Education* 13, no. 5: 471–87.

James, A., and A. James. 2004. *Constructing childhood. Theory, policy and social practice.* New York: Palgrave Macmillan.

Karlsson, L. 2009. To construct a bridge of sharing between child and adult culture with the storycrafting method. In *Arts contact points between cultures, 1st International Journal of Intercultural Arts Education Conference*, ed. H. Ruismäki and I. Ruokonen, 117–28. Research report 312. Helsinki: University of Helsinki. Department of Applied Sciences of Education. https://helda.helsinki.fi/bitstream/handle/10138/14969/RR312_verkkoversio.pdf.

Kelly, B. 2005. Chocolate ... makes you autism: Impairment, disability and childhood identities. *Disability and Society* 20, no. 3: 261–75.

Komulainen, S. 2005. The contextuality of children's communication difficulties in specialist practice. A sociological account. *Child Care in Practice* 11, no. 3: 357–74.

Komulainen, S. 2007. The ambiguity of the child's 'voice' in social research. *Childhood* 14, no. 1: 11–28.

Lämsä, A.-L. 2009. *Tuhat tarinaa lasten ja nuorten syrjäytymisestä* [A thousand stories about exclusion among children and young people]. Acta Universitatis Ouluensis E 102. Oulu: Faculty of Education, University of Oulu.

Lee, N. 1998. Towards an immature sociology. *The Sociological Review* 46, no. 3: 459–82.

Lightfoot, J., and P. Sloper. 2003. Having a say in health: Involving young people with a chronic illness or physical disability in a local health services development. *Children & Society* 17, no. 4: 277–90.

Loijas, S. 1994. *Rakas rämä elämä. Vammaisten nuorten elämänhallinta ja elämänkulku* [The life-course and control of own life of young disabled people]. Raportteja 155. Helsinki: Stakes.

MacArthur, J., S. Sharp, B. Kelly, and M. Gaffney. 2007. Disabled children negotiating school life: Agency, difference and teaching practice. *International Journal of Children's Rights* 15, no. 1: 99–120.

Mandich, A.D., H.J. Polatajko, and S. Rodger. 2003. Rites of passage: Understanding participation of children with developmental coordination disorder. *Human Movement Science* 22, no. 4–5: 583–95.

Mayall, B. 2002. *Towards a sociology for childhood. Thinking from children's lives*. Maidenhead: Open University Press.

Milner, P., and B. Kelly. 2009. Community participation and inclusion: People with disabilities defining their place. *Disability & Society* 24, no. 1: 47–62.

Nind, M., R. Flewitt, and J. Payler. 2010. The social experience of early childhood for children with learning disabilities: Inclusion, competence and agency. *British Journal of Sociology of Education* 31, no. 6: 653–70.

Patton, M.Q. 2002. *Qualitative research and evaluation methods*. 3rd rev. ed. Thousand Oaks, CA: Sage Publications.

Priestley, M. 2003. *Disability: A life course approach*. Cambridge: Polity Press.

Rainio, A. 2010. *Lionhearts of the playworld – An ethnographic case study of the development of agency in play pedagogy*. Studies in Educational Sciences 233. Helsinki: University of Helsinki. http://helda.helsinki.fi/handle/10138/19883.

Rehm, R., and J. Bradley. 2006. Social interactions at school of children who are medically fragile and developmentally delayed. *Journal of Pediatric Nursing* 21, no. 4: 299–307.

Sieppert, J.D., and Y.A. Unrau. 2003. Revisiting the Calgary Project evaluation: A look at children's participation in family group conferencing. *Protecting Children* 18, no. 1–2: 113–8.

Spitzer, S. 2003. With and without words: Exploring occupation in relation to young children with autism. *Journal of Occupational Science* 10, no. 2: 67–79.

United Nations. 1989. Convention on the Rights of the Child. http://www2.ohchr.org/english/law/crc.htm.

United Nations. 2006. Convention on the Rights of Persons with Disabilities. http://www.un.org/disabilities/default.asp?id=259.

Vandenbroeck, M., and M. Bouverne-De Bie. 2006. Children's agency and educational norms: A tensed negotiation. *Childhood* 13, no. 1: 127–43.

Watson, N., T. Shakespeare, S. Cunningham-Burley, C. Barnes, M. Corker, J. Davis, and M. Priestley. 2000. *Life as a disabled child: A qualitative study of young people's experiences and perspectives*. Final report to the ESRC. Edinburgh: University of Edinburgh, Department on Nursing Studies. http://www.leeds.ac.uk/disability-studies/projects/children.htm.

No safety net for disabled children in residential institutions in Ireland

Pauline Conroy

Independent social researcher, Dublin, Ireland

The voices of adults and children with disabilities who have experienced violence and abuse are slowly beginning to surface in the public domain. Segregated residential institutions run by religious congregations appear to be dangerous places for children with disabilities and perceived differences – according to the former residents, speaking and communicating to us today as adults in Ireland. A statutory Commission to Inquire into Child Abuse in Ireland attracted important numbers of former residents – witnesses – who recounted appalling experiences of violence as children. The UN Convention on the Rights of Persons with Disabilities contains articles concerning the prevention of cruelty, sexual assault, violence and acts of humiliation that may be useful for countries like Ireland which have been unable to ratify the Convention. The protection of children with disabilities requires legal reform in Ireland, statutory licensing, monitoring and inspection of the segregated centres where children with disabilities are living.

Points of interest

- More and more studies are revealing violence and abuse against children and young people with disabilities.
- Specific articles in the UN Convention on the Rights of Persons with Disabilities addressing freedom from abuse and cruelty remain essential.
- The voices of adults with disabilities in Ireland who have experienced extreme violence and abuse as children in residential institutions are finally being legitimised.
- Monitoring and inspection of residential institutions where children with disabilities are living is one of the crucial methods to reduce violence and abuse – be it physical, sexual, emotional or neglect.

Introduction

More than 100 countries have ratified the UN Convention on the Rights of Persons with Disabilities, which came into force in 2006. In the European Union, 18 of the 27

Member States have ratified the Convention. This group of countries includes states from northern Europe such as Sweden, the United Kingdom and Denmark, Mediterranean states such as Italy and Portugal, and newer Member States such as Latvia, Lithuania and Slovenia. Of the nine Member States that had not yet ratified the Convention by June 2011, four are recently joined members of the European Union: Malta, Bulgaria, Poland, and Estonia. Ireland, Luxembourg, Finland, Greece and the Netherlands have not signed the Convention and stand out as exceptions in that they are longstanding members of the European Union. The European Union itself ratified the Convention on 5 January 2011, the first time in history that the European Union has become a party to a human rights treaty (Europa 2011). The Convention does not create new rights for people with disabilities. Its 50 Articles spell out in detail, in a single and coherent document, the rights and freedoms of people with disabilities and the obligations of governments, which had previously been scattered across a range of international laws and instruments (United Nations 2006a).

Articles 15 and 16 are of particular interest to people with disabilities who have experienced violence and abuse. They are equally of interest to their families and supporters as well as public and private providers of services. Article 15 provides that people with disabilities will have 'freedom from torture or cruel, inhuman or degrading treatment or punishment'. Article 15 prohibits medical or scientific experimentation on any person without their free consent. Article 16 declares 'freedom from exploitation, violence and abuse'. It describes five areas of state obligation or duty towards people with disabilities. Firstly, governments must do all that is possible to protect people with disabilities from exploitation, violence or abuse at home or outside the home. Secondly, governments must take actions to prevent violence and ensure that people with disabilities are able to recognise and report violence and abuse.

Thirdly, states must ensure that facilities designed for people with disabilities are independently monitored. Fourthly, public authorities have the duty to promote the physical and mental recovery, rehabilitation and integration of persons who have experienced abuse, exploitation or violence in an environment that promotes dignity and autonomy. Fifthly, states must have legislation and policies, including gender-focused and child-focused dimensions, in order to identify, investigate and prosecute instances of exploitation, violence and abuse. The Convention on the Rights of Persons with Disabilities has to be read in conjunction with the UN Convention on the Rights of the Child of 1989 – in particular Article 19, which states that:

> States parties shall take all appropriate legislative, administrative social and educational measures to protect the child from all forms of physical or mental violence, injury or abuse, neglect or negligent treatment, maltreatment or exploitation, including sexual abuse, while in the care of parent(s), legal guardian(s) or any other person who has the care of the child. (United Nations 1989, Article 19)

Conventions are not a substitute for the social movements and shifts in power that will force forward and redress the effective exclusion of people with disabilities from major public and social forums (Barnes and Sheldon 2011). Unlike European Directives or Regulations, Member States cannot be forced to adopt Conventions. The 2006 UN Convention, while synthesising and interpreting existing human rights into a helpful programmatic summary, can nevertheless raise expectations of what ought to be delivered in public policy; and to this extent, their ratification can be a useful step in reconfiguring thinking about policy.

Children with disabilities have been identified as one of the more vulnerable groups of children among the eight million children in residential care across the world and who experience violence and abuse in care (Morris 1997; United Nations 2006b, 16). Children may be subject to abuse not only by staff, but also, as a consequence of neglect, by their peers. An International Save the Children Alliance report noted that children with disabilities are often in residential care not because they need nursing or medical care but because they have been abandoned or rejected (International Save the Children Alliance 2003, 16). Cousins, Monteith, and Kerry (2003) demonstrate that, despite policy narrative to the contrary, high proportions of disabled children spend time in residential schools, hospitals and respite centres. Morris (2001a, 2001b) has repeatedly stressed that young people with high levels of support needs rarely get a chance to give their own opinions or feel restricted less by their impairment than by the absence of supports, hence the importance of consulting with children with disabilities (Whyte, 2006).

The UN Convention has had an influence in Europe. It is shaping the European's Union's disability strategy for the period 2010–2020 to some extent (European Commission 2010, 3). The strategy proposes to support 'national efforts to achieve the transition from institutional to community-based care' (2010, 6). The strategy, however, makes no reference to the violence and exploitation experienced by adults and children with disabilities, despite long-standing support for such actions through the European Union DAPHNE programme administered by the Commission's Justice Directorate. The programme supported more than 30 large multi-country projects on violence against adults and children with disabilities between 1997 and 2006 (European Commission 2008). With implications wider than the European Union, the European Court of Human Rights, in a Swiss disability discrimination case, made reference to the UN Convention as a new standard, whether countries like Switzerland had ratified it or not, and in the case of Switzerland it had failed to ratify the Convention.[1]

The slow pace of policy change towards the rights of people with disabilities at the level of the European Union may, to an extent, be found in the unresolved past of eugenic influences on public policy in the 1930s and 1940s, and in particular in Germany, among the medical profession (Weindling 1987; Hanauske-Abel 1996). The belief that some life is unworthy of living, that some human beings have less humanity and are subhuman, spread widely and enthusiastically among European scientific and intellectual circles. The beliefs provided the rationale for wide-ranging programmes of extermination of first children and then adults who had disabilities, and in particular those with developmental disabilities and the mentally ill in Germany and Austria. Starting in 1939 tens of thousands of disabled people were put to death having been first selected by doctors, nurses and administrators. By 1941, in the first wave of killings, about 70,000 had been murdered in institutions usually without the knowledge of their families. One in four of the first wave died in Hartheim Castle near Linz in Austria. The extermination programmes continued with a variety of names and titles. Some authors consider negative eugenic concerns may be reappearing in new guises in the field of genetic testing and the treatment of certain mental illnesses (Wiener, Ribeiro, and Warner 2009).

Ignoring or neglecting the phenomena of violence against persons with disabilities, and children in particular, renders it quite invisible despite its high prevalence. The first findings of the largest known survey of crime against people with disabilities have been published in the United States by the US Department of Justice

(2009). It confirms that people with disabilities are more likely to be victims of crime. Children and youth aged 12–19 years had experienced violence at nearly twice the rate of those children and youth without a disability. Persons with a disability had an age-adjusted rate of rape or sexual assault that was more than twice the rate for persons without a disability. The National Crime Victimisation Survey is based on a sample survey of 76,000 households containing 135,300 adults, youth and children aged 12 years or more. Women and girls with a disability had a higher victimisation rate than boys and men with disabilities. The rate of victimisation of women and girls was almost twice the rate compared with women and girls with no disability. The survey found that people who had a cognitive disability had a particularly high rate of crime victimisation. This was the case for both men/boys and women/girls with cognitive disabilities. Even here the victimisation rate for women/girls with a cognitive disability was higher again than those for men/boys with such a disability; a gender bias reinforced by other studies (Nixon 2009; International Network of Women with Disabilities 2010).

The US survey is consistent with the Mencap (2007) study in the United Kingdom, which found that 82% of children with a learning disability – 280,000 children – are bullied, leaving many of them frightened to leave their own homes. Others manage to cope with the support of friends (Burke and Burgman 2010). An example of bullying cited by the Mencap study was actually a physical assault requiring 18 stitches in the forehead of a child with a learning disability (2007, 3). In this regard, the conceptualisation of violence against people with disabilities as a form of hate crime makes sense (Thomas 2011; Chakroborti 2010; Quarmby 2008).

A confluence of historic and contemporary forces have formed and modernised the disenfranchisement of people with disabilities, and of children in particular, according to McDonnell (2007, 147–179).The older separatist institutions, owned and maintained by religious orders and funded by the state, have strongly interacted with modern expertism and highly individualised pathology frameworks. This has generated new normalisation perspectives that dissipate and disperse difference into rebranded mainstream institutions. The reduction in places in residential care institutions has been frequently replaced by equally institutionalised, medicalised and sometimes overcrowded community care homes (Conroy 2010b). Despite change, the institutional power of large-scale religious-operated but state-supported services for people with disabilities remain.

The case of Ireland

The public and private treatment of children in care, and in residential care in particular, has been a highly sensitive, controversial topic and unresolved policy concern in Ireland for the last decade (Rafferty and O'Sullivan 1999). Within the context of unfolding scandals of abuse of children in residential centres run by religious orders, widespread abuse of boys by priests, as well as a systemic neglect of children in need, acceptance that abuse of disabled children actually occurred was reluctant. Bob McCormack, writing of Ireland, observed that:

> The realisation that children with disabilities were at risk of sexual abuse was slow to be acknowledged. The thought that the most vulnerable children in society were the most abused was so abhorrent as to (be) inconceivable to many. (2005, 1)

His observations are consistent with those of the NSPCC (2003) for the United Kingdom.

In a 2002 study of sexual abuse and violence in Ireland that addressed the sexual abuse of people with learning disabilities, the authors found staff or directors of two centres refused to participate in the study unless questions about reporting of cases was removed from the questionnaire or on the grounds that the study might 're-traumatise the participants' and 'no resources were available to mitigate the trauma' (McGee et al. 2002, 248). This minimisation and refusal to accept the threat of violence against children with disabilities is a persistent challenge to child protection policies. Add to this the particularity of clericalism in Ireland and a noxious mixture is created. Authoritarianism and defensiveness feed each other.

A build-up of allegations that children had been and continued to be abused in residential institutions run by Catholic religious orders mounted at the end of the 1990s. Cultural activism played an important part in generating doubt and unease among the general public concerning the *bona fides* of such charitable institutions. Cultural influences played a part in bringing the subject to a head (Smith 2007, 87–112). The UK film *Lamb* (1985) starring Liam Neeson and directed by Colin Gregg was loosely based on real events that occurred in Ireland and Scotland in 1978. Louis Lentin's 1996 film *Dear Daughter* revealed allegations of vicious treatment of girls in the care of the state in an institution run by the Sisters of Mercy. Journalist Mary Rafferty's three-part television documentary *States of Fear* in 1999 brought the systematic ill-treatment of children in care in religious-run industrial schools to a wider Irish public. Disability activist Paddy Doyle had written his autobiography 10 years earlier, recounting his treatment as a child, but few journalists reviewed it (Doyle 1988). In a similar vein, warnings that the child protection system was wholly inadequate attracted weak responses (McGrath 1996) despite efforts at law reform (The Law Reform Commission 1990).

In 2000 the Irish Government established a statutory Commission to Inquire into Child Abuse, which published a five-volume report in 2009 chaired by a judge (Commission to Inquire into Child Abuse 2009). The Commission explored the treatment of former residents in relation to physical, sexual, emotional abuse and neglect. The Commission itself travelled to the United Kingdom and the United States to hear testimony from Irish emigrants. Over the decade, 1500 adults who had lived in a variety of care settings came forward or engaged with the Commission. The Commission held public hearings where state officials and religious orders were questioned about the allegations of abuse. Some survivor witnesses opted to claim compensation at a Redress Board. Over 1000 former residents gave evidence of their experiences to a special Confidential Committee made up of Commissioners (Commission to Inquire into Child Abuse 2009, vol. III). No questionnaires were used and witnesses could tell their story in their own way. Witnesses could have an accompanying person with them, when telling their stories. Sign language interpreters were employed by the Commission.

Some 58 witnesses to the Confidential Committee reported abuse they had experienced as children in 'special schools' prior to the 1970s and up the 1990s. 'Special' schools, 'special' needs, 'special' education are the terms used in Ireland in service provision and in law for designating the separate services for children with physical, sensory, intellectual or mental health disabilities. Witnesses had often been in special residential schools for the deaf, for the blind or for pupils with mainly learning difficulties. Children with disabilities were physically, sexually, and emotionally abused in hospitals, as well as being neglected. Thirty-one former hospital residents brought their accounts to the Confidential Committee. Among these, 23 had spent periods from two to 10 years in 18 institutions described as hospitals. In addition to the witnesses who had been abused as children in schools and hospitals, there were survivors who were deaf or blind. Twenty-one complaints were made to the Commission's Investigation Committee concerning St Mary's School for Deaf Girls in the Cabra district of North Dublin. The Commission investigated in detail accounts of sexual abuse of children at St Joseph's School for Deaf Boys in Cabra, North Dublin, managed by the Christian Brothers. The complaints dated back decades and up to the 1990s. The witnesses who came to the Tribunal's Confidential Committee complained of a wide range of physical, emotional and sexual abuse and neglect.

Children's loss of identity

Of the 58 witnesses who attended segregated schools, 12 reported having no knowledge of their family of origin. All they had was their name. Their identity had been lost from the moment of their admission to an institution – a cruel forgetfulness:

> I was looking for my mother, there was no answers ... I heard girls talking about their Mammies and I had nobody to come up to see me. I knew nothing (about family) ... so I took these fits of temper, I was a handful (Commission to Inquire into Child Abuse 2009, III: 250)

Others complained of being beaten for being who they were:

> There is the whole issue of ... [mannerisms] ... people have sort of mannerisms maybe, shaking backwards and forwards, you'd be beaten for that. (Commission to Inquire into Child Abuse 2009, III: 241)

Peter Tyrell, a former child detainee at the age of eight, wrote in his memoir of the treatment of other boys at Letterfrack Industrial School, which was managed by the Christian Brothers:

> Boys who are not good looking or are in any way deformed, are laughed at, and ill-treated. Tom x a big lad for his age, has one leg, and is made to do serve duties and washing up and scrubbing floors etc. I have seen him beaten by (Brother) Vale on the stump of his bad leg (Tyrell 2006, 82)

Peter Tyrell killed himself on Hampstead Heath, London in 1966. His unpublished memoir was found in Ireland and published after his death.

One patient described her lack of personal identity:

> They used have a discussion when they were bathing me, on my head, the size of my head and I remember them saying 'this one has a very small head, I wonder will she be alright?' I remember thinking 'what am I going to do about my small head?' ... (Commission to Inquire into Child Abuse 2009, III: 340)

Pupils with learning needs, far from being treated with any care or respect, reported being humiliated, sneered at and their intelligence ridiculed. The perpetrators were not only religious and lay staff, as well as holiday home members, but also by older or stronger co-residents who were allowed to bully and molest them – a phenomena also reported by children with disabilities in Canada (Odell 2011).

Physical abuse of children

Former residents described being severely physically punished by staff as young children:

> There was a whole load of them ... who'd slap me across the face or with the strap on my legs ... they just kept slapping me the whole time and they all said I was a trouble maker. (Commission to Inquire into Child Abuse 2009, III: 241)

Among the behaviours that attracted severe physical abuse were:

> making mistakes in the classrooms or workshops, using sign language, not using disability aids properly, losing or damaging disability aids, disclosing abuse talking to co-residents and being forced by violence to carry out sexual acts. (Commission to Inquire into Child Abuse 2009, III: 241)

Some of the former residents of the special schools were traumatised by witnessing or hearing violence against other children.

> ... and you could hear the screams, the screams, he was very violent. He was a big strong fit man, I was petrified of him, it came back to me in dreams, the dreams of it returned. (Commission to Inquire into Child Abuse 2009, III: 241)

The abuse of children in hospitals was perpetrated by doctors, nurses, religious sisters and older patients. The former child patients described being used as 'exhibits' for visitors, teased, made fun of and being frightened by observing the treatments and deaths of other patients on wards and having sweets and gifts sent from home, removed from them and consumed by staff or distributed to other patients. A former child patient reported:

> I remember one morning ... I was about five and I was sat up in the bed ... and I heard a voice behind and there's a very tall nun looking down on me and she's not pleased, I can tell by her face. She said I'd offended God, she called me a cripple. I remember it's the first time I was ever called a cripple ... She said before I was fit to meet him [God] again, I'd have to be broken and she just picked me up out of the bed and she threw me down onto the ground ... she'd just kick the shit out of me, picked me up and punched and beat me ... after that I kept very, very quiet ... invisible ... (Commission to Inquire into Child Abuse 2009, III: 333)

One patient who reported being beaten to a relative was believed, and the relative confronted the religious Sister. Subsequently the mother got a letter asking her to stop the relative's visits. While 10 of the 33 hospital witnesses disclosed the abuse at the time, for others the Confidential Committee hearing in private was the first time they had recounted their experiences.

Denial of communication needs

Deaf witnesses described being forced to use oralist communication instead of sign language:

> I was very, very disappointed with myself, because I couldn't learn through oralism, and then they would hit you, if you didn't understand and so we pretended to understand to avoid being hit all the time. (Commission to Inquire into Child Abuse 2009, III: 248)

> We were punished for signing ... it was very, very difficult to control ... it was our language. It was the way we communicated. It was natural for us to use gestures. We were deaf. (Commission to Inquire into Child Abuse 2009, III: 241)

Twenty of the complaints from deaf witnesses concerned excessive physical punishments by nuns, teachers and lay staff using a variety of implements. Some of the complaints alleged the children's hands were tied behind their backs to stop them using sign language. Complaints included emotional abuse, fear, bullying and humiliation. The nuns denied to the Commission that they had 'beaten' children or used punishments for signing (Commission to Inquire into Child Abuse 2009, II: 555). Similarly, in the case of the Mary Immaculate School for Deaf Children in South Dublin the nuns denied the contents of 20 allegations against six nuns that children were beaten with a stick or ruler for using sign language, that the children were forced to use the toilet 'on demand' by systematically administering laxatives to them and that they were denied an education through the use of oralism.

Sexual abuse, rape and assaults

Many witnesses provided the Confidential Committee with graphic accounts of sexual abuse they experienced while living at special schools from the age of seven years and upwards.[2] Witnesses described being shown pornographic films, or taken to pubs and given alcohol prior to being sexually assaulted or violated. Witnesses reported bribes and inducements such as money and, cigarettes.

A resident described: 'Brother ... X used to do dirty things to me at night...He used to wake me at night and took off all my clothes ...' (Commission to Inquire into Child Abuse 2009, III: 244). Another resident remarked of a religious Brother:

> ... afterwards [the rape] he gave me a bar of chocolate and told me to keep quiet about it, I was very shocked. From the time I was 7 until I was 14, maybe three nights a week maybe 4, 2 or 3 (religious) Brothers sexually abused me ... Sometimes they would follow me behind the toilets in the day time and do it again, they would pretend to dry ... [me] ... with a towel and they would do that, mess with you. (Commission to Inquire into Child Abuse 2009, III: 245)

> There was another Brother, he brought me into his room, I didn't like it, he did things, and he hurt me. I was crying ... it was at night time, he made me do things ... he did things to me ... he hurt me ... (Commission to Inquire into Child Abuse 2009, III: 244)

A former resident described her experience as a small girl sent out to a holiday family:

> I was abused, I was sexually abused, it was a man [the father] ... I was sent out nearly every weekend and holidays and it went on for years and years of my life ... I can't get over it, it just gets to me. I was 7 years of age. (Commission to Inquire into Child Abuse 2009, III: 247)

While one Order acknowledged that individual Brothers had sexually abused deaf boys in their care, they insistently denied that it was systematic or a 'phenomenon'. The Commission concluded that:

> the management in Cabra failed to protect children from sexual abuse by staff. When complaints were made, they were not believed or ignored or dealt with inadequately. The level and extent of abuse perpetrated by one lay worker, as late as the 1990s, was an indication of the lack of proper safeguards ... the investigation revealed a pattern of physical and emotional bullying that made Cabra a very frightening place for children who were learning to overcome hearing difficulties. (Commission to Inquire into Child Abuse 2009, I: 578)

The creation of new impairments

A number of witnesses with intellectual disabilities attended the Confidential Committee and remained frightened. Some sought reassurances from the Commissioners and their accompanying persons that they would not 'get in trouble' for attending the Commission (Commission to Inquire into Child Abuse 2009, III: 253). Describing the effects on their adult lives, 49 former residents described a wide range of impacts, injuries and mental health problems they encountered. The highest number reported feeling they needed counselling, could not forget the abuse and, among men, feelings of suicide or attempting suicide (Commission to Inquire into Child Abuse 2009, III: 246).

St Conleth's Reformatory School at Daingean in County Offaly closed in 1973 but its name still causes a shiver for its notorious brutality towards the boys who were sent there because they had been taken into care or by the Courts. It was managed by the Catholic Congregation of the Oblates of Mary Immaculate. The Commission heard that the Oblates were aware that severely psychiatrically disturbed children ended up in Daingean via the courts. They also accepted that they had failed to meet the needs of pupils with psychological or emotional difficulties (Commission to Inquire into Child Abuse 2009, I: 620) The Commission found that children were sexually abused at Daingean and that the most cruel punishments were administered to the boys, including flogging the children. Far from being an educational or childcare facility, the Commission determined that it had neither a remedial or reformatory practice. Because it was not officially a prison, the Commission stated that there was an absence of legal and administrative protections for detainees. The Commission noted that an earlier report on the Daingean boys found that, after Daingean, 'a surprising number went to Britain, where they finished up sleeping rough and declining into alcoholism. A large proportion went to other places of detention in Ireland or Britain' (Commission to Inquire into Child Abuse 2009, I: 689). A Brother who had worked at Letterfrack Industrial School in County Galway remarked pithily to the Commission:

> The boys in Letterfrack were disturbed. How will I say this? If they weren't disturbed before they got to Letterfrack, they were disturbed when they got there ... the very fact of sending them there, they did become disturbed, they became sort of unhappy

and quiet – not quiet – into themselves, introverted. (Commission to Inquire into Child Abuse 2009, I: 380)

In this regard, the system of residential institutions and industrial schools injured and damaged the children. They literally impaired the children, generating disabilities where none had been present before. In that sense, the treatment of children with disabilities cannot be confined to the 'special' schools to which children are sent but to all institutions, be they hospitals or reformatories, where children are confined. The children were treated cruelly despite the various schools being managed by separate religious orders and congregations. Addressing the Report, President of Ireland Mary McAleese described the treatment of the children as 'cruel, inhuman and degrading' (McGarry 2009, 8). The meagre inspection system of the state failed to identify the abuse, and where it was reported to them generally ignored the reports. This response is not unique to Ireland; it can be found also in Italy and the United States.

Conclusions

Answers to the questions of how and why did such an appalling catalogue of abuse against children continue for so long are still a cause for reflection. At least some of the answer must lie in the culture of secrecy that typifies closed segregated institutions. The secrecy was and is bolstered by the significant status attributed to members of religious congregations combined with exaggerated deference on the part of the laity including public servants, politicians and parents (Hegarty 1995, 10; Coldrey 2000; Callaghan 2010). The absence of respect for the dignity and rights of the child that renders their protection superfluous is manifest in the vicious violence which victims described. The ideology of normalisation and the consequent effacing of difference are patently clear in the domination and subordination of the children to unfettered power. The continuing refusal of the Irish State to introduce monitoring and inspection into centres where children with disabilities are separated from their families suggests that, despite discourse on the social model, children with disabilities obtain no particular protection from neglect or predation. Apart from secrecy, a deeper cause may be found in a widespread societal tolerance of violence and abuse towards children, a flawed belief in the unerring goodness of those declaring themselves pledged to do the work of God and a view of the perpetrators as rogue exceptions. Overall, the psychological effects of the violence have been compounded by their envelopment in religious belief.

The standards established by the UN Convention on the Rights of Persons with Disabilities do not remove inequalities of class, ethnicity and social origin. The standards nevertheless constitute an important benchmark for countries like Ireland that have not yet ratified the Convention. They provide legitimation for those who seek radical reform, such as a regime of monitoring and inspection, even though the standards are not enforceable in any Member State of the United Nations. To ratify the Convention, the government states that it needs to publish and enact a Mental Capacity Bill. Such a bill was listed as number 40 on the legislative programme of the Government in mid-2011 and so could not be considered a priority for that period. It would also need an accountable and resourced inspection regime for the places where children with disabilities live. The new government in 2011 decided to establish a full Ministry for Children and a Minister for Children within the Cabinet. The parliament (Oireachtas) was presented with the *Fourth Report of the Special Rapporteur on Child Protection* in May 2011 (Shannon 2010). No comment arose on the rights or risks facing children with disabilities in the discussion of the 300-page report in the Upper House of Parliament in June 2011 (Seanad 2011).

Children diagnosed with acute mental illness and believed to be at risk to themselves or others continue to be placed and detained in adult psychiatric hospitals by the state. During 2010, 91 admissions of children under the age of 18 years took place to adult wards of psychiatric hospitals. Of these, 11 children were aged 15 years or less on admission (Bonnar 2010). Attempts to investigate reports of sexual and physical abuse in a residential service managed by a religious congregation for persons with intellectual disabilities during the period of the 1970s to the 1990s, when the residents were children, drifted into disarray in 2008 (McCoy 2007; Hynes 2008).

The absence of monitoring and inspection

Children with disabilities in Ireland have experienced violence and cruel, inhuman and degrading treatment. In terms of the need for monitoring and vigilant inspection, the 150 residential institutions where more than 300 children with disabilities are living remain without inspection in 2011. The government would not agree to an inspection regime despite being asked to do so by the state body responsible for social service inspections – the Health Information and Quality Authority. The Act providing for inspection of children's care homes specifically excludes homes for children with disabilities. Section 59(c) of the Child Care Act 1991 provides for the exclusion of inspection of: 'an institution for the care and maintenance of physically or mentally handicapped children'. This provision, in place for 20 years, has not been repealed. The Child Care Act was amended in 2007 (Health Act 2007, Schedule 2), but the exclusion of institutions caring for children with disabilities was retained. The matter was raised in the Dáil (Parliament) in an exchange between the (then) opposition and the Minister of State, Deputy Andrews in 2010:

> Deputy David Stanton: Will the lack of statutory guidelines and inspection services have an impact on our ability to ratify the UN Convention on the Rights of Persons with Disabilities, given the Irish Human Rights Commission has said that the standards relating to the right to health, education and so on are not being met adequately in the State today?
>
> Deputy Barry Andrews: With regard to the rights of people with disabilities under the UN Convention, clearly the ambition of the Government to provide a statutory basis for the guidelines is directed towards complying with the convention. (Parliamentary Debates 2010, 19–21)

The right of children to a safe environment and to have their voices officially heard continues to be denied, and the attachment to untrammeled institutional containment remains.

There is a definite need for new legislation or the amendment or commencement of existing legislation that would allow for the entire range of services for children with disabilities to be subject to enforceable standards, rigorous inspection and the sanctioning of breaches of standards of services. This would go some way towards redressing the balance of power between state and children with disabilities.

What has been unique to developments of the last decade in Ireland has been the slow emergence of the voices and associations of those adults with disabilities or perceived differences, who have lived in, endured and been survivors of residential institutions as children (Conroy 2010a). Their decision to speak out has broken the public forgetfulness of the cruelty they endured. The failure of Ireland to ratify the UN Convention has provided renewed energy to activists and policy-makers to lobby for standards of accountability in service provision and for legal change to underpin the human rights of people with disabilities,

Notes

1. Mr Sven Glor, a 21-year-old Swiss lorry driver, took a case to the European Court of Human Rights concerning the refusal of the Swiss army to allow him to do his military service on the grounds that he had diabetes and their subsequent sanctions against him for failing to serve. The judgement against Switzerland mentioned (paragraph 53) the UN Convention on the Rights of Persons with Disabilities (Affaire Glor c. Suisse – Requête no 13444/04 30 avril 2009).
2. Very extensive and precise detail of this is in the Commission to Inquire into Child Abuse Report Volume III.

References

Barnes, C., and A. Sheldon. 2011. Disability, politics and poverty in a majority world context. *Disability and Society* 25, no. 7: 771–82.
Bonnar, S.E. 2010. *Report for the Mental Health Commission on admission of young people to adult mental health wards in the Republic of Ireland*. Dublin: Mental Health Commission.
Burke, S., and I. Burgman. 2010. Coping with bullying in Australian schools: How children with disabilities experience support from friends, parents and teachers. *Disability and Society* 25, no. 3: 359–71.
Callaghan, B. 2010. On scandal and scandals, the psychology of clerical paedophilia. *Studies: An Irish Quarterly Review* 99, no. 395: 343–56.
Chakroborti, N., ed. 2010. *Hate crime: Concepts, policy, future directions*. Cullompton: Willan Publishing.
Coldrey, B. 2000. A mixture of caring and corruption – Church orphanages and industrial schools. *Studies: An Irish Quarterly Review* 89, no. 353: 7–18.
Commission to Inquire into Child Abuse. 2009. *Commission to Inquire into Child Abuse report*. Dublin: Stationary Office.
Conroy, P. 2010a. Comparative issues in the field of disability. In *Comparing welfare states, a symposium of the Irish Social Policy Association, 2*. Dublin: School of Applied Social Science UCD.
Conroy, P. 2010b. *Disability, difference and democracy – Some rights and wrongs*. Dublin: TASC.
Cousins, W., M. Monteith, and N. Kerry. 2003. Living away from home: The long term substitute care of disabled children. *Irish Journal of Applied Social Studies* 4, no. 1: article 6. http://arrow.dit.ie/ijss/vol4/iss1/.
Doyle, P. 1988. *The god squad*. Dublin: Ravens Art Press.
Europa. 2011. EU ratifies UN Convention on disability rights. Press releases of the European Union, no. IP/11/4, 5 January, Brussels.
European Commission. 2008. *Violence and disability – Daphne*. Luxembourg: European Communities.

European Commission. 2010. *Communication from the Commission to the European Parliament, the Council, the European Economic and Social Committee and the Committee of the Regions*. COM(2010) 636 final. Brussels: European Commission.

Hanauske-Abel, H.M. 1996. Not a slippery slope or sudden subversion: German medicine and National Socialism in 1933. *British Medical Journal* 313, no. 7070: 1453.

Hegarty, K. 1995. Foreward. In *Betrayal of trust – The Father Brendan Smyth affair and the Catholic Church*, ed. C. Moore, 5–13. Dublin: Marino Books.

Hynes, J. 2008. *Review of the circumstances surrounding the elapse of time in bringing to completion the Western Health Board Inquiry into allegations of abuse in the Brothers of Charity Services*. Galway: Health Service Executive.

International Network of Women with Disabilities 2010. Document on violence against women with disabilities. http://groups.yahoo.com/group/inwwd.

International Save the Children Alliance. 2003. *A last resort: The growing concern about children in residential care*. London: Save the Children.

McCormack, B. 2005. The power relationship in sexual abuse: An analysis of Irish data relating to victims and perpetrators with learning disabilities. Paper presented to the Seminar of the National Disability Authority 'Violence against disabled people', November 29. www.nda.ie.

McCoy, M. 2007. *Report of Dr Kevin McCoy on the Western Health Board Inquiry into the Brothers of Charity Services in Galway, November*. Dublin: Health Service Executive.

McDonnell, P. 2007. *Disability and society – Ideological and historical dimensions*. Dublin: Blackhall Publishing.

McGarry, P. 2009. Findings demand focus on children – McAleese. *Irish Times*, June 26. http://www.irishtimes.com/newspaper/ireland/2009/0626/1224249571926.html.

McGee, H., R. Garavan, M. De Barra, J. Byrne, and R. Conroy. 2002. *The SAVI report – Sexual violence and abuse in Ireland*. Dublin: Royal College of Surgeons in Ireland, Liffey Press with Dublin Rape Crisis Centre.

McGrath, K. 1996. Protecting Irish children – investigating protection and welfare. In *Administration*, vol. 44, ed. H. Ferguson and T. McNamara, 7–72. Dublin: Institute of Public Administration.

Mencap. 2007. *Bullying wrecks lives: The experiences of children and young people with a learning disability*. London: Mencap.

Morris, J. 1997. Child protection and disabled children at residential schools. *Disability and Society* 12, no. 2: 241–58.

Morris, J. 2001. *That kind of life? Social exclusion and young disabled people with high levels of support needs. Report*. London: SCOPE.

Morris, J. 2001. Social exclusion and young disabled people with high levels of support needs. *Critical Social Policy* 21, no. 2: 161–83.

Nixon, J. 2009. Domestic violence and women with disabilities: Locating the issue on the periphery of social movements. *Disability and Society* 24, no. 1: 77–89.

NSPCC. 2003. *It doesn't happen to disabled children: Report of the National Working Group on Child Protection and Disability*. London: NSPCC.

Odell, T. 2011. Not your average childhood: Lived experience of children with physical disabilities raised in Bloorview Hospital, Home and School from 1960–1989. *Disability and Society* 26, no. 1: 49–63.

Parliamentary Debates. 2010. *Dáil Éireann* 713, no. 1, 22 June: 10.

Quarmby, K. 2008. *Getting away with murder – Disabled people's experiences of hate crime in the UK*. London: SCOPE.

Rafferty, M., and E. O'Sullivan. 1999. *Suffer the little children: The inside story of Ireland's industrial schools*. Dublin: New Island.

Seanad. 2011. Vol. 28, no. 4, June 7: 6.

Shannon, G. 2010. *Fourth report of the Special Rapporteur on Child Protection*. Dublin: Government Publications.

Smith, J.M. 2007. *Ireland's Magdalen laundries and the nation's architecture of containment*. Manchester: Manchester University Press.

The Law Reform Commission. 1990. *Report on sexual offences against the mentally handicapped*. Dublin: The Law Reform Commission.

Thomas, P. 2011. 'Mate crime': Ridicule, hostility and targeted attacks against disabled people. *Disability and Society* 26, no. 1: 107–11.
Tyrell, P. 2006. *Founded on fear*. Dublin: Irish Academic Press.
United Nations. 1989. *Convention on the rights of the child*. New York: United Nations.
United Nations. 2006. *Convention on the rights of persons with disabilities*. New York: United Nations.
United Nations. 2006b. *Report of the independent expert, Paulo Sérgio Pinheiro, for the United Nations study on violence against children*. Sixty-first session, document A/61/299. New York: United Nations, General Assembly.
US Department of Justice. 2009. *National crime victimization survey – Crime against people with disabilities, 2007*. Washington, DC: Bureau of Justice Statistics.
Weindling, P. 1987. Compulsory sterilisation in national socialist Germany. *German History – The Journal of the German History Society* 5, no. 1: 10–24.
Whyte, J. 2006. *Consulting with children with disabilities as service users: Practical and methodological considerations*. Dublin: Social Services Inspectorate and Children's Research Centre, Trinity College.
Wiener, D., R. Ribeiro, and K. Warner. 2009. Mentalism, disability rights and modern eugenics in a 'brave new world'. *Disability and Society* 24, no. 5: 599–610.

Conclusion
Sarah Beazley and Val Williams

Concluding comments

Readers will have approached this collection in various ways, but as editors we hope you have been inspired to follow up ideas, revisit references and pursue new lines of enquiry, as we ourselves were stimulated to do when selecting the papers for this book. We would like to conclude with just a few reflections, from the experience of choosing and reading these papers, and to raise some questions for readers to consider further.

The collection of papers in this book has made clear that, over the two decades of work represented, much has shifted in the world of disability studies and subsequently in the way in which studies of childhood and disability are framed. Long before the first paper in the book, the social model of disability had been introduced by one of the journal's founders, Mike Oliver (Oliver, 1983) and during the 1990s a linked notion of emancipatory and participatory research for dismantling disabling barriers was rapidly evolving (Zarb, 1992) alongside fast developing, perpetually shifting theoretical contestations (Oliver, 1990; Thomas, 2004; Shakespeare, 2006; Oliver & Barnes, 2012). Ground-breaking ideas, which are still key underpinning values of the journal, coalesced during the decades we have been reflecting upon in this book and were firmly based on the right of disabled people to be active in making their own knowledge, and in exerting control over research and dissemination agendas.

Despite these developments, some groups of disabled people have found it much harder to gain a foothold in emancipatory processes and children in particular, whose sense of autonomy and personal power can be constrained by others, have found it much harder to have a voice in the world of disability studies generally. Nevertheless, it is now widely recognised that children, including disabled children, can be active meaning-makers, while having support to participate, a principle that underpins the move towards inclusive research with people with learning disabilities (Walmsley & Johnson, 2003; Williams, 2011) and informs changing practice with disabled children (Beazley & Chilton, 2013; Beazley et al., 2012). In particular, disabled young people themselves have started to take a more active role as researchers, as for example in the Viper Project (2013) and it is our aim to encourage such contributions for publication in *Disability & Society*. We want to endorse the importance of disabled children becoming the researchers of the future through the work of the journal.

Reading the papers for this book challenged us, both as academics and practitioners, to consider how we could engage with disabled children to greater effect. We agree with a persistent message in this book calling for more opportunity to be opened up for conversations between disabled children, disability activists and researchers and their allies. There are questions to hold in the light about what happens beyond listening to children, and we wish to pose some for readers to address themselves. These include:

- Having read these papers, what changes are you inspired to make to your own interactions with disabled children?
- How can you expand good practice for listening to children in all contexts, allowing children greater agency at every opportunity?
- How can you act on what you are told by disabled children?
- Can you ensure any actions taken based upon what children tell you are monitored and reviewed by children, with flexibility for children to add in new directions?
- In what ways can disabled children take on active roles as researchers, adding further power to their messages?
- Why is it important that disabled children are the principal architects of studies and publications concerned with childhood and disability?

Of course aspirations for involving disabled children in our efforts to understand their lives are circumscribed differently in relation to the context in which those lives are lived. At the time of writing, disabled children in the UK may be denied a bedroom of their own, if threatened welfare reforms prevail, none of which has consulted with disabled children. Research conducted in Kenya, Zambia, Uganda, India and Nepal has highlighted the enormous requirement for capacity building to increase sustainable inclusion of disabled children in international development initiatives concerned with health, access to water, poverty and education (Groce et al., 2011). The life and times of disabled children caught up in conflict in Iraq, Syria and Egypt are seldom glimpsed and issues of disability and childhood in war require much further attention (Alborz, 2013; Miles, 2013).

It is our collective responsibility in the years ahead to ensure that *Disability & Society* continues to present and reflect on disabled children's experiences, by including them as active partners in developing not only dialogue, but action. There is no room for complacency concerning the urgency and complexity of new understandings of childhood and disability issues.

References

Alborz, A. 2013. Environmental characteristics and prevalence of birth defects among children in post-war Iraq: implications for policies on rebuilding the Iraqi education system. *Medicine, Conflict and Survival* 29, no. 1: 26–44.

Beazley, S., and H. Chilton. 2013. Theory of mind: are there wider implications from working with d/Deaf people. *Disability & Society.*

Beazley, S., R. Merritt, and J. Halden. 2012. Working with deaf children. In *Speech and Language Therapy*, eds. M. Kersner and J. Wright. London: Taylor Francis. eScholarID:195172.

Groce, N., M. Kett, R. Lang, and J.F. Trania. 2011. Disability and Poverty: the need for a more nuanced understanding of implications for development policy and practice. *Third World Quarterly, Special Issue: Disability in the Global South* 32, no. 8: 1493–1513.

Miles, S. 2013. Education in times of conflict and the invisibility of disability: a focus on Iraq. *Disability & Society, Special Issue: Global Conflicts & Crises* 28, no. 6: 798–811.

Oliver, M. 1983. *Social Work with Disabled People*. Basingstoke: Macmillan.

Oliver, M., and C. Barnes. 2012. *The New Politics of Disablement.* Basingstoke: Palgrave.
Shakespeare, T. 2006. *Disability Rights and Wrongs.* Abingdon: Routledge.
Thomas, C. 2004. How is disability understood? An examination of sociological approaches. *Disability & Society* 19, no. 6: 569–583.
'Viper' Project. 2013. *Voices, Inclusion, Participation, Empowerment, Research*, The Children's Society. http://www.childrenssociety.org.uk/what-we-do/research/research-areas/disabled-children-and-young-people/viper accessed 31/07/2013
Walmsley, J., and K. Johnson. 2003. Inclusive Research with People with Learning Disabilities: Past, Present and Futures. London: Jessica Kingsley.
Williams, V. 2011. Disability and Discourse: Analysing Inclusive Conversation with People with Intellectual Disabilities. Chichester: Wiley-Blackwell.
Zarb, G. 1992. On the road to Damascus: first steps towards changing the relations of research production. *Disability, Handicap & Society, Special Issue: Researching Disability* 7, no. 2: 125–138.

Index

abandonment and rejection: inclusion/exclusion 24; looked after children 13; residential institutions 18, 20, 26, 150, 157, 179; wishes, views and experiences of children 90

abuse and violence: Bloorview Hospital, Home and School, Toronto 150; communication 91–2; Convention on the Rights of the Child 1989 (UN) 178–9; emotional abuse 3–4, 154–5, 181–2; gender 180; hate crimes 180; Ireland, religious institutions in 3–4, 180–8; physical abuse 3–4, 154–5, 181–5, 187; peers, by 3, 111–12, 130, 168, 179; psychiatric treatment, lack of 20; reprisals 156; sexual assault 3–4, 154–5, 180–2, 184–7 *see also* bullying

accommodation, definition of 12

actors, children as social 40, 87–91, 95–6, 120, 162–74

Adam, Barbara 73

Adams, J 43

adoption 16–17

adult surveillance 78

advertising 74

agency of children: actorness, differentiated from 163; attitudinal factors 167–70; barriers 162–74; bullying 171, 172–3; carers 135, 141–2; choice-making 168–70; communication 163, 169–73; Convention on the Rights of the Child 1989 (UN) 1, 163; culture 167, 171, 173; definition 163, 164, 173; disablism 76; education and schools 163, 172–3; facilitating agency 162–74; identity formation 89; India 118–19, 128–31; institutional factors 169, 171–3; professionals, relationships with 164–74; residential institutions 162–74; social model of disability 113; structural issues 169, 171–3; wishes, views and experiences of children 167, 171–2, 174

Ainscow, M 53

Alan, S 52

Alderson, P 40, 51

Aldridge, J 135, 143

Ali, Z 102

Andrews, Barry 187

Appadurai, Arjun 82

appropriate behaviour, notions of 43, 49, 51

armed conflict, children in 192

Armstrong, D 52

Aroni, Rosalie 2, 171

assessments 20, 29, 31, 45

attitudinal factors 167–70

Australia 45, 53, 58 *see also* Victoria, Australia, wishes and views of children with cerebral palsy in

Baldwin, Sally 17

Ball, S 44

Bandura, A 163

barriers: agency 162–74; being, to 104, 110–11, 114; carers 2, 143; cerebral palsy in Victoria, Australia, children with 5, 58; consumption 74, 76–80; doing, to 104, 112, 114; identity 76–7; India 117, 123, 128; innovation 45–6, 53; oppression 87, 97; participatory research 191; reaction to others 107, 111–12; residential institutions 162–74; social and cultural exclusion in special and mainstream schools 39–47, 52–3; social model of disability 6, 36, 102–4, 110–14; wishes, views and experiences of children 5, 90, 94–5, 97–8

Baudrillard, Jean 74

Bauman, Zygmunt 76

Becker, J 135, 143

behavioural problems 8, 10–11, 14

Beresford, Bryony 8

Berry, JW 125

best interests test 30, 33–4

blame 24–5, 28, 126, 129, 141, 157

Bloorview Hospital, Home and School, Toronto, experiences of 3, 147–61: 1960–1989 149; 1960–1975 cohort 150–3, 160; 1975–1989 cohort 150, 153, 160; abuse and

INDEX

victimization 153, 154–6; communication 150, 159; emotional, physical and sexual abuse 154–5; family relationships, attitudes to 157–8; history of Bloorview 149; length of stays 149, 150–2; mixed experiences 150, 152–3; negative experiences 150, 152–5, 160; other residents, abuse by 153–4; peer relationships 153–5; positive experiences 150, 152–3, 159–60; profiles 151–2; reasons for admission 150; rebellious, finding ways to be 155–6; recreational programs, attitudes to 158–9; reprisals in form of abuse 156; sexuality, expressing 155, 156; success factors 160–1; technology, resource for 159–60; therapeutic interventions, attitudes to 158

boarding schools *see* residential education
Booth, TA 45
Brown, H 118
bullying: agency 171, 172–3; Bloorview Hospital, Home and School, Toronto 155; education and schools 43–4, 111–12, 155; India 129, 131; Ireland, abuse in religious institutions in 183; parents, protection of 129; peer relationships 43–4, 92, 111–12, 129, 131, 139, 183; professionals, relationships with 172–3; residential institutions 155, 171, 183; statistics 180; wishes, views and experiences of children 92
Burns, J 118

Cameron, L 170–1
Canada *see* Bloorview Hospital, Home and School, Toronto, experiences of
capacity building 192
captive customers 79
care and living away from families, children in 5–21: behavioural or emotional problems as a disability 10–11, 14; care orders 12–13; Department of Health guidelines 12–13; formally in care, children not being 15–17; hospitals 5, 13, 14–16; leave care, lack of opportunity to 19–20; life stories 12–21; living away from home, definition of 12–15; looked after children 12–14; medical model of disability 6–8, 21; OPCS research 9–12, 16–17; recording and measurement 13; research 5–21; residential institutions 5–21; respite care 5, 14–15; statistics 9–10, 13–14, 16
care orders 12–13
carers *see* young carers
Castells, M 73
causes of disability 107–8, 114, 123, 125, 131–2
Cavet, J 79, 109

charity/pity model 43, 76, 118–19, 128
Cheston, R 90
child-centred approach 1, 2, 4, 78, 162–3, 174
childhood, definition of 2
Children Act 1989 5, 12, 14–15, 19, 51
children first principle 5, 6, 77
Children First policy (Wales) 77
children living away from home, definition of 12
Children (Scotland) Act 1995 51
children's voices *see* wishes, views and experiences of children
China 45
choice-making 6, 31, 33, 48, 74–5, 168–70
civil movements 149
Clark, C 45
class 41, 53, 74, 76, 87, 103, 131, 186
Cocks, A 172, 174
Code of Practice on the Identification and Assessment of Special Educational Needs 31
communication 170–1, 191–2; abuse 91–2; agency 163, 169–73; benefits 57–8, 67; Bloorview Hospital, Home and School, Toronto 150, 159; cerebral palsy in Victoria, Australia, children with 57–68; continuity of care 66–7; diagnosis, of 25, 31, 59, 64; disabilities, discussions of 92–4, 97; drawings 2, 120–1, 125–6; gender 65–6; home-school partnerships 28–9; Ireland, abuse in religious institutions in 184; professionals, relationships with 26, 28, 57–68, 93, 98–9, 169–74; research, invisibility in 2, 8–9; social model of disability 105–6, 112; time, lack of 172; training 93–4; wishes, views and experiences of children 2, 57–68, 91–4, 97–9
Connors, Clare 2, 102–3, 107
Conroy, Pauline 3
consultation 1, 5–6, 90, 96
consumption 72–84: barriers 74, 76–80; captive customers 79; discrimination 77–8, 82; flawed consumers 76, 80–2; globalisation 75; home-school partnerships 34; identity 72–7, 79, 83; immobilization 72–83; inclusion/exclusion 74, 76–7, 80, 83; leisure activities, access to 77–80; mobile or liquid identities 72–7, 79, 83; projects of self-identity 74–80; residential institutions 77–8, 80; segregation 74, 77–80, 83; signifiers of disability 74, 81–2; signifiers of youth and perfection 74, 81–2; social model of disability 112–13; spoiled identity 81
continuity of care 66–8
Convention on the Rights of the Child 1989 (UN) 1, 5, 51, 56, 97, 163, 177–9, 186–8

196

INDEX

Corbett, J 52
Corbin, J 60
Corker, M 51
Cousins, W 179
Crane v Lancashire 30–1
critical disability studies 160
culture 81–3, 88: agency 167, 171, 173; carers 135, 137–8, 143–4; consumerism 74; cultural construction of childhood 118–20; cultural activities 77, 144; inclusion/exclusion 42–3; Ireland, abuse in religious institutions in 181, 186; normalcy 167; sociocultural factors 160; youth culture 3, 7, 76–9, 81–2, 112–13
cure and treatment, focus on *see* medical model of disability

Dalal, A 125
DAPHNE programme 179
Davies, C 89–90
Davis, JM 120, 167–8, 170
Dear Daughter (film) 181
defensiveness 48, 181
deficit/defect thinking 24–5, 28–9, 81, 118, 120, 127
definitions *see* terminology and definitions
Department of Health (DOH) guidance 12–13
dependency: carers 135–6, 141; fixed dependency 3; India 118–19, 121, 123–4, 128–30; parents 78, 135–6, 140–1; social and cultural exclusion in special and mainstream schools 42–3
developmental psychology 135, 138–44
diagnosis: communication 25, 31, 59, 64; parents, reaction of 31–2
difference: agency 167; carers 135; essentialism 39–40, 45, 52, 104; India 118–21, 126; institutionalisation 40–2, 44, 52; peer relationships 42–3, 78, 94, 109, 111, 135; professionals 46–9, 53; social model of disability 103, 104, 109–14; wishes, views and experiences of children 94–5
Disabilities Convention 3–4, 163, 178
disability, definition of 6, 7, 14, 103–4, 118, 121–3, 130
disability movement 6, 53, 76, 79, 84, 102
Disability Studies 73, 83, 103–4, 160, 174, 191
disablism 76, 81, 104, 107, 163
discrimination and prejudice: class 53, 56, 186; consumption 77–8, 82; Convention on the Rights of the Child 1989 (UN) 56; Disability Discrimination Act 1995 77; disablism 76, 81, 104, 107, 163; education and schools 6, 40, 44, 51, 53; ethnicity 53, 56, 186; gender 53, 180; inclusion/exclusion 76; parents, relationship with 24–5, 32; religion 53, 56; social model of disability 6–7, 36, 87; wishes, views and experiences of children 56, 90, 99; youth culture 7
diversity 76, 97, 103–4, 136, 138, 144–5, 162–4, 167, 169, 173–4
docile subjects 76, 80
dominant discourses, impact of 89–95
Doyle, Paddy 181
drawings 2, 120–1, 125–6
dual experience of living as child and disabled person 3, 88, 131
Durkheim, Emile 72–3
Dyer, B 26

Edgerton, RB 113
Education Act 1981 29–30, 51
Education Act 1993 31
education and schools: agency 163, 172–3; Bloorview Hospital, Home and School, Toronto 159; bullying 43–4, 111–12, 155; Code of Practice on the Identification and Assessment of Special Educational Needs 31; inclusion/exclusion 35, 39–53, 77, 110, 168; India 120, 128, 131; ineducable, removal of idea of 27; integrated education 29–30, 45, 107, 110, 120, 131, 159; Ireland, abuse in religious institutions in 181–2, 186; mainstream schools 2, 7, 16, 29–30, 39–53, 107–14, 168; peer relationships 30, 42–5, 54, 120, 135, 155; professionals 2, 23–36, 40–53, 60, 110, 114 ; residential institutions 11, 12–13, 15, 17–19, 159, 180–2, 186; segregation 32, 43–5, 51, 77, 107, 109–12, 111, 159, 182; social model of disability 109–12, 114; special schools 2, 9, 18, 31, 39–53, 109–10, 113, 159, 181–6 *see also* home-school partnerships; social and cultural exclusion in special and mainstream schools
Education Reform Act 1988 31
emancipatory research 73, 83, 120, 149, 191
embarrassment 26, 90, 97
emotional problems 10–11, 20, 30, 128, 185
epistemology 73–4, 83–4
essentialism 39–40, 45, 52, 104, 127
ethnicity and race 53, 56, 76, 87, 103, 106, 138, 186
eugenics 25, 81, 179
European Union (EU) 178–9
exclusion *see* inclusion/exclusion
experiences of children *see* wishes, views and experiences of children
expert model 34, 58, 65

families: Bloorview Hospital, Home and School, Toronto 157–8; construction of

197

INDEX

families 140–2; home, role within the family 95; India 122, 124, 128; oppression 24; siblings 94–5, 105, 107, 129–31, 137, 155; support, provision of 16–17; wishes, views and experiences of children 1–2 *see also* parents, relationships with; parents, views of
fathers, role of 60, 66
feminism 103, 137
Finkelstein, V 103
flaneurs 83
flawed consumers 76, 80–2
Ford, M 59, 63
fostering 16–17
Framework for Social Justice (Scotland) 77
Franklin, A 167–8, 172
Fulcher, G 24
Fullagar, S 79–80
future, aspirations for the 2, 97, 105, 109, 123–5, 127–8, 168

Gallagher, DJ 121
Galloway, D 52
Garth, Belinda 2, 171
gatekeepers 60, 171
gender 53, 65–6, 76, 87, 103, 137–8, 167, 178, 180
genetic testing 179
Ghai, Anita 2, 120, 125–8, 130
globalisation 75
Goffman, E 81
Gone Missing 12, 15–20
Goodey, C 40, 51
Goodley, D 119–20
Gregg, Colin 181
guilt 26–8, 124, 141–2

handicap, definition of 7
Hannam, C 27
Hargreaves, A 44
hate crimes 180
hierarchy and status 2, 44, 52, 153
Higgins, S 172
Hirst, Michael 17
holidays 18–19 *see also* respite care
home-school partnerships 23–36: best interests test 33–4; chief partner, child as 24, 34–5; communication 28–9; consumer model 34; *Crane v Lancashire* 30–1; Education Act 1981 29–30; Education Act 1993 31; Education Reform Act 1988 31; expert model 34; failing pupils 28–9; future 35; information, provision of 34; integrated education in mainstream schools 29–30; models 33–4; negotiating model 34; parents, experiences of 31–3; partnership, meaning of 24, 33–5; past experience 25–7; post-war legislation 27–31; power 30–1, 34–5; professionals 24, 31–3; resources 30–1; selection 31; transplant model 34; Warnock Report 28–9, 33
home, role within the 95
hospices 15
hospitals: agency 163; care and living away from families, children in 5, 13, 14–16; community-based institutions, moves to 27; extended stays 14–15; Ireland, abuse in religious institutions in 181–2; larger institutions 25–7; life stories 15–16; normalcy 27; parents, relationship with 25–7; social aspects of hospital visits 2, 63
Hubert, Jane 150
Hughes, Bill 3, 113
human rights 77, 163–4

identity: agency 89; barriers 76–7; carers 2; consumption 72–7, 79, 83; dominant discourses, impact of 91–4; formation 76, 80, 88–9, 114, 120, 131; immobilisation 76, 77–80; Ireland, abuse in religious institutions in 182–3;
loss of identity 4, 182–3; mobile or liquid identities 72–7, 79, 83, 97; multi-dimensional identities 87–8; nomadic identity 74, 83; parents, negative impact of 94; professionals 32–3; self and personal identity 73–80, 88–92, 97–8, 120, 121–8, 182; social identity 74; social model of disability 114; spoiled identity 81; wishes, views and experiences of children 88–95, 96–9
immobilisation 72–83
impairment, definition of 7, 88
inclusion/exclusion: abandonment and rejection 24; agency 164; blame 24–5; capacity-building 192; cerebral palsy in Victoria, Australia, children with 57; consumption 74, 76–7, 80, 83; education and schools 35, 39–53, 77, 110, 168; home, role within the 95; India 127; social model of disability 104, 110, 113; wishes, views and experiences of children 1, 57, 92, 94–5
independence 20, 51, 78, 92, 96, 98, 109, 160
India, lived realities of children in 2, 117–31: agency 118–19, 128–31; attributions of disability 123–6; barriers 117, 123, 128; bullying 129, 131; causes of disability 123, 125, 131–2; definition and comprehension of disability 118, 121–3, 130; dependency 118–19, 121, 123–4, 128–30;difference 118–21, 126; discrimination 128; drawings 120–1, 125–6; education 120, 128, 131; familial experiences 124, 129–32; future, aspirations for the 127–8; identity 120, 121–8, 131;

INDEX

inclusion/exclusion 127; karma or God 118, 125; labels 121, 127, 129, 130–1; medical model of disability 121; National Trust Act 1999 117–18; normality, discourses of 119–23, 127, 131; parents 126, 129–31; Persons with Disabilities (Equal Opportunities, Protection of Rights and Full Participation) Act 1995 117; reactions of others 128–31; Rehabilitation Council of India (RCI) 117; self-identity 120, 121–8; siblings, reaction of 130, 131
individualisation 45, 135, 140, 142–5
infanticide 80
informal care 15–17
information, provision of 34, 64–7, 93–4
inspection 186, 187–8
international perspectives: Bloorview Hospital, Home and School, Toronto 3, 147–61; India, lived realities of children in 2, 117–31; Ireland, abuse in religious institutions in 3–4, 180–8; Victoria, Australia, children with cerebral palsy in 2, 5, 56–68
InterViews approach 149
Ireland, abuse in residential institutions run by religious orders in 180–8: authoritarianism 181; bullying 183; Commission to Inquire into Child Abuse report 182–6; communication needs, denial of 184; Convention on the Rights of the Child 1989 (UN) 186–8; Disabilities Convention 3–4, 186–8; defensiveness 181; emotional abuse 3–4, 181–2; hospitals 181–2; identity, loss of 182–3; Ministry for Children 186–7; monitoring and inspection 186, 187–8; new impairments, creation of 185–6; physical abuse 3–4, 181–5, 187; secrecy, culture of 186; segregated schools 181–2, 186; sexual abuse and rape 3–4, 180–2, 184–7

Jenkins, R 89
Jones, C 34
Joshi, P 130

Keith, L 136–7
Kelly, B 3, 102–3, 168, 172
Kenworthy, J 51
Kerry, N 179
Khanna, R 120
King, RD 7
Kvale, Steinar 149

labels:
 agency 168; essentialism 127; impairment, definition of 88; India 121, 127, 129, 130–1; learning difficulties 89; social and cultural exclusion in special and mainstream schools 40–1, 45, 47, 49, 52; social model of disability 110, 114
Lamb (film) 181
language: brokers 136–7, 143–4; education and schools 52
learning disabled children, definition of 88
learning from disabled children 3–4
leave care, lack of opportunity to 19–20
Lee, Frances 18
Leicester, M 52–3
leisure activities 77–80, 109, 112, 158–9
Lentin, Louis 181
life stories 2–3, 12–21, 105–6
looked after children 12–14, 20
loss of childhood 135, 139–40, 142
Loughran, F 10
Lyon, Christina 16

MacArthur, J 170, 172
magic wand wishes 95, 97, 106, 108
Mahabharata 118
Marchant, Ruth 8
market-based education 39–40, 52
martyrs and saints, parents as 25
Mayall, B 163
McAleese, Mary 186
McCormack, Bob 180–1
McDonnell, P 180
medical consultations 57–68
medical model of disability: care and living away from families, children in 6–8, 21; cerebral palsy in Victoria, Australia, children with 58–9; India 121; oppression 59; social model of disability 113; WHO International Classification of Impairment, Disabilities and Handicaps 6–7; wishes, views and experiences of children 58–9, 83
Meeuwesen, L 67
Mencap 180
methodological naturalism 73
Middleton, S 90
mistakes, learning to make 5–6
mocking 128–9
models of disability *see* medical model of disability; social model of disability
modernism 72–3, 80
monitoring 178, 186, 187–8
Monteith, M 179
Morris, Jenny 1, 3, 77, 104, 136–7, 179
Murch, M 11
Murphy, J 170–1
Murray, Pippa 1, 77
Myerscough, P 59, 63

National Crime Victimisation Survey 180
Nazi Germany 25, 179

INDEX

Neeson, Liam 181
negotiating model 34
New Social Movements 83
New Zealand 2, 45
Newman, T 136
normalcy 2, 42–4, 51: Bloorview Hospital, Home and School, Toronto 153; carers 135, 138–9, 143–4; diversity 167; hospitals 27; India 119–23, 127, 131; parents 140–1
Northern Ireland 90–9
Norway 45

objectification 44
Odell, Tracy 3
Oliver, Mike 58, 191
Olli, Johanna 2
Olsen, R 136
oppression 1, 3, 24, 32, 53, 59, 73, 83, 87–8, 97, 99
otherness 2, 81, 167
out-of-country placements 14
over-protection 51, 89, 129–31, 153–4, 168
Owler, K 79–80

parentified children 136
parents *see* parents, relationships with; parents, views of
parents, relationships with: blame 24–5, 126; bullying 129; dependency 78, 135–6, 140–1; diagnosis, reaction to 31–2; fathers, role of 60, 66; home-school partnerships 23–36; hospitals, institutionalization in 25–7; identity 94; India 126, 129, 130–1; medical consultations 2, 59–68; over-protection 51, 89, 129–31, 153–4, 168; partnerships 23–36; past experience 25–7; prejudice 24–5, 32; protection of parents by children 129
parents, views of: carers 135; causes of disability 107; cerebral palsy in Victoria, Australia, children with 2, 57, 59, 64–6, 68; communication 91–3; dominant discourses, impact of 93–4 8; social model of disability 105, 109, 111, 113–14; wishes, views and experiences of children 57, 59, 64–6, 68, 91–4, 97–9
Parker, G 136
paternalism 58, 68, 173
partnerships 23–36, 58, 66–8
peer relationships: abuse and bullying 3, 111–12, 130–1, 168, 179; agency 171–3; barriers 95; behaviours, development of particular 92, 168; Bloorview Hospital, Home and School, Toronto 153–5; carers 135, 139–40, 142–3; difference 42–3, 78, 94, 109, 111, 135; education and schools 30, 42–5, 53–4, 120, 135, 155; siblings 94–5, 105, 107, 129–31, 137, 155; similarities, focus on 3, 5,

108–9, 113; youth culture 7, 77–8, 80, 112–13
perspectives of children *see* wishes, views and experiences of children
pity/charity model 43, 76, 118–19, 128
Plowden report 27–8
policy 5–6, 27–8, 39–42, 45–53, 77, 135–6, 178–9
postmodernism 3
poverty 76, 118, 145, 192
power 34, 44, 47–8, 52–3, 89–90, 97
prejudice *see* discrimination and prejudice
Priestley, M 89, 121
Prilleltensky, O 145
professionals, relationships with 24, 31–3: agency 164–74; attitudinal factors 167–70; bullying 172–3; communication 26, 28, 57–68, 93, 98–9, 169–74; defensiveness 48, 181; difference 46–9, 53; dominant ideology, preservation of 24; education and schools 2, 23–36, 40–53, 60, 110, 114; expert model 34, 58, 65; gatekeepers 171; identity 32–3; oppression 32, 99; own actions and influence, attitudes to 168–70; personal and cultural values 2; reflexive practitioners 41, 45–6, 52–3, 90, 97–8; social model of disability 105, 107–8, 113; subjectivity, attitudes to 167–8; time, lack of 172; vested interests 46, 53; wishes, views and experiences of children 93–4, 97–9
psychiatric treatment, lack of 20

Quality Protects Programme (England) 77

Rafferty, Mary 181
Ramayana 118
Raynes, NV 7
reactions of others: barriers 107, 111–12; India 128–31; parents, from other 25; siblings 105, 107, 124, 130, 131; social model of disability 111–12, 114; wishes, views and experiences of children 107, 124, 128–30
recreational activities 77–80, 109, 112, 158–9
reflexive practitioners 41, 45–6, 52–3, 93–4, 97–9
rejection *see* abandonment and rejection
religion: discrimination 53, 56; Ireland, abuse in religious institutions in 180–8
research: 16 and 19, exclusion of children aged between 10–11; communication issues 8–9; design 2, 57, 60–1, 137; emancipatory research 73, 83, 120, 149, 191; guidance 6; invisibility of children 6, 8–9, 11; methodology 2, 8, 11, 60–1, 72–3, 104–7, 120, 136–8, 149, 165–6, 170–1; OPCS 9–12, 16–17; participatory research 120, 191;

INDEX

policy guidance 6, 106; WHO International Classification of Impairment, Disabilities and Handicaps 7; wishes, views and experiences of children 2–9, 21, 44, 56–68, 78, 88–9, 96–9, 103–6, 113–14, 118–20, 164, 191–2

residential institutions 3–4: 5 and 15, children between 11; 16 and 19, exclusion of children aged between 10–11; actors, children as social 162–74; agency, barriers to 162–74; abandonment and rejection 18, 20, 26, 150, 157, 159; barriers 162–74; bullying 155, 171, 183; care, children in 5–21; community-based institutions, moves to 27; consumption 77–8, 80; discrimination 6; education and schools 11, 12–13, 15, 17–19, 159, 180–2, 186; Ireland, abuse in religious institutions in 180–1; large institutions 25–7; medicalisation 180; normalisation 27; religion 180; warehousing 77–8 *see also* Bloorview Hospital, Home and School, Toronto, experiences of; hospitals

resources 30–1, 45–6, 53, 172

respite care 5, 14–15, 80, 96, 171

restraints 42

Riddell, S 45, 52, 79

risk 78, 91, 95, 106, 180, 187

Robinson, C 14–15

Rowley, D 42

Russell, Philippa 9, 18

safety issues 51

sameness/similarities 2–3, 5, 103, 108–10, 112–13, 167

schools *see* education and schools

Scotland 77, 102–14, 181

Scott-Hill, M 104

segregation: agency 172, 174; consumption 74, 77–80, 83; education and schools 32, 43–5, 51, 77, 107, 109–12, 111, 159, 182; Ireland, abuse in religious institutions in 180–2, 184–7; policy 27; social model of disability 36, 87; streaming and units, through 44; warehousing 77–8

self-esteem 88, 90, 147, 158–9

self-reactiveness 163

self-reflectiveness 163

sexual assault and abuse 3–4, 154–5, 180–2, 184–7

sexuality, expressing 155, 156

Shakespeare, T 81, 104

shame 26–7, 122, 124–5, 128, 130

siblings 94–5, 105, 107, 129–31, 137, 155

Sieppert, JD 173

sign systems 93, 106–7, 181, 183–4

signifiers of disability 74, 81–2, 121

signifiers of youth and perfection 74, 81–2

similarities/sameness 2–3, 5, 103, 108–10, 112–13, 167

Singh, Vanessa 2

Slee, R 52–3

Sloper, P 167–8, 172

social actors, children as 40, 87–91, 95–6, 120, 162–74

social and cultural exclusion in special and mainstream schools 39–53: appropriate behaviour, notions of 43, 49, 51; barriers to inclusion 39–47, 52–3; dependency, narrative of 42–3; different adults 46–9, 53; discrimination 40, 44, 51, 53; essentialism 39–40, 45, 52; experiences of children 40, 49–51, 53; hierarchy and status 44, 52; informal exclusion from mainstream schools 45; innovation, barriers to 45–6, 53; institutionalisation of difference 40–2, 44, 52; institutionalisation of normality 42–4, 51; labelling 40–1, 45, 47, 49, 52; language practice, changing 52; market-based education 39–40, 52; medical model of disability 45, 53; peer relationships 42–5, 53; power 44, 47–8, 52–3; practice and policy 39–42, 45–53; reflexive practitioners 41, 45–6, 52–3; segregation 43–4, 51; streaming and units, segregation through 44; structural issues 44–7, 52; teachers, experiences of 2, 40, 47–9, 51, 52–3; vested interests of teachers 46, 53; Warnock Report 45, 53

social care, residential education as 18–19

social construction of childhood 118–19

social model of disability 6, 73, 102–14, 191: barriers 6, 36, 102–4, 110–14; bullying 111–12; causes of impairment 107–8, 114; cerebral palsy in Victoria, Australia, children with 58–9; communication 105–6, 112; consumerism 112–13; difference 103, 104, 109–14; disability or impairment, discussions of 107–8, 113; discrimination 6–7, 36, 87; education 109–12, 114; identity 114; inclusion/exclusion 104, 110, 113; India 121; interviews 105–7; leisure, activities, access to 109, 112; life stories 105–6; medical model of disability 113; oppression 97; parents, perspectives of 105, 109, 111, 113–14; professionals, relationship with 105, 107–8, 113; reactions of other people 111–12, 114; sameness, focus on 103, 109, 112–13; Scotland 102–14; segregation 87; siblings, perceptions of 105; social relational model 103–4, 113–14; special needs assistants 110; wishes, views and experiences of children

INDEX

58–9, 87–8, 97, 102–14; youth culture 112–13
social relational model of disability 103–4, 113–14
sociology 73–5, 83–4, 87, 96–7, 103–4
special, disabled children as 111
Spitzer, S 170
Stalker, Kirsten 2, 14–15, 102–3, 107
States of Fear (documentary) 181
statistics 9–10, 13–14, 16
stigma 26, 128
Strauss, A 60
Street, R 65
structural issues 169, 171–3
sub-human, disabled people as 25
subjectivity 41, 52, 167–8
support workers 24, 110
suspended childhood 118

Taanila, A 67
Tannen, D 59
Tates, K 67
teenage subculture 7
terminology and definitions: accommodation, definition of 12; agency 163, 164, 173; Australia 58; care orders, definition of 12; carers 134–5; childhood 2; Children Act guidance 12; disability 6, 7, 14, 103–4, 118, 121–3, 130; handicap 7; impairment 7, 88; India 118, 121–3, 130;
learning disabled children 88; living away from home, definition of 12–15; looked after children, definition of 12; oppression 88
Thomas, C 88, 90, 97, 103–4, 108, 110–14
time, lack of 172
Tizard, J 7
Toronto *see* Bloorview Hospital, Home and School, Toronto, experiences of
torture, inhuman or degrading treatment or punishment 4, 178
tragedy model of disability 79, 81, 91, 97, 108, 121
training 93–4
transplant model 34
transport 77–9, 104, 112, 153
Tregaskis, C 127
Trickett, Sue 18
Tyrell, Peter 182

UN Convention on the Rights of the Child 1989 1, 5, 51, 56, 97, 163, 177–9, 186–8
United States 45, 179–80
universal childhood, notion of 135–6
Unrau, YA 173
Urry, John 73, 81, 83–4

Victoria, Australia, wishes and views of children with cerebral palsy in 2, 5, 56–68: abandonment and rejection 90; agency 167, 171–2, 174; barriers 5, 58; care and living away from families, children in 6, 8–9, 15–21; communication 2, 57–68; continuity of care as means of developing partnership 66–8; diagnosis, communication of 59, 64; discrimination 56; doctors, interaction with 57, 58–68; expert model of professional practice 58, 65; fathers, role of 60, 66; gender issues 65–6; included and informed in medical consultation, desire to be 62–3, 68; inclusion/exclusion 57; information, lack of 64–7; medical consultation 2, 57–68; medical model of disability 58–9; parents' perspective 2, 57, 59, 64–6, 68; partnerships 58, 66–8; social and cultural exclusion in special and mainstream schools 40, 49–51, 53;
social aspects of hospital visits 2, 63; social model of disability 58–9; State Disability Plan (Victoria) 57
views of children *see* wishes, views and experiences of children
Villa, RA 129
violence *see* abuse and violence
Viper Project 191
voices of children *see* wishes, views and experiences of children

Wales 77
Wallat, C 59
warehousing 77–8
Warnock Report 28–9, 33, 45, 53
Watson, N 77, 81, 90, 102–4, 113, 120–1, 126, 167–8, 170
Whittaker, J 51
WHO International Classification of Impairment, Disabilities and Handicaps 6–7
wishes and views *see* parents, views of; wishes, views and experiences of children
wishes, views and experiences of children 1–3, 87–99, 191; age and maturity of child 5, 163; Australia, children with cerebral palsy in 56–68; barriers 5, 90, 94–5, 97–8; Bloorview Hospital, Home and School, Toronto 147–61; bullying 92; cerebral palsy, children with 56–68; communication 2, 57–68, 91–4, 97–9; consultation with children 1, 90, 96; continuity of care 66–8; different, feeling 94–5; disability or impairment, discussions of 92–4, 97; discourse of disability and identity 94–5; discrimination 56, 90, 99; dominant discourses, impact of 89–95; education and

INDEX

schools 2, 147–61; home, role within the family 95; identity 88–94, 96–9; inclusion/exclusion 1, 57, 92, 94–5; India 1, 117–31; information, lack of 64–7, 93–4; life stories 2–3, 12–21, 105–6;

measurement 7–8; medical consultations 2, 57–68; medical model of disability 7–8, 58–9, 83; mistakes, learning to make 5–6; multi-dimensional identities 87–8; parents, perspectives of 57, 59, 64–5, 68, 91–4, 97–9; partnerships 58, 66–8; power 89–90, 97; professionals, relationship with 2, 57, 58–68, 93–4, 97–9; reaction of others 107, 124, 128–30; reflexive practice 90, 97–8; research 2–9, 21, 44, 56–68, 78, 88–9, 96–9, 103–6, 113–14, 118–20, 164, 191–2; respite care 96; reviews 93–4, 96; self-esteem 88, 90; self-identity 88–92, 97–8; social actors, children as 87–9, 91, 95–6; social and cultural exclusion in special and mainstream schools 46; social model of disability 58–9, 87–8, 97, 102–14; sociology 87, 96–9; theoretical reflections 96–9

work 136–7

working-class boys, discrimination against 53

young carers 2, 134–45: abnormal parents 140–1; agency 135, 141–2; barriers 2, 143; Carers Act 1995 134–5; culture 135, 137–8, 143–4; definition 134–5; dependency 135–6, 141; developmental psychology 135, 138–44; difference 135; families, construction of 140–2; gender 138;

individualization 135, 140, 142–5; language brokers 136–7, 143–4; loss of childhood 135, 139–40, 142; negative construction 135, 140–1, 143–5; normal childhoods 135, 138–9, 143–4; parentified children 136; parents, wishes of 135; peer relationships 135, 139–40, 142–3; psychological effects 135, 140; research 134–45; socialization with peers 135, 139, 143; statistics 135; universal childhood, notion of 135–6; work 136–7

youth culture 3, 7, 76–9, 81–2, 112–13

www.routledge.com/9780415693530

Related titles from Routledge

The Sociology of Disability and Inclusive Education
A Tribute to Len Barton

Edited by Madeleine Arnot

Len Barton's intellectual and practical contribution to the sociology of disability and education is well-known and highly significant. This collection addresses the challenge that the social model of disability has presented to dominant medicalised concepts, categories and practices, and their power to define the identity and the lives of others. Expert scholars explore a wide range of topics, including difference as a field of political struggle; the relationship of disability studies, disabled people and their struggle for inclusion; radical activism: organic intellectuals and the disability movement; discrimination, exclusion and effective change; inclusive education; the 'politics of hope', resilience and transformative actions; and universal pedagogy, human rights and citizenship debates.

This book was originally published as a special issue of the *British Journal of Sociology of Education*.

February 2012: 246 x 174: 160pp
Hb: 978-0-415-69353-0
£85 / $145

For more information and to order a copy visit
www.routledge.com/9780415693530

Available from all good bookshops

www.routledge.com/9780415834377

Related titles from Routledge

Diverse Spaces of Childhood and Youth: Gender and socio-cultural differences
Edited by Ruth Evans and Louise Holt

Diverse Spaces of Childhood and Youth focuses on the diverse spaces and discourses of children and youth globally. The chapters explore the influence of gender, age and other socio-cultural differences, such as race, ethnicity and migration trajectories, on the everyday lives of children and youth in a range of international contexts. These include the diverse urban environments of Istanbul, Copenhagen, Helsinki, Toronto, London, and Bratislava and the contrasting rural settings of Ghana and England. The analyses of children's, young people's, parents' and professionals' experiences and discourses provide critical insights into how gender and other socio-cultural differences intersect. Overall, the book provides an original contribution to geographies of children, youth and families and research on diversity and difference in global contexts.

This book was published as a special issue of *Children's Geographies*.

August 2013: 246 x 174: 240pp
Hb: 978-0-415-83437-7
£85/$145

For more information and to order a copy visit
www.routledge.com/9780415843377

Available from all good bookshops

Printed in Great Britain
by Amazon